MEMPHIS *Delivering the Future*

URBAN TAPESTRY SERIES
TOWERY PUBLISHING, INC.

Introduction by FREDERICK W. SMITH

Art Direction by BRIAN A GROPPE

MEMPHIS

Delivering the Future

MEMPHIS

CONTENTS

MEMPHIS

Introduction by Frederick W. Smith

Perhaps it's the aviator in my blood. Or maybe it's my life's work at FedEx. But for me, one image of Memphis that comes readily to mind is the view of the city you get from the air. As you're coming in to land here, you're struck immediately by two dominant features. One is how green the city is. The trees are thick and bountiful, something you don't see in other major cities. In Memphis, especially in the older parts of town, trees are everywhere—huge stands of trees. That canopy of trees, especially as viewed from above, has always stuck in my mind as one of Memphis' greatest assets.

The city's other dominant feature is, of course, the Mississippi River—the root of the city, the source of its initial prosperity. My grandfather was a captain on riverboats back in the Mark Twain era. Most people think that my father was my grandfather because I came along very late in his life, just as my father came along late in his father's life. But my grandfather was actually operating up and down the river at a time when it was the city's major source of transportation.

As someone whose livelihood depends directly on transportation, I find this bit of family history gives me a strong connection to the river. Along with the Nile and the Amazon, the Mississippi is one of the most amazing water systems in the world.

The river has had, and still does have, a tremendous impact on all aspects of this city's life. I think the heritage of being a river port—and all that entails, from the standpoint of culture, from Beale Street and Cotton Row on Front Street, on out to the eastern fringes of the metropolitan area—has been profound. ▶

What's more, the river dictated that the city would evolve into the important transportation hub that Memphis has become for the modern world. The river reminds me that Memphis started as a transportation hub, and that it has always exploited its geographic location and its natural amenities. Transportation has been a central focus for the entire business segment, and obviously the social fabric of the community underpins that. The river is central to everything Memphis ever was, and to everything that it now represents.

But the overwhelming thing I see when I enter the air lanes that lead into Memphis is something both personal and unique: the city I call home.

PEOPLE SOMETIMES ASSUME THAT I COULD HAVE FOUNDED AND BUILT FEDEX anywhere in the country. We're such a huge corporation these days—in terms of operations, resources, personnel, and facilities—that it seems like we're located everywhere, all at once. And that's how the company had to evolve if it was to become a global enterprise.

But the truth is that when I looked for the ideal location to start FedEx, I was fortunate to be a Memphian. If you want to connect all the points in the 48 contiguous states together, you're limited by the speed of the jet airplane, as well as by the circadian rhythm of the economy—that is, the times when businesses close and open. People want

to pull goods off the shelf late in the day and package them up so that they can have them delivered the following morning.

If you take those two limitations—the speed of jet planes and the business rhythm—you have to locate the hub of the delivery system someplace in a square that goes from Memphis to Indianapolis to Columbus, Ohio, to south of Nashville near the Tennessee-Alabama state line.

In addition to its prime location, Memphis also has incredibly good weather. In nearly 30 years of operations, I can count on the fingers of one hand the times we've been delayed at the hub here, and it's always been for extremely aberrant reasons, like rare ice storms that would have been hard for anyone to deal with.

And Memphis had a tremendous airport with a lot of space available. The Air Force Reserve had moved out, and a progressive airport commission—headed up by a very forward-thinking individual named Ned Cook—was willing to take a risk on us and let FedEx have the space it needed to grow and prosper. ▶

And, it didn't hurt that I was from here and was very familiar with the city. You put all those factors together and it's almost tailor-made for a company like FedEx.

There has, throughout the company's evolution, been a happy association between FedEx and the city of Memphis. For some reason, Memphis seems to have always been a good place for entrepreneurs. True, my own thinking is that entrepreneurs sort of happen without regard to the political or socioeconomic landscape. Now, maybe that's not true of some of the scientific endeavors that are centered around one university or another. For instance, a lot of the nuclear initiative arose around the University of Chicago during World War II. But entrepreneurs can appear anywhere.

Memphis, however, seems to have had a disproportionate number of them, or at least of those who have attained some prominence in their field. We've had people like Kemmons Wilson, who founded Holiday Inns here; Clarence Saunders, who revolutionized the grocery business; Billy Dunavant, who came in and changed the cotton business into a global enterprise; and Jim Barksdale, who worked for FedEx before going on to become the CEO of Netscape, which was of course vital to the emergence of the Internet.

So I'd have to say that Memphis is a location that is conducive to business enterprises. I don't think it's because of anything that Memphis overtly does. Instead, I think it might have a lot to do with what Memphis *doesn't* do—there's nothing here working against

entrepreneurs. It's an environment in which, for whatever reason, people feel free to try all sorts of innovations, not just in business, but in music and other areas as well.

Maybe, in the end, you have to just shrug your shoulders and say that it's something in the water. We do, after all, have great water here, with artesian wells that filter it naturally. Or maybe it has to do with being in a central location, at a cultural and economic crossroads, where a person is not limited by his or her vision, or by boundaries.

Whatever the reasons—identifiable and intangible alike—Memphis has been an ideal place for innovators, and it remains a culture where the art of the possible seems to be a way of life.

I DON'T RECALL FEELING THIS WAY WHEN I WAS GROWING UP. I SUPPOSE THAT like almost all young people, I just assumed that the place I lived had developed by accident, and that its character was predetermined in some sort of mysterious way. ▶

I do recall feeling that there were some very nice things about being young in Memphis, but I also had strong feelings that there was a lot about the community that needed to be changed. Obviously, Memphis was a totally segregated place, and from this segregation there arose a lot of negative aspects, to put it mildly.

Today, of course, things have improved tremendously. Memphis is quite an integrated community. I think it has developed a reasonable degree of racial harmony, far better than many communities.

And I think that experience has been very good for the city of Memphis. We've still got a number of problems, and a number of hurdles when it comes to race, but I'm gratified to see the level and degree of interaction between the races—in business, in social situations, in the arts, everywhere you look.

I mention this both to counter the stereotype that Memphis is a city with many racial problems, and also to point out that the city's approach to racial harmony is an indication of just how cosmopolitan and mature a city it has become. The Memphis I grew up in was a very traditional Southern city marked by extreme cleanliness—the city was very proud of the fact that it had won national prizes in terms of city beautiful competitions. The trees, as today, were abundant. I remember Memphis' dominant characteristic being that it was a very *pleasant* place. There were lots and lots of churches. The traditional values held. The political powers maintained a stable government.

It certainly was a good place for me to grow up, and when I think of the expansion of FedEx, and all the people who have moved here to take advantage of our growth, I'm gratified to know that this notion still holds true. Memphis is, perhaps more than ever, a good place for a person to come of age, or raise a family, or relocate to take up a new job. And that, in the grand scheme of things, says a lot about this city's attributes and its character.

TODAY, THERE'S A GREAT DEAL OF ATTENTION BEING PLACED ON WHAT, FOR want of a better term, is called e-commerce. There's a common misapprehension that e-commerce can only flourish in places like Silicon Valley and Route 128 in Boston. But what we've found here in Memphis is that the skill sets and resources to facilitate this "new" world of doing business are available just about everywhere.

It's like medical technology. Thirty years ago, you could only have an operation like a coronary artery bypass done in Houston or New York. Now, those skill sets have migrated

16

into almost every reasonably sized city in the country. The medical center here is one of the best in the nation, and it's something that the city needs to exploit more.

The same thing is true of information technology (IT) and e-commerce skills, because a lot of these are available here in Memphis. FedEx has a major IT campus in Collierville, which houses about 3,000 folks. We have other IT campuses that allow us to avail ourselves of the talent pools that are out there in Colorado, Texas, and Florida, as well as on the West Coast. But there's no doubt in my mind that Memphis can attract and retain adequately trained people to work in the IT and e-commerce area. We've made a number of investments at the University of Memphis and Christian Brothers University to train people in these areas. I think there's a little bit of a myth that e-commerce is this esoteric skill set that you can possess only if you live someplace between San Jose and San Francisco.

NOT THAT YOU'D BE ABLE TO GUESS THIS FROM THE AIR APPROACH TO THE CITY. One of the more common approaches directs planes into the airport from the north, bringing flights in right over East Parkway. I always feel something special when I see this part of the city—the older residential areas—from this vantage point.

I grew up on the Parkways. When I was young, the Parkways didn't have curbs, and in the center was a grass strip that was a bridle path. If there was a prettier street in any city

in America, I don't know where it would have been. You could walk over to the Fairgrounds, just a few blocks from where I grew up. You could either rent or board a horse at the Fairgrounds, and go get it and ride it all the way around the perimeter of the city. And what still marks these beautiful streets in my mind are those huge trees along the way. It's so shady that, even when it's blistering hot, it seems cool out there.

Now, when I arrive back in Memphis from one of my travels, and when we make our approach from the north, I can see the ring of the Parkways, and the broad span of trees that carpet the neighborhoods of my hometown, and I'm reminded that I'll soon be on familiar paths once again. ■

MEMPHIS

Photo-Essay

M EMPHIS IS ONE OF THE few cities in the country to have two governing executives. Jim Rout (LEFT), who was elected Shelby County mayor in 1994, and Dr. Willie W. Herenton (OPPOSITE), who was elected city mayor in 1991, both work to promote economic development and increase the quality of life throughout the region.

I N 1541, STANDING ON THE bluffs just south of Memphis, Spanish explorer Hernando de Soto became the first European to set eyes on the Mississippi River. Today, his legacy remains prominent throughout the area, commemorated in local artist Burton Callicott's 1934 murals at the Pink Palace Museum (BOTTOM) and in the Hernando de Soto Memorial Trail in Mississippi.

THE STORY OF THE CIVIL War can be read in the local monuments honoring Southern politicians and soldiers like Jefferson Davis (OPPOSITE) and General Nathan Bedford Forrest (TOP). Recounting this history in a different medium is Shelby Foote (BOTTOM LEFT), a native Memphian who has written several definitive texts on the war between the states.

Music born of hardship, politics born of power: In 1909, E.H. "Boss" Crump—memorialized with a bronze statue at the entrance to Overton Park (ABOVE)—was elected mayor of Memphis, launching his controversial four-decade political career. Considered by many to be the father of the blues, W.C. Handy (OPPOSITE), after whom Handy Park on Beale Street is named, penned his famous "Memphis Blues" while playing for Crump's first mayoral campaign.

I T JUST KEEPS ROLLING ALONG: The mighty Mississippi River has had an overarching influence on Memphis' industry and culture. Steamboats like the *American Queen* once brought cotton and other goods—not to mention travelers—to and from the city. Considered by many to be Ol' Man River himself, James Hyter (OPPOSITE) sang the *Showboat* tune at the Memphis in May International Festival's Sunset Symphony for more than 20 years—often with multiple encores prompted by enthusiastic applause—before retiring in 1998.

AS MORE LOCALS CONSIDER the area for business, residence, and recreation, downtown Memphis is experiencing a renaissance, restoring its buildings while maintaining its natural surroundings. Its efforts have not gone unnoticed: The National City Beautiful Commission has named Memphis the cleanest city in the country five times—more than any other metropolis.

Y LAND, SEA, OR AIR: MEMPHIS' central location, along with its easy access to every mode of transportation, has helped it become America's Distribution Center. In addition to being the second-largest inland port on the Mississippi River, Memphis also boasts the world's busiest cargo airport.

Quality of water is one of the many attributes that help draw major industries to Memphis. With its atmosphere of innovation and entrepreneurship, the region attracts a variety of successful businesses, including those in the food, power, technology, and health care industries.

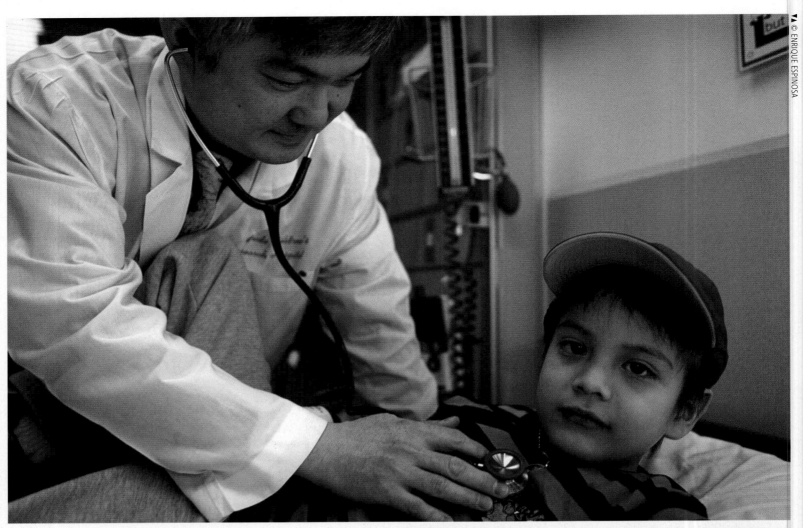

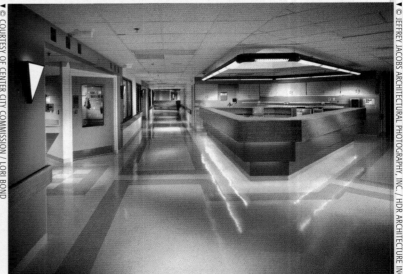

Founded by actor Danny Thomas in 1962 and named after the patron saint of lost causes, St. Jude Children's Research Hospital cares for more than 4,000 children each year. Devoted to researching and treating serious childhood diseases, the hospital maintains several laboratories staffed by highly skilled medical staff like Dr. Peter Doherty (OPPOSITE), who was awarded the 1996 Nobel Prize in Physiology or Medicine for his work in T-cell recognition and cell-mediated immunity.

Moon over Memphis: Many of the city's most distinctive structures reflect Middle Eastern architectural styles, including the Great American Pyramid (ABOVE) and the Danny Thomas/ALSAC (American Lebanese Syrian Association Charities) Pavilion at St. Jude (OPPOSITE).

Memphis takes its name from an ancient city near the Nile, and these origins fuel an ongoing fascination with all things Egyptian. Founded in 1984, the Institute of Egyptian Art and Archaeology at the University of Memphis maintains a popular collection of more than 150 artifacts (ABOVE), and in 1987, the *Ramesses the Great* exhibit (OPPOSITE) drew more than 650,000 visitors from around the country.

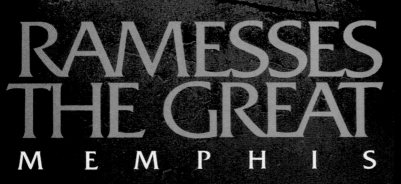

SEE THE EXHIBITION EMPERORS WERE DYING TO GET INTO.

RAMESSES THE GREAT
MEMPHIS

EGYPT 1290-1224 BC   TENNESSEE APRIL 15-AUGUST 31 1987 A.D.

TITANIC
The Exhibition

APRIL 3 - SEPT 30, 1997 • THE PYRAMID, MEMPHIS

ANCESTORS OF THE INCAS

THE LOST CIVILIZATIONS OF PERU

April 16 - September 16, 1998 · The Pyramid, Memphis

Presented by WONDERS: The Memphis International Cultural Series in association with Instituto Nacional de Cultura and PromPerú

AFTER THE SUCCESS OF THE
Ramesses the Great show,
local businessmen and
city leaders formed Wonders: The

the Pyramid, the Wonders series—
which has showcased Catherine the
Great, the *Titanic*, and the Imperial
Tombs of China, among many

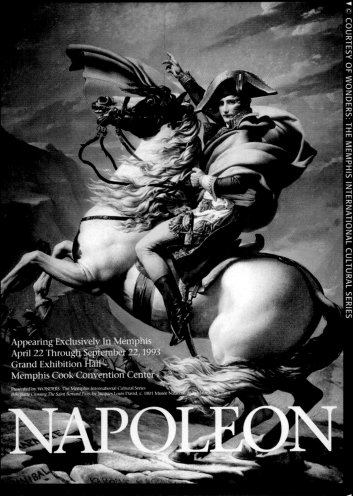

Appearing Exclusively In Memphis
April 22 Through September 22, 1993
Grand Exhibition Hall
Memphis Cook Convention Center

Presented by WONDERS: The Memphis International Cultural Series
Bonaparte Crossing The Saint Bernard Pass by Jacques Louis David, c. 1801 Musée National du Château, Paris

NAPOLEON

Splendors
of the **Ottoman**
Sultans

WWII
THROUGH
RUSSIAN EYES

T H E
ETRUSCANS
LEGACY OF A LOST CIVILIZATION
FROM THE VATICAN MUSEUMS
MEMPHIS PINK PALACE MUSEUM • MAY 1 - AUGUST 31, 1992
WONDERS

ETERNAL EGYPT

MASTERWORKS OF ANCIENT ART
FROM THE BRITISH MUSEUM

JUNE 28 – OCTOBER 21, 2001

THE PYRAMID / MEMPHIS, TENNESSEE

PRESENTED BY:

WONDERS

FOR TICKET INFORMATION CALL 901/754-ARTS

MEMPHIS ROYALTY KNOWS how to get around in style. While Elvis took care of business in his flashy Cadillac, Russia's Catherine the Great—the subject of a popular Wonders exhibit that attracted more than 600,000 visitors in 1991—rode around in her horse-drawn Grand Coronation carriage, which was specially restored for the Memphis show.

F ROM AN AWKWARD TEENAGER singing "That's All Right, Mama" at Sun Studios in 1954 to an international superstar, Elvis Presley stands—well, gyrates—as a true emblem of Memphis and its creative spirit. Buried at Graceland, but sighted around the world, the King of Rock and Roll has strummed up a booming tourism business— including his namesake restaurant on Beale Street (BOTTOM)—and makes every December a blue Christmas.

© ENRIQUE ESPINOSA

© JUDI PARKS

MEMPHIS' STREETS AND neighborhoods shine brightly, whatever the occasion—be it a holiday or birthday celebration or just a night on the town.

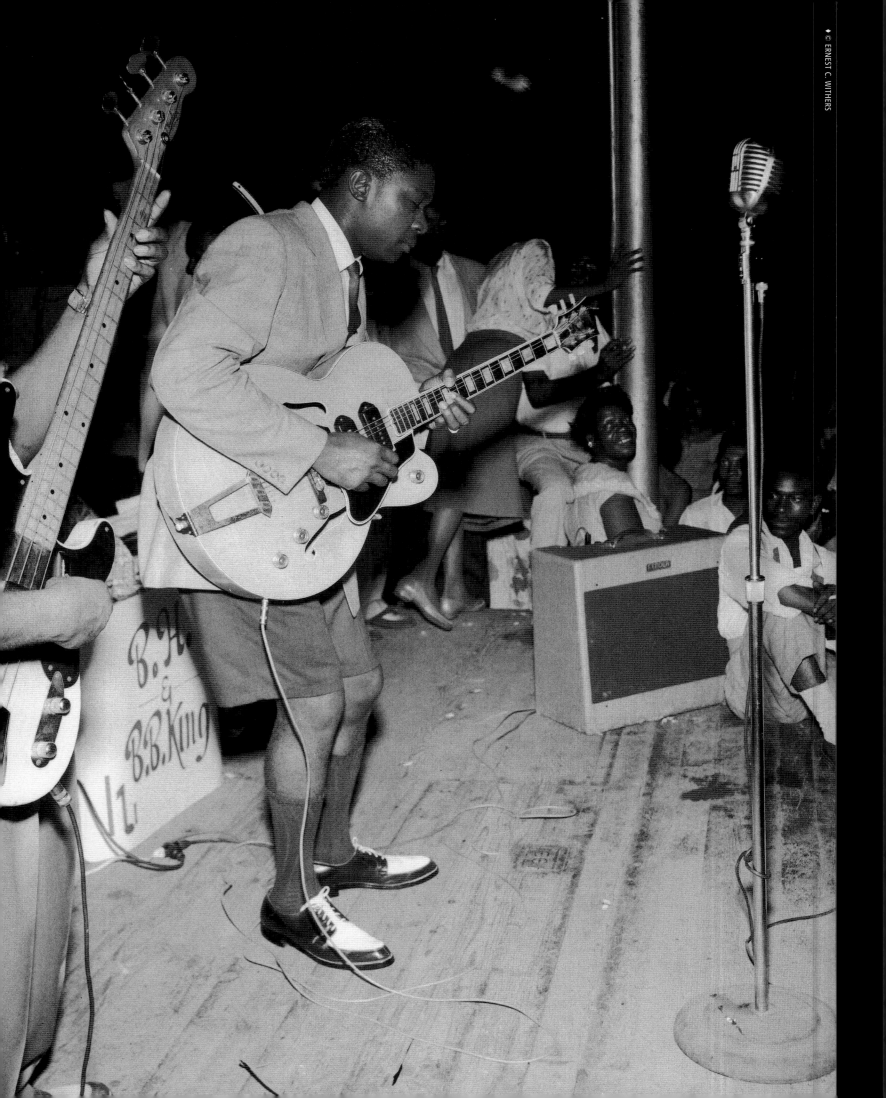

THE MEMPHIS BLUES

SUCCESSFULLY FEATURED BY ED. V. CUPERO'S BAND AND ORCHESTRA

IN GEO. EVANS' "HONEY BOY" MINSTRELS

A SOUTHERN RAG BY W.C. HANDY

GEO A. NORTON'S SONG FOUNDED ON W.C. HANDY'S WORLD WIDE BLUE MELODY

JOE MORRIS MUSIC CO.
Sole Selling Agents
145 West 45th Street
New York.

HANDY PARK

GIVE MY REGARDS TO BEALE Street: One of the city's top tourist attractions, Beale Street reverberates with music and activity day or night. Home to numerous bars and clubs, as well as Handy Park (TOP), the historic thoroughfare has hosted performances by such local legends as B.B. King (PAGE 52) and Elvis Presley (PAGE 53), among many others.

E ACH YEAR, MORE THAN 2,000 attendees from around the country get all dolled up to hear the blues and have a ball at the Blues Ball. Founded in 1994 and organized by internationally recognized fashion designer Pat Kerr Tigrett (OPPOSITE), the event raises hundreds of thousands of dollars for local charities and musicians' funds, and has featured such legends as Jerry Lee Lewis (TOP RIGHT), the late Carl Perkins (BOTTOM LEFT), official Blues Ball artist Leroy Neiman (TOP LEFT), and—in spirit—Elvis himself.

ONE OF THE CITY'S PREMIER cultural institutions, Ballet Memphis has been gracefully gaining national exposure, earning a grant from the Ford Foundation in 2000 and performing in New York City in 2001. Founded by current Artistic Director Dorothy Gunther Pugh (OPPOSITE BOTTOM) in 1985, the organization performs four full-length productions annually at the Orpheum Theatre (OPPOSITE TOP), in addition to several smaller shows around the region and an extensive touring schedule.

Since 1952, the Memphis Symphony Orchestra has been serenading the city with the music of Brahms, Mozart, Vivaldi, and Ellington, among many other composers. Led by the wand of David Loebel (OPPOSITE BOTTOM), music director and conductor since July 1999, the orchestra features more than 80 musicians—including violinist and concertmaster Susanna Perry Gilmore (RIGHT).

AT THE FOREFRONT OF the ongoing downtown renaissance is the Peabody Hotel. With a reputation for luxury, elegance, and fine dining—including the award-winning Chez Philippe restaurant and Master Chef José Gutierrez (TOP LEFT)—the Peabody is perhaps best known for its ducks, who get top bill at the hotel, swimming in the Grand Lobby fountain and living in the rooftop Duck Palace—all under the watchful eye of Duck Master Toby Carter (BOTTOM LEFT).

Memphis' fun-loving, gregarious personality shows through at downtown block parties sponsored by Belz Enterprises, where locals enjoy a brew or two and the music of entertainers such as salsa sensations Orquestra Caliente (bottom) and Jason D. Williams (opposite top).

WITH ITS FRANTIC PACE and its M-shaped Hernando DeSoto Bridge, downtown Memphis provides a perfect backdrop for every kind of activity, from celebrations like the Beale Street Music Festival and the Fourth of July, to a quite evening's midriver meditation.

Hog heaven: Each year during Memphis in May, more than 100,000 hungry barbecue fans flock to Tom Lee Park for the World Championship Barbecue Cooking Contest, the largest event of its kind in the world. More than 250 teams from across the globe cook up savory barbecue to compete for a large cash prize and, more important, bragging rights.

W HETHER THEY ORDER wet or dry, on the bone or in a sandwich, Memphians pig out on barbecue. Known as the Pork Barbecue Capital of the World, the city boasts upwards of 100 restaurants specializing in the delicacy.

CATFISH FARMERS ARE cultivating big business and netting increasingly large profits in the Mid-South. In Mississippi alone, more than 110,000 water acres produce approximately 50 million pounds of catfish each day, accounting for more than half the national production.

© WILLIAM E BARKSDALE

CONCRETE AND STEEL FORM the foundation of many of Memphis' new buildings, spurring the city's continuing expansion. Located near the Pyramid, the Lone Star Industries cement terminal (OPPOSITE BOTTOM) ships more than 400,000 tons of cement each year, making it one of the busiest such facilities in the country.

NEITHER RAIN NOR SLEET nor gloom of night will keep hats—whether for shade, warmth, or protection—off the heads of working Memphians. At Mr. Hats, Alvin Lansky (OPPOSITE TOP) makes sure all his customers brim with fashion and style. Today, his store is one of the largest hat shops in the South, with more than 10,000 chapeaus in stock.

The country's largest three-service municipal utility company, Memphis Light, Gas & Water keeps the city lit and running, supplying energy to more than 400,000 customers throughout Shelby County. The growing number of construction projects around the city has sparked business for several electric sub-contractors, including Thomas & Betts Corp. and TAM Electric, which together installed more than 550 floodlights during the building of AutoZone Park in 1999 (OPPO-SITE TOP).

ALWAYS
WEAR
YOUR
GLOVES
AND
SLEEVES

© LISA WADDELL BUSER

© JUDI PARKS

© JONATHAN POSTAL / TOWERY PUBLISHING, INC.

Beautiful AutoZone Park, home to Memphis' Triple-A Redbirds, championed the redevelopment of the city's downtown. The 14,500-seat stadium was designed by the local firm Looney Ricks Kiss Architects.

© LARRY T. INMAN

© LARRY T. INMAN

© COURTESY OF KRISTI JERNIGAN

Take me out to the ball game: Cheered on by thousands of fans of all ages—not to mention mascot Rockey the Redbird—the Memphis Redbirds prepare minor-league players for spots on the St. Louis Cardinals' roster. Along with her husband, Dean, Kristi Jernigan (BOTTOM RIGHT) truly went to bat for Memphis, helping to finance the park and locate it downtown, as well as cofounding the nonprofit Memphis Redbirds Baseball Foundation.

THE BLENDING OF OLD and new architecture makes Memphis a mosaic of development. Rounding out the city's modern skyline are landmarks like Peabody Place (LEFT), Hampton Inn & Suites, and the Louis T. Fogelman YMCA.

MEMPHIANS DEMONSTRATE a strong work ethic while performing jobs requiring technical skill, business savvy, and creative juices. It's little wonder the city has gained a reputation as a top spot for starting and growing a company.

F ROM 1891 UNTIL 1947, some 75 electric streetcars traveled more than 100 miles of routes throughout the city, but were eventually made obsolete by automobiles and buses. In 1993,

Memphis got back on track: Operated by the Memphis Area Transit Authority, a fleet of vintage trolleys resumed carrying Memphians around downtown.

THE MAIN STREET TROLLEY line has proven a popular mode of transportation for locals and visitors alike. For a true taste of the city, nothing beats a nighttime trolley ride along Main Street and around the Riverfront Loop.

THE BELL RANG, AND WE ANSWERED...

IN MEMORIAM

As dusk descends, Memphis lights up dramatically, high-lighting tributes to local civil servants. In October 2000, the old Memphis Police Station (ABOVE) shone vividly as part of Light It Up: The Downtown Illumination Project, a collaboration between the UrbanArt Commission and the Center City Commission. Located in the former Fire Engine House No. 1 on Adams Avenue, the Fire Museum of Memphis contains interactive and historical exhibits, as well as the Memorial Wall (OPPOSITE), which lists the 48 local firefighters who have lost their lives since 1880.

THE HALLS AND WALLS of justice find a home in downtown Memphis, where the seats of city, county, and federal governmental bodies hold sway.

From South Main to the Pinch District at downtown's northern tip—and everywhere in between—trolleys transport passengers engaged in both work and leisure, offering unique glimpses of city life.

Mud Island is neither made of mud nor technically an island: Built of silt, it connects to Memphis at its northern end. But it does house the extensive Mississippi River Museum and the five-block-long Mississippi River Walk, a recreational water park that traces the lower 1,000 miles of the crooked-letter waterway past Memphis and into the Gulf of Mexico swimming pool.

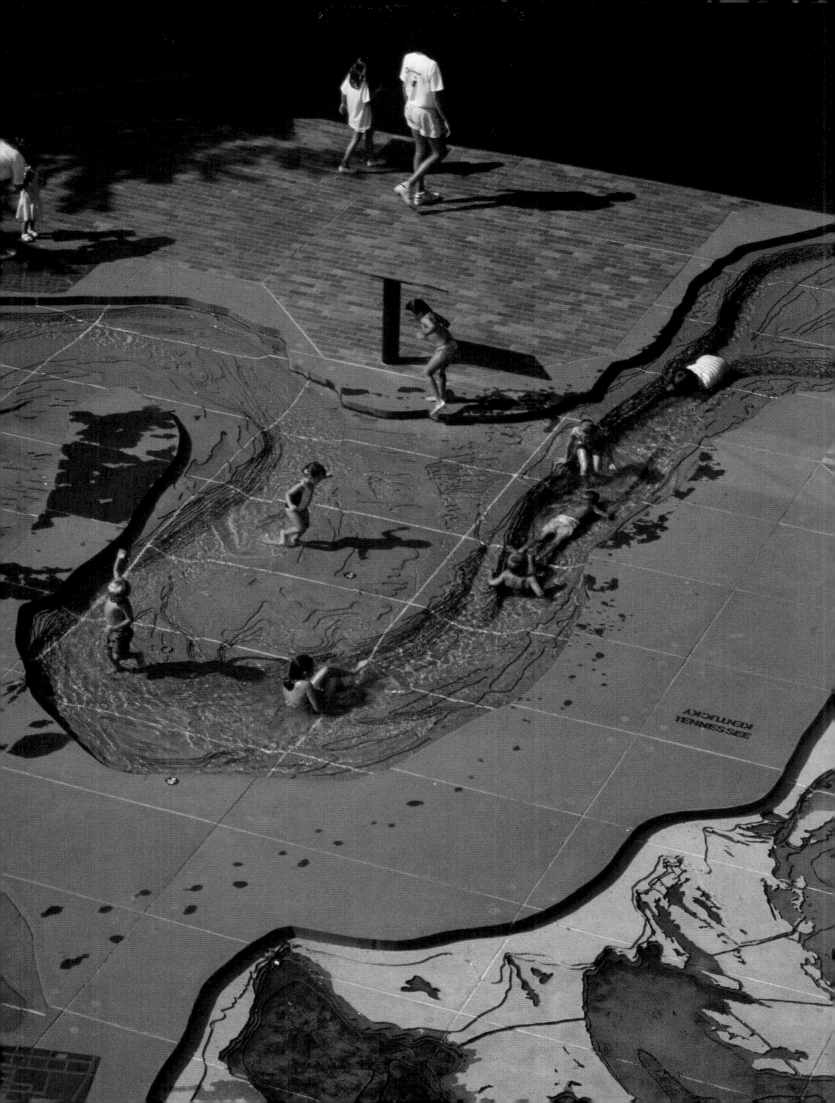

WHETHER COVERED FROM head to toe with water or with mud, youthful Memphians display a joie de vivre infused with the city's own zest for life.

ONE OF FOUR PUBLIC AREAS created in the original 1819 city plans, Court Square provides an oasis amid the urban landscape. At its center stands an ornate fountain dedicated in 1876 and topped with the figure of Hebe, the Greek goddess of youth.

At the heart of the city, scenic Court Square bustles with people, many enjoying a brief work break from offices such as the Burch, Porter & Johnson law firm (TOP), located in the former Tennessee Club building adjacent to the park. For those needing directions from the park to anywhere in Memphis, the Blue Suede Brigade (BOTTOM LEFT) patrols downtown six days a week.

CLASSIC FACES AND FIXTURES on the Memphis scene join forces with newcomers to form an urban core rich in history and promise. One retail old-timer, Carter's Seed Store, sadly closed its doors in early 2001 after more than 80 years of service.

Several Memphians are making sound investments in the area's culture. A Loverly recording artist, Lamar Sorrento (BOTTOM)—a.k.a. James Eddie Campbell—has gained local and national acclaim for his folk art portraits, which hang in establishments like the Center for Southern Folklore (TOP). Run by Executive Director Judy Peiser (OPPOSITE), the restaurant/museum/musical venue, located in Peabody Place, hosts musical acts including Mose Vinson, DiAnne Price, and Blind Mississippi Morris.

FORTUNE OFTEN SMILES ON the many men and women who operate businesses downtown. Abe Schwab (ON RIGHT) became the third generation of his family to don an apron and hawk merchandise from the Beale Street staple A. Schwab Dry Goods. For several years, glass designer Dan Oppenheimer (ON LEFT) headed Rainbow Studio, a popular stained-glass company whose product-filled windows lend a colorful air to South Main's thriving arts and residential district.

FOR DECADES, BEALE STREET served as the active center for Memphis' black community, hosting parades and concerts and fostering all types of music—from blues to jug band to soul. Now one of the city's top tourist draws, Beale still reverberates with hot tunes and reflects the contributions of African-American culture to the city's identity.

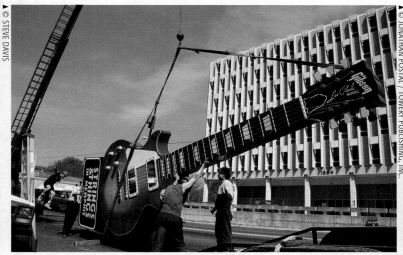

Gibson FACTORY

Guitars both new and vintage strike a familiar chord in Memphis. Gibson Guitar Corp. Chairman and CEO Henry Juszkiewicz (bottom right) paid tribute to the city's musical heritage when he picked a spot just south of Beale Street for a factory. The Gibson facility also includes the Smithsonian Institute's Rock 'n' Soul Museum, overseen by Director of Operations Jimmy Ogle (opposite). Scores of classic stringed instruments line the walls of Rod and Hank's Vintage Guitars, owned and operated by Rod Norwood and Hank Sable (bottom left).

A MUSICIANS' PARADISE, Memphis and its many venues reverberate with rockin' tunes played by a cast of colorful characters. Known far and wide as the Grandmother of Rock 'n' Roll, Cordell Jackson (BOTTOM) has strummed up a lot of applause in her more than 50 years in the local music business: Not only did she establish Moon Records in 1956, she also was one of the first women to write, play, sing, record, and produce her own debut album. Infamous for his fast wit and faster fretwork, Monsieur Jeffrey Evans (OPPOSITE BOTTOM) recorded his 2001 debut, *I've Lived a Good Life*, live at Shangri-La Records.

ARKED BY ITS FAMOUS rooster logo, Sun Studio has risen to legendary status. During the 1950s, owner Sam Phillips (OPPOSITE)—whom A&E's *Biography* called the Man Who Invented Rock and Roll—recorded an impressive roster of musicians, including artists such as Johnny Cash, Carl Perkins, and, of course, Elvis Presley.

DURING THE 1960s AND early 1970s, in a former movie theater on McLemore Avenue, Stax Records produced a vast catalog of sweet soul music by David Porter (OPPOSITE, BOTTOM LEFT), Isaac Hayes (OPPOSITE, BOTTOM RIGHT), Willie Mitchell (BOTTOM LEFT), and Rufus Thomas (BOTTOM RIGHT), among many others. Sadly, the building was razed in 1989, leaving only a historical marker to commemorate the site. But a change is gonna come: Plans call for the construction of the Stax Museum of American Soul Music and the Stax Music Academy.

A FAMILY AFFAIR: An accomplished studio musician who has worked with such artists as Bob Dylan and the Replacements, Jim Dickinson (TOP) has passed along his love of regional music to his sons, Cody and Luther Dickinson, who, along with bassist Chris Chew, comprise local faves the North Mississippi All-Stars (BOTTOM). A native of Clarksdale, Mississippi, and a frequent performer at the Center for Southern Folklore with his band the Pocket Rockets, Blind Mississippi Morris (OPPOSITE) has been blowing Delta blues on his harmonica for decades.

© ENRIQUE ESPINOSA

© JONATHAN POSTAL

© CENTER FOR SOUTHERN FOLKLORE

FROM THE CROSSROADS where Robert Johnson is said to have sold his soul to the devil, to the porches and doorsteps where musicians pick their guitars, the Memphis region has long been a stomping ground for the Delta blues. A former medicine show entertainer, Walter "Furry" Lewis (OPPOSITE, BOTTOM RIGHT) helped create the "Memphis Sound" with his signature bottleneck slide. He died in 1981, but continues to influence generations of musicians.

Born in 1907, Lillie Mae Glover (RIGHT) belted the blues in Memphis as Ma Rainey II, taking her stage name from the famed singer whose powerful style she emulated. Glover died in 1985 and, after a funeral procession through Beale Street, was laid to rest in historic Elmwood Cemetery (OPPOSITE).

MEMPHIS

MEMPHIS BEST

BEAUTY OF THE BLU

BECKWITH

S OUTH MAIN SHALL RISE again: In decline for years, South Main is fast becoming Memphis' chief arts district. Many of its historic buildings are being renovated and upgraded for use as galleries, studio and loft apartments, and retail space, while its longtime businesses continue to flourish.

Broadcasting from South Main, WEVL FM90 (TOP)—the only listener-supported, independent, volunteer radio station in the country—airs more than 70 unique programs a week featuring an eclectic range of musical styles and genres.

OPEN DOORS AND OPEN arms greet newcomers to the burgeoning South Main District. Ephraim Urevbu (BOTTOM LEFT) has added to the success of his Art Village Gallery with Zanzibar, a popular café and coffee shop. Just across Main Street, artist Jay Etkin (OPPOSITE) owns and operates Jay Etkin Gallery, while artistic furnishings occupy the space in Carnevale, owned and operated by Michael Moreau and John Simmons (BOTTOM RIGHT, FROM LEFT).

© ENRIQUE ESPINOSA

© SAL CRONE

DAN BALL

I HEAR THAT TRAIN A-COMIN': Built in 1914, Central Station underwent a $23.3 million renovation that restored it to the splendor of its glory years. In addition to loft apartments, the building houses a police precinct and the local offices for Amtrak, which brings two daily trains through the station. Located at the southern end of Main, the historic site lies a mere trolley ride from the attractions of downtown.

W HILE MUCH OF SHELBY County displays an urban flair, the area never forgets its roots. As the spot where the Delta begins, Memphis has risen from rural surroundings.

AT THE WHEEL OF HIS 1955 Cadillac, Tad Pierson (ABOVE) conducts personalized tours of Memphis and the Mississippi Delta through his company American Dream Safari. Along the way, Pierson points out historic locations and old-fashioned juke joints as he expounds on the region, its music culture, and such locals as Elvis Presley and Memphis Minnie, as well as lesser-known— but no less influential—musicians like the Al Jackson Band (OPPOSITE).

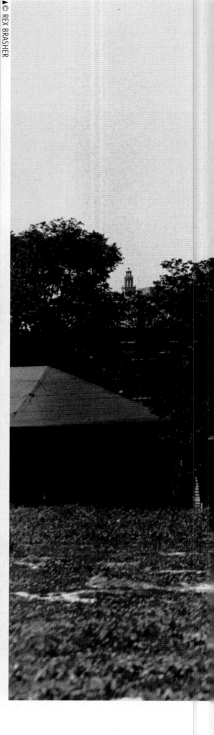

IME WAS WHEN COTTON was king in the Mid-South, bringing with it an agricultural lifestyle that has significantly changed. Today, one is more likely to find casinos than cotton in the shadows of the city's skyline.

THROWING A HOE DOWN: Mid-South farmers and gardeners must work tenaciously to protect their plants from the dreaded kudzu vine, which can grow nearly 60 feet during one season. Indigenous to Asia, the vine was transplanted to North America in an effort to prevent soil erosion, but today covers everything in its path.

Seas of white blanket the fall landscape as farms around the area reap the plentiful harvest of a profitable cotton crop. As the green plants turn brown and the bolls open, cottom farmers look for new and more efficient methods of tracking production and fighting harmful pests in order to maintain the plant's importance to the regional economy.

© CINDY STUART

© ENRIQUE ESPINOSA

© STEVE DAVIS

© ENRIQUE ESPINOSA

NEWS OF THE REGION'S agricultural accomplishments comes straight from the horse's mouth. From farmers' markets to wineries to simulated farms at the Memphis Zoo, the sweat of the brow has long been a local way of life.

A HOME WHERE THE BISON roam occupies 4,500 acres in East Memphis. Shelby Farms, the largest urban park in the country, offers outdoor recreation for hundreds of Mid-Southerners who take advantage of its walking and biking paths to view its lakes, woods, and wildlife. The farms are also headquarters to locally based Ducks Unlimited Inc. (OPPOSITE BOTTOM), a wetlands conservation organization with some 500,000 members.

D EDICATED TO PRESERVING Memphis' natural assets and chronicling its rich history, the Pink Palace Family of Museums maintains seven facilities throughout the city, including the 65-acre Lichterman Nature Center (TOP AND BOTTOM), which boasts a 10-acre lake, miles of hiking trails, and a wildlife hospital. The Pink Palace Museum and the Pink Palace Mansion (OPPOSITE) emphasize extensive, interactive exhibits on Memphis history and natural science.

CHUCALISSA, AN ARCHAEO-
logical museum operated by
the University of Memphis
Department of Anthropology, hosts
the Spring Powwow, an April event
with dance, crafts, and food. In addition, Chucalissa—which means "lost
village"—features a reconstruction
of a 15th-century Native American
settlement.

9TH ANNUAL MEMPHIS
POW-WOW AND CRAFTS FAIR
FRI, SAT, SUN, JUNE 19, 2021

MEMPHIS annual POWWOW

S ENDING IN THE CLOWNS, Memphis' many festivals and circuses—including the handmade model at the Pink Palace Museum (BOTTOM)—reflect the population's fun-loving spirit and outgoing nature.

MID - SOUTH
FAIR

HONORABLE
MENTION

HONEY & BEESWAX

To bee or not to bee? That is the question posed by Memphis' sun-saturated gardens. Whether 'tis nobler for locals to grow their own herbs and flowers or to buy them from vendors at venues like the Mid-South Fair, such garden-grown treats never get old.

GROW ALONG WITH ME THE BEST IS YET TO BE

Mᴇᴍᴘʜɪꜱ Bᴏᴛᴀɴɪᴄ Gᴀʀᴅᴇɴ provides quiet sanctuary from the urban hubbub, giving visitors a peaceful place to ponder. With a sensory garden, a Japanese Garden of Tranquility, and a shady cherry tree orchard, the picturesque 96-acre site offers educational programs and hosts a full calendars of concerts and events. Nearby, the Dixon Gallery and Gardens (ᴛᴏᴘ ʀɪɢʜᴛ) is nestled among its own lush gardens, decorated with statuary and sculpture. Opened in 1976 in the former residence of Hugo and Margaret Dixon, the small, private museum exhibits an impressive collection of French and American Impressionists.

Each year, more than 750,000 visitors go wild for the Memphis Zoo, located in Overton Park. Founded in 1905 and sporting an Egyptian architectural theme, the zoo is home to more than 2,800 animals representing 400 species of mammals, birds, and reptiles—including some 50 endangered species like the Pere David deer and the Przewalski horse.

N O COOKIE-CUTTER HOTEL, the small Talbot Heirs Guesthouse combines attentive service with whimsical decor, making it popular with corporate travelers as well as just-marrieds and second-honeymooners. Owned and operated by Jamie and Phil Baker (ABOVE), who bought the property in 1995 and renovated it themselves, the hotel has nine spacious rooms, each with its own distinct personality that blends modern and retro flourishes.

M AKING SURE THAT brand-new Memphians get a good start on life, neonatal facilities around town— such as BirthPlace (RIGHT) at Regional Medical Center, known locally as the MED—strive to provide the most skilled and attentive patient care in the most comfortable setting possible. One of the oldest and largest neonatal intensive care units in the country, the MED's Newborn Center—founded in 1968 by Medical Director Dr. Sheldon Korones (OPPOSITE TOP)—treats more than 1,300 premature or critically ill newborns each year.

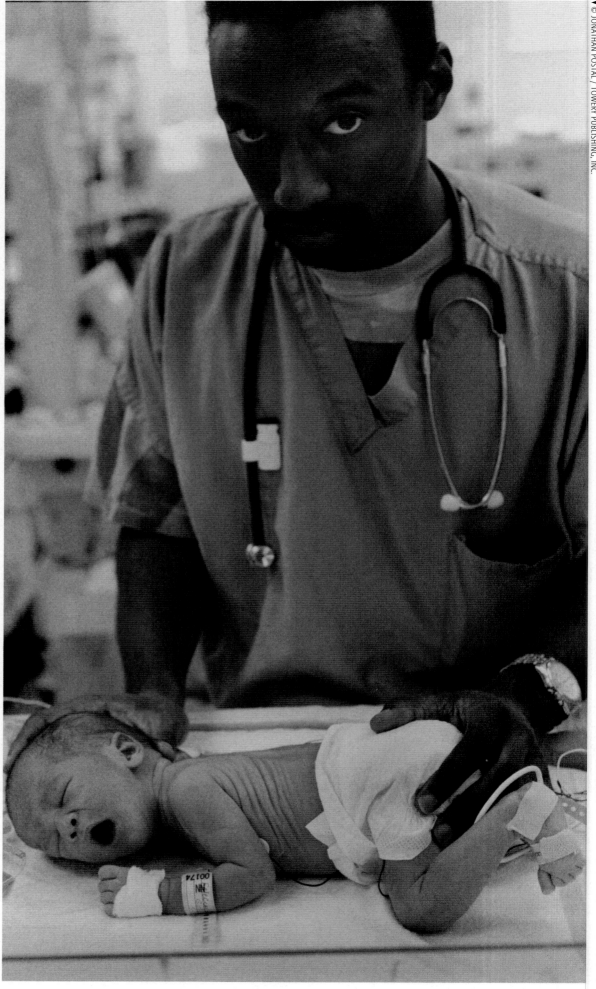

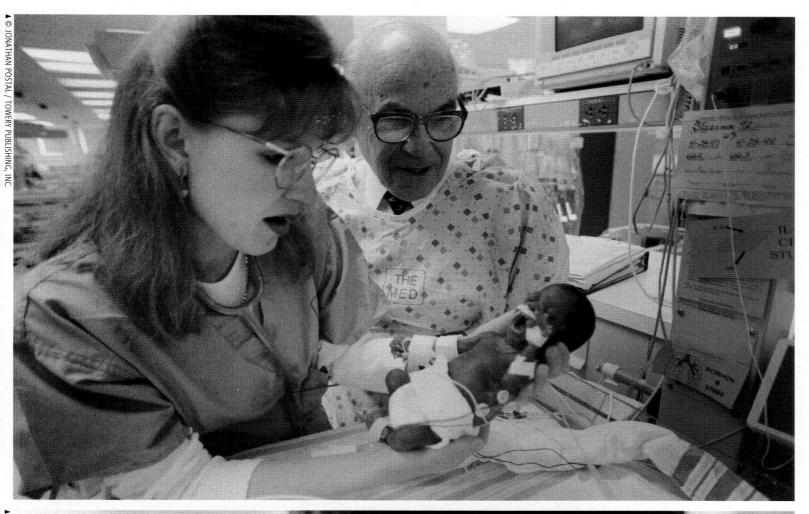

CHALK IT UP TO INNOVATIVE educational programs and numerous artistic outlets: Memphis encourages budding imaginations by providing children opportunities to learn and create.

ITH ITS REPUTATION AS
a growing biomedical and
research center, Memphis
puts its heart into creating affordable
health care programs like the Church
Health Center (BOTTOM), founded by
Methodist minister and physician Dr.
Scott Morris (OPPOSITE BOTTOM). The
center provides medical, optometric,
and dental attention to working
Memphians. The Memphis Children's
Museum (TOP) lets kids play doctor
in its interactive exhibits, and the
nonprofit International Children's
Heart Foundation, established by
Dr. William M. Novick (OPPOSITE
TOP), provides medical care for
children in Third World countries.

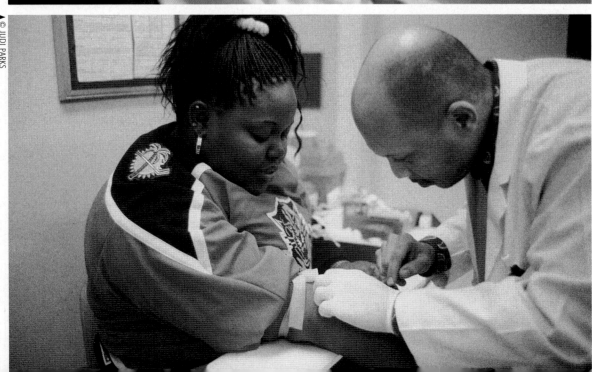

Taking a step in the right direction, the Hope and Healing Center, established by the Church Health Center, ministers to both the body and the spirit. A health club with state-of-the-art equipment and facilities, it promotes spiritual awareness among its more than 3,000 members.

PEDAL POWER PROPELS many Memphians, who opt to wheel around town in style. Selling bikes both big and small, local stores keep avid riders well equipped, while area schools and clubs make sure cyclists of all ages have a good handle on safety.

A REA YOUTHS TAKE THE field in a variety of sports that bolster their competitive spirits and help them get a leg up on life. Memphis is home to several state-of-the-art athletic facilities—such as the Mike Rose Soccer Complex (TOP) and the USA Stadium (OPPOSITE BOTTOM)— where young players from across the nation score goals and hit homers.

BIG WHEELS AND EVEN bigger dreams: Inspiring a little racing fever in fans, drivers rev up for action at Memphis Motorsports Park, which hosts numerous events throughout the year, including the National Hot Rod Association's AutoZone Nationals (BOTTOM).

A DOG DAY AT THE RACES:
Whether vying for breed or
speed, competitors at area
tracks go full circle to be the leader
of the pack. NASCAR drivers watch
for the checkered flag at Memphis
Motorsports Park (OPPOSITE, TOP AND
BOTTOM RIGHT), but at Southland
Greyhound Park (TOP), racing is for
the dogs. In addition to sponsoring
the annual Germantown Charity
Horse Show (OPPOSITE, BOTTOM
LEFT), the Germantown Horse Show
Arena hosts the Running of the
Weenies (BOTTOM), which features
more than 50 hot dogs a year.

AUTHORITY

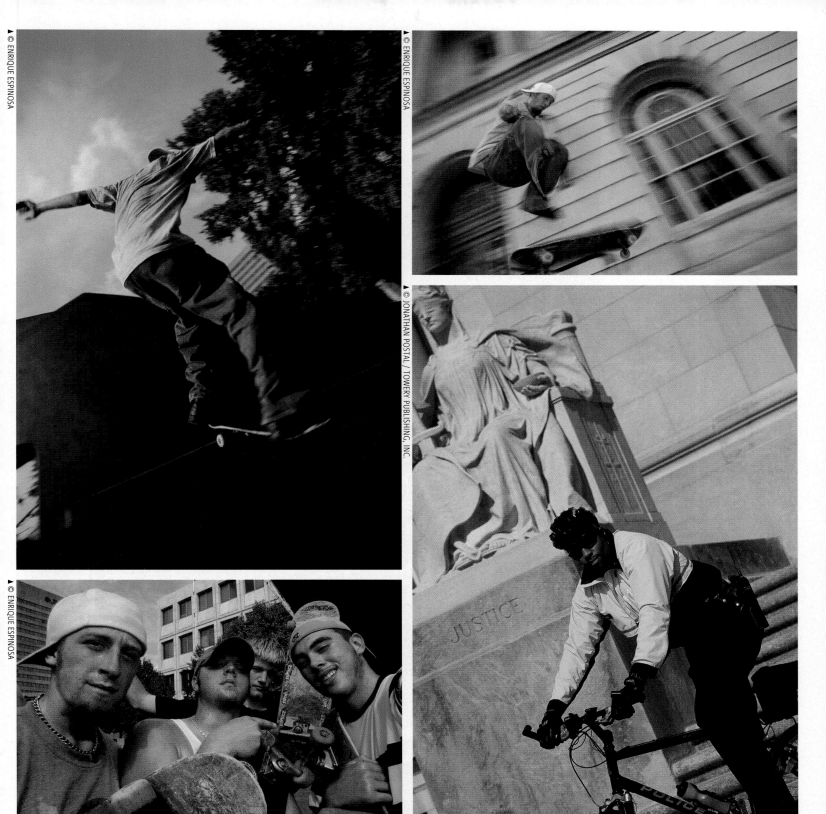

JUSTICE

T RAVERSING THE CITY'S streets and sidewalks, Memphians find fun in monumental proportions. And while justice may be blind, the beat cops who bike through local neighborhoods keep a steady eye on fighting urban crime.

From West Memphis, Arkansas, to DeSoto County in north Mississippi, to the inner-city and suburban schools, education rings in the ears of local kids. Active in the classroom, as well as in extracurricular events, area students are attuned to excellence.

D EGREES OF EXCELLENCE: Memphis' academic institutions encourage concentration and contemplation through rigorous courses. Graduating hundreds of well-prepared students each year are Rhodes College (LEFT), University of Memphis (OPPOSITE TOP), and Christian Brothers University (OPPOSITE BOTTOM).

THE RACE IS AFOOT FOR sports-minded Memphians. Courts and arenas across the city boast a range of athletic competitions on both the collegiate and professional levels—often involving skilled players like international tennis star Monica Seles (OPPOSITE, BOTTOM RIGHT). Local favorites packing in fans range from University of Memphis basketball teams to the Central Hockey League's Riverkings.

MEMPHIS

Local football fans went crazy for the Maniax (ABOVE), Memphis' XFL team, until the beleaguered league folded after only one season. But the crowds still roar loudly for the University of Memphis Tigers (OPPOSITE), who score their touchdowns at the 62,380-seat Liberty Bowl Memorial Stadium, which stands as a tribute to area veterans.

STEP IN THE RING: Boxing and wrestling pack a punch in Memphis, as up-and-coming pugilists train hard in local gyms for the big bout. Jerry "The King" Lawler (OPPOSITE LEFT) arguably reigns as the city's most famous fighter. He started his career wrasslin' in Memphis in 1970, went on to host his own local talk show, and ran for mayor in 1999.

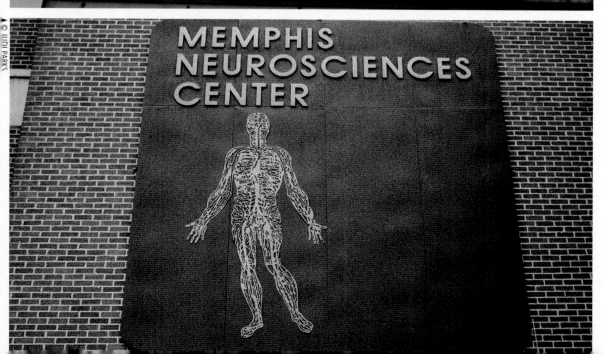

Normal
BEAUTY
SHOP
324·2101

MEMPHIS
NEUROSCIENCES
CENTER

HEADS UP: ICONS OF historic Memphis blend with newer additions as the city reshapes itself for the future. Long-established businesses from old neighborhoods like Normal coexist with modern research facilities such as the Memphis Neurosciences Center at Methodist Hospital. Watching over it all since 1940, the infamous shrunken head has been on display at the Pink Palace Museum, a landmark of the city's past in its own right.

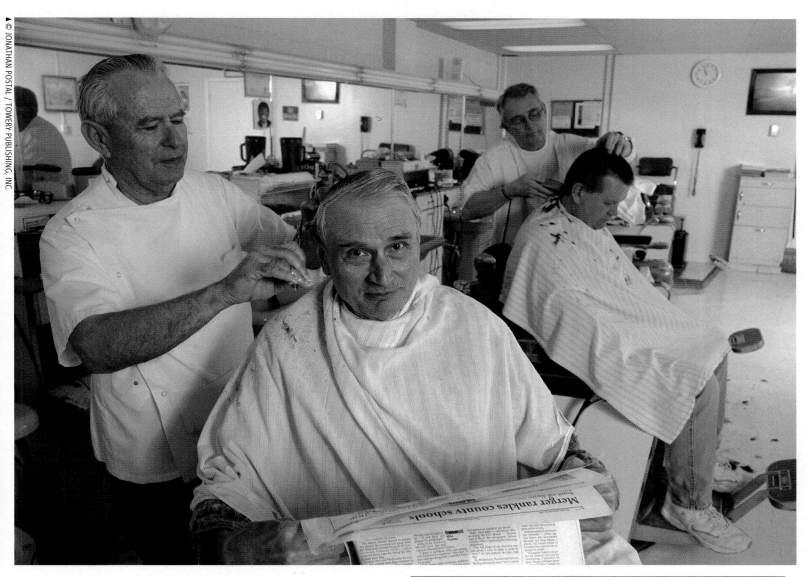

THE CHAIRS, RAZORS, AND red-white-and-blue barber's pole at Mid-City Barber Shop (ABOVE) may be old-fashioned, but the talk often concerns topics straight from the day's newspaper. Discussing current events with a much larger audience, Mike Fleming (OPPOSITE LEFT) hosts *The Mike Fleming Show* on NewsRadio 600WREC, and George Lapides (OPPOSITE RIGHT) airs his views on WHBQ-AM's *Sportstime*, one of the city's most popular sports talk programs.

E LVIS IS A WAY OF LIFE FOR many Memphians living in the King's shadow. Whether donning the gold lamé jacket of his youth or the rhinestone-sparkling jumpsuit of his later years, impersonators around town prove that imitation is the sincerest form of flattery.

D RESSED UP IN STYLIN' duds by their that's-all-right-mamas and don't-cry-daddies, local youngsters get all shook up over Memphis music and start their careers early as rock-a-hula babies.

Every August, Elvis Week attracts thousands of die-hard fans from around the world to pay tribute to the King of Rock and Roll. The event culminates with the Candlelight Vigil, during which devotees—including many impersonators—light candles or erect personal shrines to Elvis' memory.

The University of Memphis area attracts students and locals alike to its many nightspots. A reflection of high-tech culture, Café Apocalypse (ABOVE) lures patrons who get wired not only on its strong coffee, but also via the numerous computer terminals accessing the Internet. A fixture along the nearby Highland Strip since computers were the size of entire rooms, the Highland Cue (OPPOSITE) favors beer and billiards over caffeine and keyboards as means of entertainment.

JOE'S

FEAST PILGRIMS!
ON YOUR EYES
NEW OUR
HOLIDAY ARRIVALS

I T'S A GAS! NEON LIGHTS
up the night in Memphis,
from the spinning Sputnik sign
advertising Joe's Liquors (ABOVE), to
the Overton Park Shell (OPPOSITE,

TOP LEFT) painted by local artist
Burton Callicott, to the towering
Pop Tunes sign (OPPOSITE, TOP
RIGHT) on Summer Avenue.

U NDER THE DIRECTION of President Jeffrey Nesin and Graduate Dean Alonzo Davis (TOP, FROM LEFT), the Memphis College of Art forms the epicenter of the city's vigorous visual arts scene. Longtime contributors such as puppeteer Jimmy Crosthwait (BOTTOM) and young painters like James Stark (OPPOSITE) generate works that demonstrate the creative wealth of the community.

As director of the Memphis Brooks Museum of Art, Kaywin Feldman (THIS PAGE) helps to drive the city's national reputation. Also wielding a world of influence, Kate Gooch (OPPOSITE) serves as president of the Memphis Arts Council, a funding arm for numerous local organizations.

FOUNDED IN 1916, THE Memphis Brooks Museum of Art merges the visual and the performing arts. In addition to showcasing its extensive permanent collection and several traveling exhibitions each year, the museum sponsors film series, concerts, lectures, and dance performances.

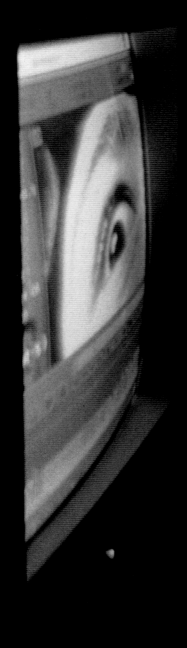

Working in still and moving pictures, local artists William Eggleston (THIS PAGE) and Chris Reyes (OPPOSITE) each have a good eye for visuals. Credited with being the first photographer to make color images an art form, Eggleston has garnered international acclaim by documenting the landscape and people of the Mid-South. Reyes' work in video media has made him one of the city's most sought-after young artists.

Local actors whip audiences into a frenzy with their stage antics. Preformances both dramatic and comical occur weekly in venues such as Playhouse on the Square and Circuit Playhouse—the city's professional repertory venues—and award-winning community troupes like Theatre Memphis and Germantown Community Theatre.

PUTTING THE CITY UP ON the big screen is a role played by many Memphis movie stars. Through his production company Big Broad Guerrilla Monster Inc., John Michael McCarthy (RIGHT) has captured the area's unique personality in films like *Teenage Tupelo* and *The Sore Losers*. Working to promote the city as a film location, Linn Sitler, executive director of the Memphis and Shelby County Film, Tape & Music Commission, and Shelby County Film Commissioner Richard Ranta (OPPOSITE TOP, FROM LEFT) have helped draw top Hollywood talent to the area. Once a resident of nearby Oxford, Mississippi, writer John Grisham (OPPOSITE, BOTTOM LEFT) has set many of his books in Memphis; the film adaptation of his novel *The Firm* brought celebrities like Tom Cruise and Gene Hackman to town. But at least one hometown celebrity turned the tables, taking a little Memphis to Hollywood. Cybill Shepherd (OPPOSITE, BOTTOM RIGHT) began her career in films and starred in two long-running television series.

A LOCAL ICON, WANDA Wilson (LEFT) coproduced and appeared in *The Poor and Hungry*, a digital film about auto theft and cello players that took its title from the bar of the same name, better known as the P&H Cafe. Directed by Craig Brewer (OPPOSITE), the locally produced digiflik won the award for Best Digital Feature at the 2000 Hollywood Film Festival.

GIMME SHELTER: Through Estival Place Life Skills School (TOP), the Metropolitan Inter-Faith Association (MIFA) helps people like Pat Eichols and her son, T.C. Harper (BOTTOM), regain their independence by providing a year of rent-free housing and job training courses. Similarly, the Seek for the Old Path Home for the Homeless (OPPOSITE TOP) provides shelter for some 40 homeless women and their children. Going beyond its normal duties, the home arranged for the Shiloh Baptist Church to pay for the wedding of resident Diane Barne and Lester Jones (OPPOSITE BOTTOM), with Seek for the Old Path founder and director Reverend Barbara Moment officiating.

PLACING A HIGH PREMIUM on reading, the Memphis Literacy Council battles local illiteracy by offering free courses to adults and collecting books for children. Each year through the nonprofit organization, nearly 500 local volunteers help some 700 Memphians to start new chapters in their lives by improving their reading and writing skills.

From historic shops like Burke's Book Store (TOP LEFT) to coffeehouses like the Deliberate Literate (RIGHT), Memphis is a bibliophile's paradise. For those who speak Spanish, the city is home to *La Prensa Latina*, a free weekly for Memphis' growing Hispanic community. Edited by Juan Romo (OPPOSITE), the paper reaches beyond Memphis with a circulation of more than 30,000 readers in four states.

S ERVING SOME OF THE CITY'S best hamburgers, Huey's (LEFT) has become a Midtown institution not only for its menu, but also for its ceiling, which is riddled with thousands of toothpicks shot through straws by diners. Serving up tasty fare in a unique environment, Hattley's Garage (OPPOSITE TOP) occupies a former auto repair shop and gas station, while Wiles-Smith Drug Store (OPPOSITE BOTTOM) is a throwback to the small soda shop lunch counters of the 1950s.

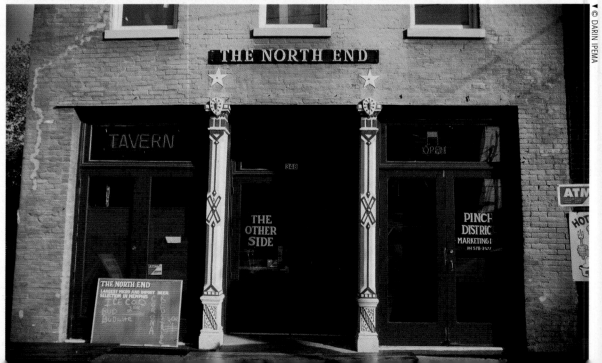

TRAVELING ITS DOWNTOWN route, the Main Street Trolley Line rumbles past many popular eateries in the Pinch District. Serving fruit, frittatas, and coffee, Café Francisco (LEFT) brings the flavor of the Golden Gate City to the Bluff City. Hungry for dessert, diners head to the North End (OPPOSITE BOTTOM) for a plate of its famous hot-fudge pie.

MEMPHIANS START THE day off right with a cuppa joe, the morning paper, and a good breakfast. Located near the University of Memphis, Brother Juniper's (TOP) is regularly voted Best Breakfast in Town in the *Memphis Flyer*'s annual Best of Memphis poll, while the Arcade Restaurant (BOTTOM AND OPPOSITE), a downtown favorite, has been serving Southern-style meals since 1919.

BAR·B·Q RIBS
ChiTTERLING
To.Go PLATE To.Go
BAR·B·Q·ShoULDER
COLD·BEER·CoLD·DRINKS

HOT TAMALES

W HETHER IT'S A HEAPING plate of soul food, a spicy tamale, or just a quick bite to eat, Memphis provides the perfect food for any occasion. Small eateries like Sadie's Soul Food Restaurant (BOTTOM LEFT) have been dishing out hearty home-cooked meals for years, while snack-food companies such as Brim's (OPPOSITE, TOP RIGHT) make sure Memphians have plenty to munch on.

MEMPHIANS GET ALL FIRED up for both deliciously spicy Vietnamese stir-fry and works of art forged from metal. For a taste of the Orient, Memphians visit Pho Pasteur or one of the many other excellent Vietnamese, Thai, or Chinese restaurants in the city. Located on the banks of the Mississippi River, the National Ornamental Metal Museum is the only museum in the United States dedicated exclusively to the exhibition and preservation of fine metalwork.

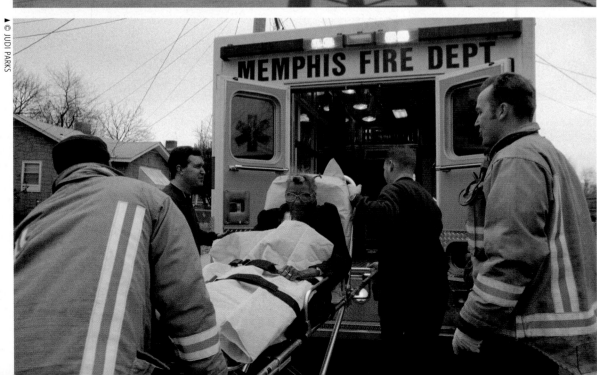

Keeping Memphis and its surrounds safe from blazes, area fire departments deploy the latest equipment and regularly conduct intense training. Founded in 1846, the Memphis Fire Department maintains 52 stations around town, with more than 1,600 firefighters on call.

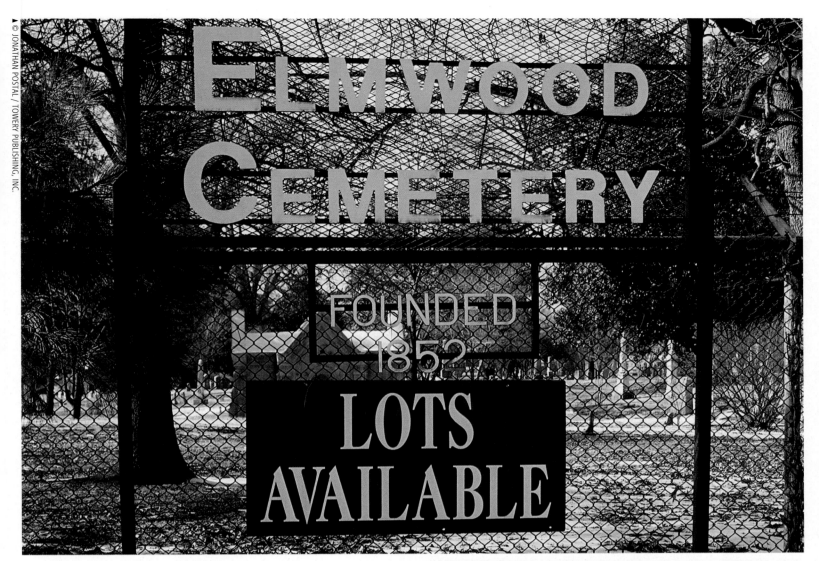

ELMWOOD CEMETERY

FOUNDED 1852

LOTS AVAILABLE

S TRAIGHT FROM THE HEARSE'S mouth: Death is a grave matter in Memphis, but many locals work to delay passing on to their final resting places for as long as possible. John W. "Jay" Biggert (OPPOSITE TOP)—a former smoker himself— crusades against deadly cigarettes by posting signs reading "Tobacco Kills" all over the Memphis region. Once a haven for local and national death metal bands and alternative acts, the Last Place on Earth (OPPO-SITE, BOTTOM RIGHT) held its last show on Earth in June 2001.

JAMES W SCRUGGS
PVT
US ARMY
WORLD WAR II
JAN 1 1921
JUN 11 1989

ABE
WILKINS JR
PVT
US ARMY
KOREA
FEB 13 1932
DEC 16 1988

UNKNOWN SOLDIER
CONFEDERATE STATES ARMY

PETE REPEAT

MILITARY MIGHT FROM the past to the present is on display throughout the region. From historic grave markers to the men and women stationed at the Naval Support Activity Mid-South base in Millington, the armed forces play an active role in the area.

BUILDING A BETTER MOUSE-trap: Rounding up rodents is a job best left to the professionals, and the folks at Atomic Pest Control on Elvis Presley Boulevard have no doubt run more than a few rats out of town since the company opened in the 1950s.

In Shelby County, junkyards can be treasure troves, rusting signs become rustic art, and automobiles are elevated to the level of advertisements. J.B. Curtis (TOP) opened the J.B. Curtis Trading Post in 1958, and today, his collection of odds and ends covers a full acre in Munford.

S PANNING SEVERAL NEIGH-
borhoods in the center of
Memphis, Midtown includes
a mix of the everyday and the exotic.
A 65-foot row of miniature houses,
stores, and gazebos—created by local
metalsmith Jill Brogdon (OPPOSITE,
BOTTOM LEFT)—adorns the Cooper

Street train trestle and marks the
entrance to the trendy Cooper-Young
district. At Flashback, proprietor
Millett Vance (BOTTOM RIGHT) sells
retro furnishings and clothes, while
Anderton's (OPPOSITE, BOTTOM
RIGHT) serves oysters and cocktails
in a time-capsule atmosphere.

HOMEGROWN BUSINESSES like the Lake Cormorant, Mississippi-based Gutterman Co. give Memphians a lift as they put the finishing touches—no matter how small—on their cozy abodes.

WIMMING POOLS AND
sidewalks, porches and car-
ports dot the Mid-South's
tree-lined neighborhoods. Whether
a historic home in the middle of the
city or a new house out in the suburbs, Memphis residences not only
reflect a diversity of architectural
styles, but also provide comfort
and splendor in varying degrees
(PAGES 250-253).

© DON REBER

LIVING IN VIEW OF THE Mississippi River is the toast of the town. Located on Mud Island, Harbortown (TOP) has a unique community atmosphere despite its proximity to the urban center. Farther down the river, the South Bluffs neighborhood (OPPOSITE BOTTOM) overlooks Riverside Drive and Tom Lee Park, while further inland, Victorian Village (OPPOSITE TOP) contains clusters of some of the city's unique and most elaborate residences.

© DAN BALL

MEMPHIS

Take a hike: Perfect for a leisurely stroll in the afternoon or an invigorating jog in the morning, trails in Harbortown (top) treat walkers to a scenic view of the Mississippi River, while the Riverwalk (opposite) runs through downtown, along the South Bluffs, and around to Tom Lee Park.

MEMPHIS MARTYRS

In August, 1878, fear of death caused a panic during which 30,000 of 50,000 Memphians fled this bluff city. By October, the epidemic of yellow fever killed 4,204 of 6,000 Caucasians and 946 of 14,000 Negroes who stayed. With some outside help, citizens of all races and walks of life, recognizing their common plight in a devastated, bankrupt community, tended the sick and buried the dead. As a result many of them lost their lives, becoming in their service to mankind.

WHETHER LIVING TRIBUTES or memorials carved in stone, reminders of Memphis' tumultuous history abound. Located on the South Bluffs, Martyrs Park (ABOVE) commemorates the legacy of the many locals who fought the devastating yellow fever epidemic during the late 1800s. Since 1988, Jacqueline Smith (OPPOSITE) has been protesting the conversion of the Lorraine Motel—the site of Dr. Martin Luther King Jr.'s assassination—into a museum.

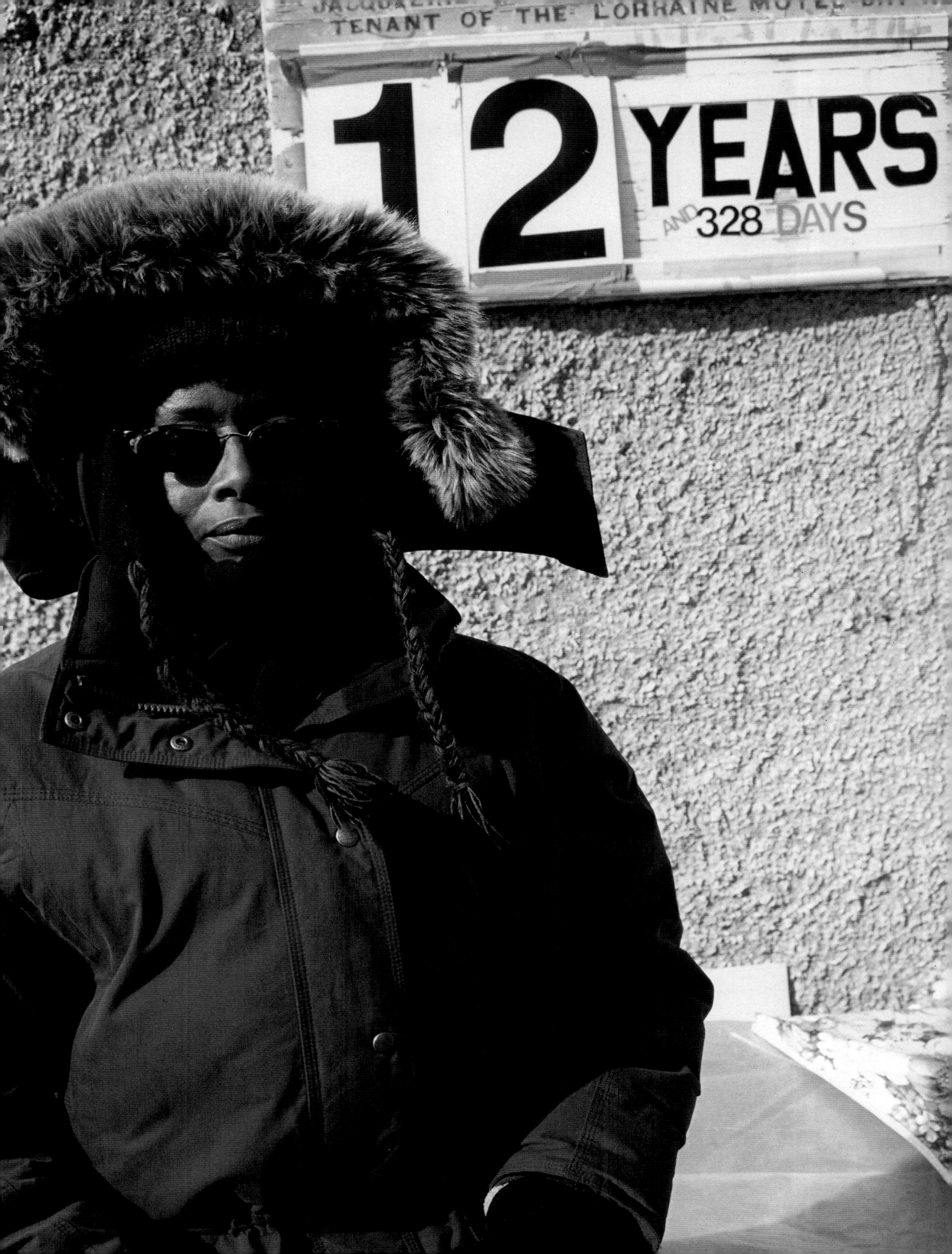
TENANT OF THE LORRAINE MOTEL
12 YEARS
AND 328 DAYS

On April 4, 1968, Dr. Martin Luther King Jr.—in Memphis for the sanitation workers' strike—was shot and killed just outside his room at the Lorraine Motel. Occupying the historic building today, the National Civil Rights Museum honors the sacrifices made by King and many others, as well as the strides being made by present generations, with interactive walk-through installations and exhibits by African-American artists.

© ERNEST C. WITHERS

FOLLOWING DR. MARTIN Luther King Jr.'s assassination, thousands of African-Americans walked down Main Street in a peaceful show of unity. As vice chairman of Community On the Move for Equality, Reverend H. Ralph Jackson (OPPOSITE RIGHT) helped organize many such marches. Today, this spirit of remembrance lives on in Memphians like Samuel H. Pieh (OPPOSITE LEFT), who served as dialect coach for and acted in Steven Spielberg's historical film *Amistad.*

DELIVERING THE FUTURE 263

264   MEMPHIS

On March 28, 1968, African-American sanitation workers, on strike, for equal pay and better treatment, convened at Clayborn Temple for a march through downtown. Organized by locally based Community On the Move for Equality and the nationally active American Federation of State, County, and Municipal Employees, an estimated 20,000 people marched down Main Street carrying signs reading "I AM A MAN"—a phrase that came to symbolize the local civil rights movement.

DADDY, I WANT TO BE FREE

EMERGENCY SQUAD

POLICE 81 CITY OF MEMPHIS

Freedom and equality were always the themes and goals of the Memphis civil rights movement, from the quiet protests in the early 1960s (ABOVE) to the first anniversary of Dr. Martin Luther King Jr.'s assassination, which closed the decade by bringing thousands of mourners, along with members of the national media, to Memphis (OPPOSITE).

FROM THE CITY TO THE suburbs, women are moving to the front ranks of the Memphis area's judicial and law enforcement agencies. In 1998, local attorney Dorothy "Dottie" Pounders (TOP) became the first woman elected president of the Memphis Bar Association, and Maria Alexander (OPPOSITE TOP) upholds the law as Germantown's first female chief of police. Such inclusion extends to African-Americans as well. Memphis swore in its first African-American judge, Ben Hooks (BOTTOM, FAR RIGHT), in September 1965, more than 15 years after the first African-American cops—including (OPPOSITE BOTTOM, FROM LEFT) Wendell Robinson and Ernest Withers—began patrolling the streets. Withers is perhaps known better as a photographer than as an officer: Armed with a camera instead of a pistol, he captured some of the city's most historic civil rights moments on film.

MEMPHIS PROVIDES MANY opportunities to celebrate diversity and individuality, from the Liberty Bowl Parade down Beale Street (TOP) to the full calendar of festivals honoring the city's multifaceted cultural makeup.

MEMPHIS' MANY RELIGIONS are as varied as their solemn ceremonies. Hundreds of parishioners attend mass at Immaculate Conception Cathedral (TOP), while at Beth Sholom Synagogue, Rabbi Peter R. Light (OPPOSITE BOTTOM) serves part of the city's growing Jewish community. At the Ngoc Phuoc Temple (BOTTOM AND OPPOSITE TOP) in Midtown, members of the Vietnamese Buddhist Association of Memphis and Vicinity come from all over the city to study the Buddha's teachings.

Hands reaching for heaven, faithful Memphians react to spiritual fervor in very different ways, resulting in a wealth of local religious denominations. The city claims almost 2,000 houses of worship, and three of the largest Protestant denominations—Church of God in Christ, the Christian Methodist Episcopal Church, and the Cumberland Presbyterian Church—are based in Memphis.

TAKE ME TO THE RIVER: Religion flows through Memphis' history and its people. Since 1977, the Reverend Al Green (THIS PAGE)—well known for secular songs like "Let's Stay Together" and "Love & Happiness"—has ministered to the soul at the Full Gospel Tabernacle Church in Whitehaven.

A T THE CROSSROADS: TRAVELERS in East Memphis can't miss the immense white-steel crosses standing tall at Bellevue Baptist Church. With the central cross rising some 150 feet high and the two flanking it measuring 120 feet high, the installation can be seen from as far away as Germantown Parkway. Devotees of Elvis Presley once crossed the country to hold their Circle of Friendship services on his ranch near Walls, Mississippi (ABOVE).

THE COUNTRYSIDE AROUND Memphis branches out into a mixture of natural beauty and urban upbuild. As commuters make the daily drive from East Memphis to downtown, they pass through a range of lanscapes, from peaceful morning fields to stripped-bare construction zones to frustrating traffic jams (PAGES 280-285).

Gʀᴏᴡɪɴɢ ꜰʀᴏᴍ ᴀ sɪᴍᴘʟᴇ settlement into a thriving community, Germantown mixes big-city amenities—including modern shopping complexes and the expansive Germantown Public Library (ᴛᴏᴘ)—with loads of suburban charm. At the heart of the town's historical district stands the old Germantown Depot (ᴏᴘᴘᴏsɪᴛᴇ), as well as the Germantown Commissary (ʙᴏᴛᴛᴏᴍ ʟᴇꜰᴛ), which serves up racks of ribs in an old general store.

WITH TRAIN TRACKS running through their storied histories, the small towns surrounding Memphis offer a wealth of unexpected treasures (PAGES 290 AND 291). Antiques are big business in Collierville (TOP, CENTER, AND OPPOSITE), where reminders of the community's railroad origins adorn the town square and create an air of Southern tradition. Tunica, Mississippi, erected the Millennium Clock (BOTTOM) on a section of track to honor the railroad's significant impact on the city's prosperity.

© STEVE DAVIS

SOUTHAVEN
HOME OF THE CHARGERS
CAPEWOOD PL.
GREENBROOK PKWY.
PLAY STREET
SPEED LIMIT 5

H OPING FOR BIRDIES OR par or the elusive hole in one, avid golfers young and old tee off at public and private links throughout the Mid-South. One of the oldest stops on the PGA tour, the annual FedEx St. Jude Classic (BOTTOM) brings some of the country's top golfers—along with national sports media and some 150,000 spectators—to take a swing at Southwind Golf Course.

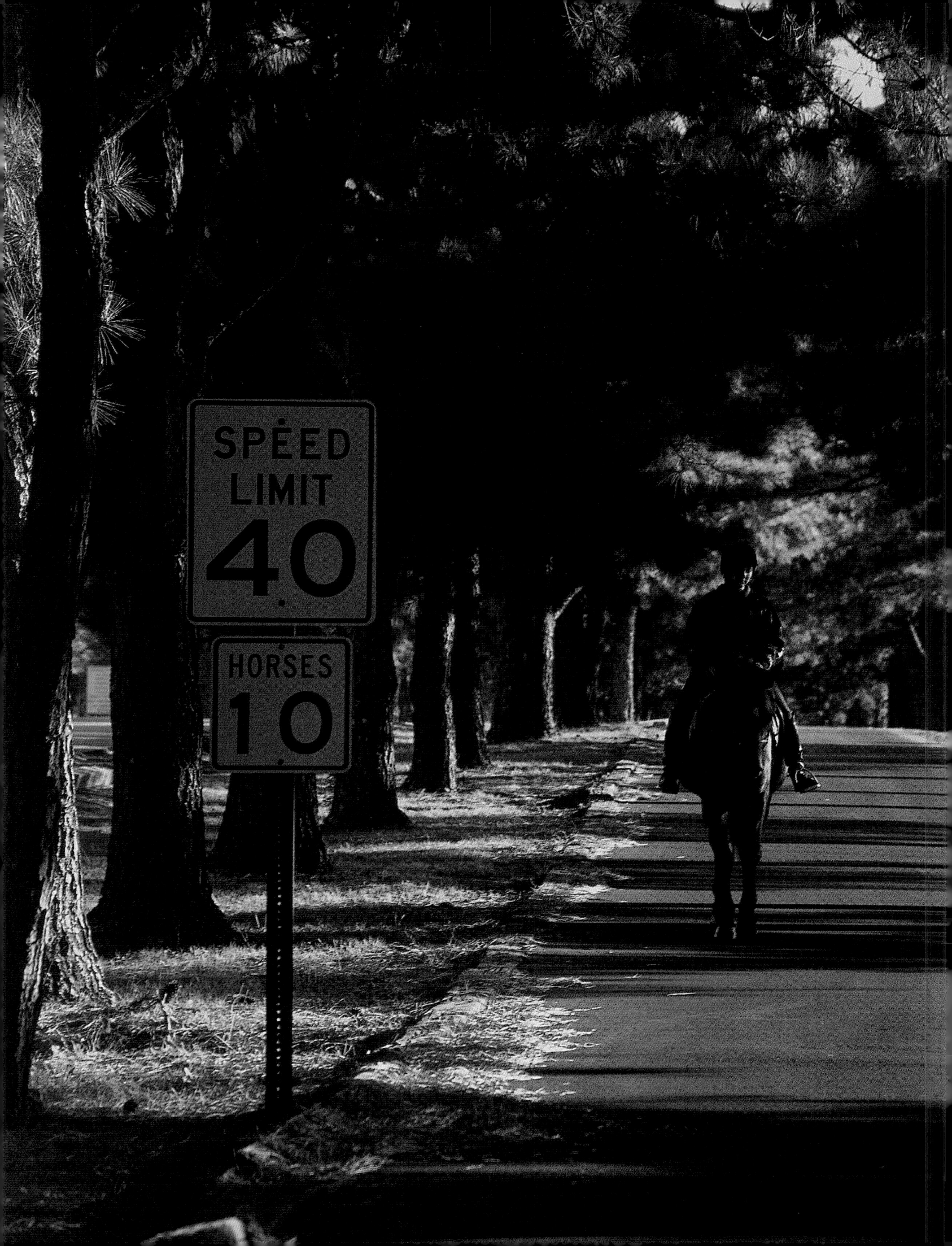
SPEED
LIMIT
40
HORSES
10

From the Carousel Court at Wolfchase Galleria (TOP AND BOTTOM RIGHT) to the streets of Germantown, no one hoofs it when a horse is around. A very neighborly place, Shelby County has more horses per capita than any other county in the United States.

I T'S A SCREAM: LOCATED ON the Mid-South Fairgrounds, Libertyland gives visitors the freedom to choose from a multitude of rides, games, and events. One of its most popular attractions, the Zippin' Pippin (TOP) was built in 1912 and today stands as the oldest wooden rollercoaster in the country. Each September, the Mid-South Fair (OPPOSITE) adds to the fun with 10 days of concerts, contests, and lots of food.

Rushin' roulette: Serious and leisure gamblers alike hurry south of Memphis to place their bets at the casinos in Tunica County, Mississippi, where the sparkling marquee lights and multicolored collection of chips brighten up the night. The annual Mid-South Fair (opposite) offers its nearly 500,000 visitors a unique view of Memphis from atop its brilliantly lit Ferris wheel.

DESPITE SCORCHING HEAT and occasional droughts, agriculture remains a growth industry in the Mid-South, with soybeans (ABOVE) and rice (OPPOSITE) two of the most profitable cash crops.

T HE OLD ADAGE "IF YOU don't like the weather, wait a while" holds true for Memphis, where deluges can interrupt sunny days and fall turns abruptly to winter. From its offices at Agricenter International in East Memphis, the National Weather Service (ABOVE) forecasts weather throughout the Mid-South, predicting precipitation and issuing storm warnings for North Mississippi, West Tennessee, Northeast Arkansas, and the Missouri Bootheel.

FALL

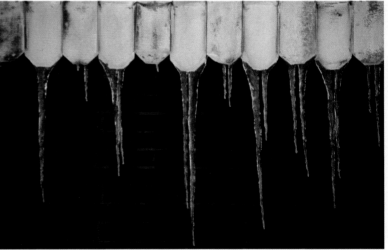

ACH SEASON OF THE YEAR casts its own spell on the Mid-South. Statues at the Memphis Brooks Museum of Art (TOP LEFT AND OPPOSITE TOP) stand as allegories for spring, summer, and fall, but only Elvis can reveal how cold-hearted winter can be.

Making the most of the weather, Memphis immerses itself in winter. While some take to the hills on their sleds, many Memphians take the annual Polar Bear Plunge into Patriot Lake at Shelby Farms—then warm up in hot tubs or with hot chocolate—to raise money for the Special Olympics. In January 2001, local police officers also took a dip, riding their bicycles into the icy waters to benefit St. Jude Children's Research Hospital.

Autumn in Memphis is a walk in the park. From Overton Park in Midtown to the Wolf River Nature Area (ABOVE AND OPPOSITE) and Shelby Farms in East Memphis, the city's parks provide perfect opportunities to enjoy the crisp weather and scenic vistas.

Rollin' on the river: The Mississippi sees constant activity on its waves and along its shores, whether it's busy with commercial or recreational endeavors. With the river as the cornerstone of a storied history of success, Memphis continues its quest to deliver the future.

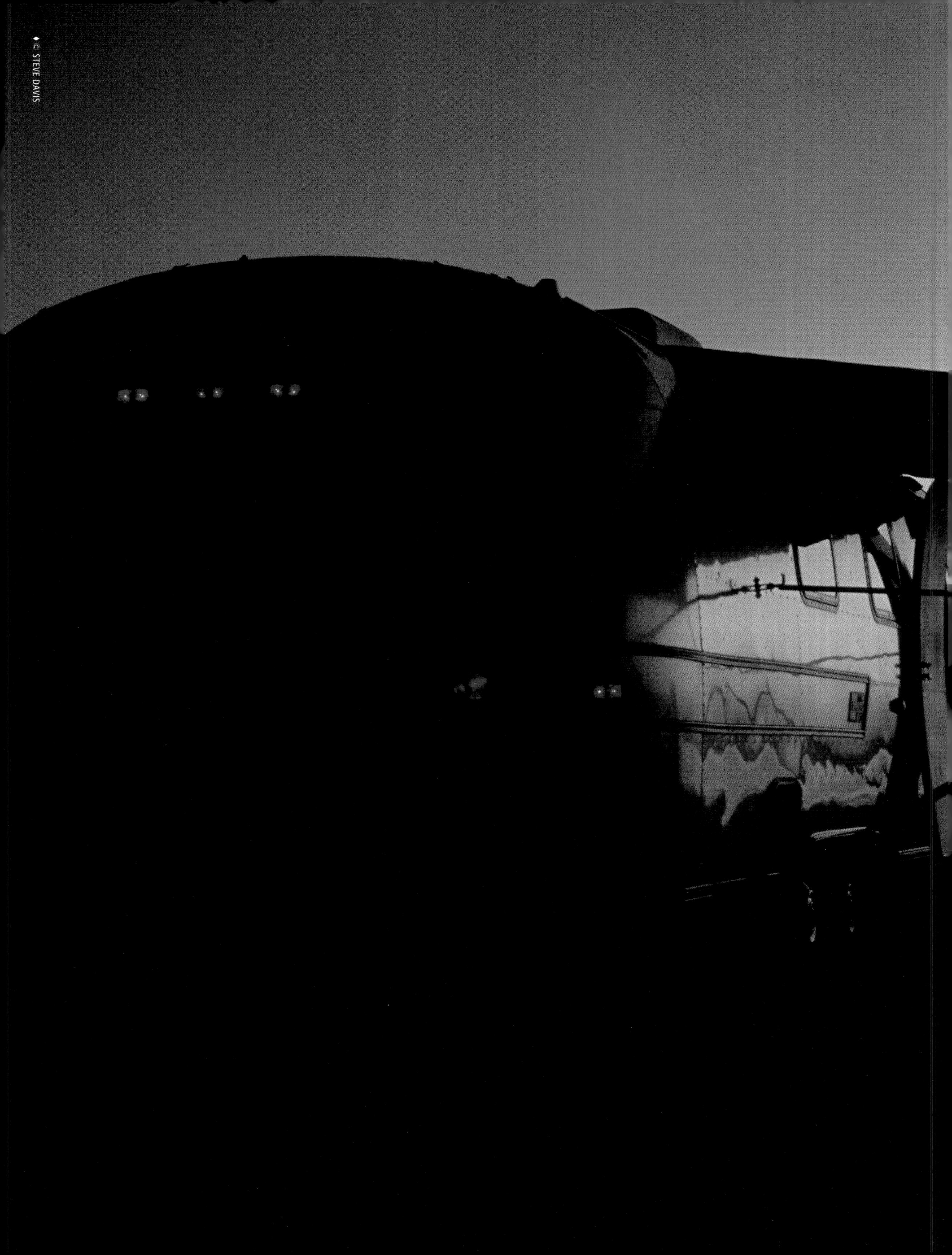

MEMPHIS

Profiles in Excellence

A look at the corporations, businesses, professional groups, and community service organizations that have made this book possible. Their stories—offering an informal chronicle of the local business community—are arranged according to the date they were established in the Memphis area.

ALLEN & O'HARA, INC. ▲ APAC TENNESSEE, INC. MEMPHIS DIVISION ▲ API PHOTOGRAPHERS/FILM & VIDEO ▲ AUTOZONE ▲ BAKER, DONELSON, BEARMAN & CALDWELL ▲ BAPTIST COLLEGE OF HEALTH SCIENCES ▲ BAPTIST MEMORIAL HEALTH CARE ▲ BAXTER HEALTHCARE CORPORATION ▲ BELLSOUTH ▲ BELZ ENTERPRISES ▲ BILL HEARD CHEVROLET ▲ BORDERS BOOKS ▲ BOSTON BASKIN CANCER GROUP ▲ BOYLE INVESTMENT COMPANY ▲ BROTHER ▲ BUCKEYE TECHNOLOGIES INC. ▲ THE BUYER'S AGENT ▲ CATHOLIC SCHOOLS OF THE DIOCESE OF MEMPHIS ▲ CHRISTIAN BROTHERS UNIVERSITY/CHRISTIAN BROTHERS HIGH SCHOOL ▲ CLARK & CLARK ▲ CLEAR CHANNEL COMMUNICATIONS ▲ COLEMAN-ETTER, FONTAINE REALTORS ▲ COMPASS FINANCIAL ADVISORS, LLC ▲ COORS ▲ CUSTOMIZED STAFFING SERVICES ▲ DREXEL CHEMICAL COMPANY ▲ DUNAVANT ENTERPRISES, INC. ▲ ELVIS PRESLEY'S GRACELAND ▲ ENSAFE INC. ▲ EXHIBIT-A, INC. ▲ EXPANETS ▲ FAXONGILLIS HOMES, INC. ▲ FEDEX CORPORATION ▲ FLINN BROADCASTING COMPANY ▲ FRED L. DAVIS INSURANCE AGENCY ▲ GOLD STRIKE CASINO RESORT ▲ GRACE-ST. LUKES EPISCOPAL SCHOOL ▲ GRAFCO, INC. ▲ GRAPHIC SYSTEMS, INC. ▲ GUARDSMARK, INC. ▲ HUTCHISON SCHOOL ▲ INTERNATIONAL CHILDREN'S HEART FOUNDATION ▲ INTERNATIONAL PAPER ▲ JAMESON GIBSON CONSTRUCTION COMPANY, INC. ▲ THE KROGER COMPANY ▲ LEDIC MANAGEMENT GROUP, INC. ▲ LEGACY WEALTH MANAGEMENT ▲ THE MALLORY GROUP INC. ▲ MEDNIKOW JEWELERS ▲ MEMPHIS AREA TEACHERS' CREDIT UNION ▲ MEMPHIS CONVENTION & VISITORS BUREAU ▲ THE MEMPHIS GROUP, INC. ▲ MEMPHIS LIGHT, GAS AND WATER ▲ MEMPHIS UNIVERSITY SCHOOL ▲ METHODIST HEALTHCARE ▲ MID-SOUTH COMMUNITY COLLEGE ▲ MID-SOUTH MARKING SYSTEMS ▲ MID-SOUTH SPECIALTIES, INC. ▲ NATIONAL BANK OF COMMERCE ▲ NEW HORIZONS COMPUTER LEARNING CENTERS ▲ NORTHWEST AIRLINES ▲ OAK HALL ▲ THE PALLET FACTORY, INC. ▲ PATTON & TAYLOR ▲ PRICEWATERHOUSECOOPERS ▲ PUTT-PUTT FAMILY PARK ▲ PYRAMID LOGISTICS GROUP ▲ RADISSON HOTEL MEMPHIS ▲ RHODES COLLEGE ▲ RUNNING PONY PRODUCTIONS ▲ SAM'S TOWN TUNICA ▲ SCHERING-PLOUGH HEALTHCARE PRODUCTS ▲ SHARP MANUFACTURING COMPANY OF AMERICA ▲ SHEA-HUBBARD ENT CLINIC, PC ▲ SHELBY COUNTY GOVERNMENT ▲ SMITH & NEPHEW ORTHOPAEDICS ▲ SOUTHWEST TENNESSEE COMMUNITY COLLEGE ▲ ST. AGNES ACADEMY-ST. DOMINIC SCHOOL ▲ SAINT BENEDICT AT AUBURNDALE ▲ ST. FRANCIS HOSPITAL ▲ ST. JUDE CHILDREN'S RESEARCH HOSPITAL ▲ SUMMERFIELD ASSOCIATES, INC. ▲ SUPREME DISTRIBUTION SERVICES ▲ TOWERY PUBLISHING, INC. ▲ TUNICA CONVENTION AND VISITORS BUREAU ▲ UNION PLANTERS BANK ▲ UNIVERSITY OF TENNESSEE HEALTH SCIENCE CENTER ▲ UT MEDICAL GROUP, INC. ▲ WALKER-J-WALKER, INC. ▲ WONDERS ▲ WRIGHT MEDICAL GROUP, INC.

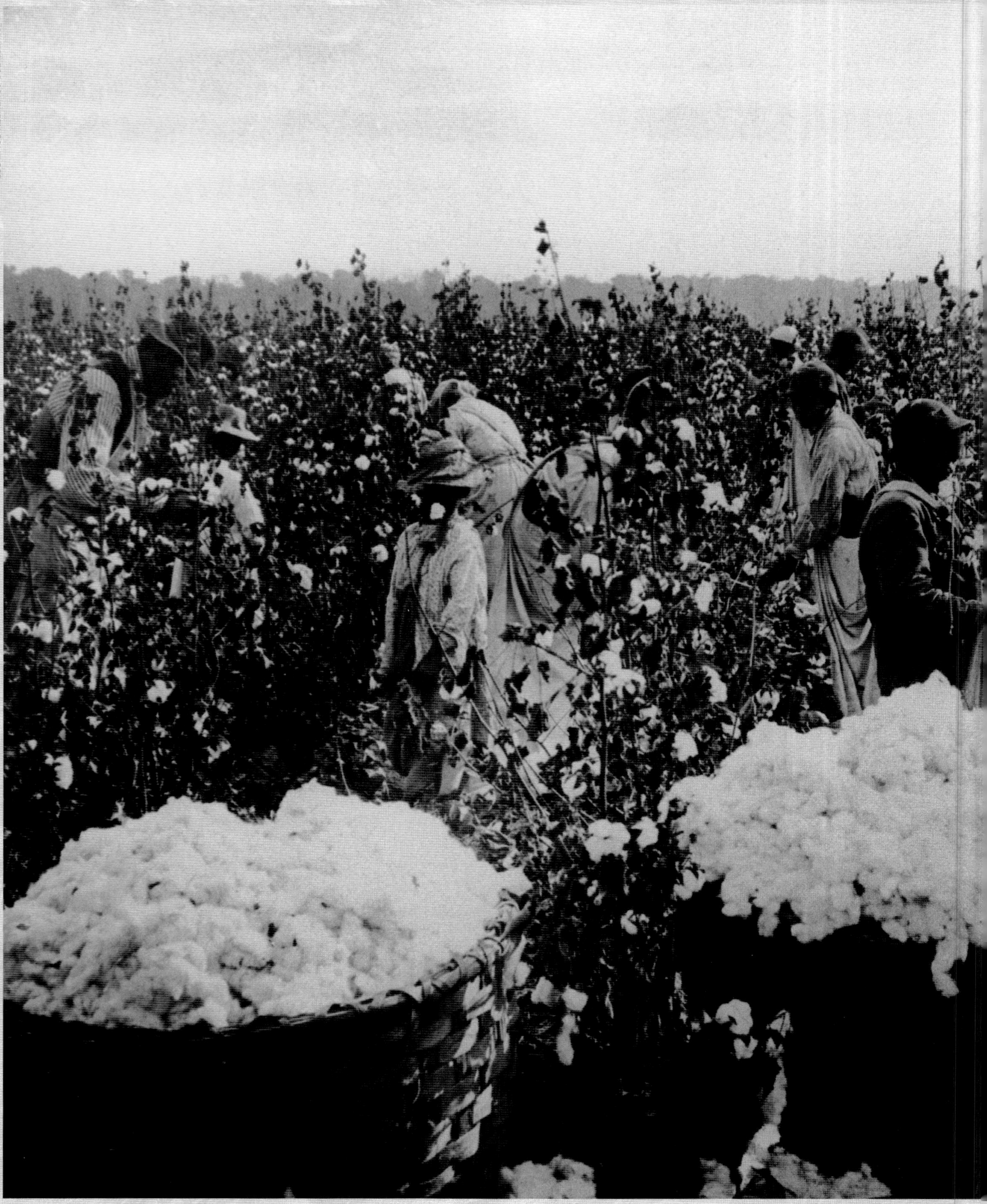

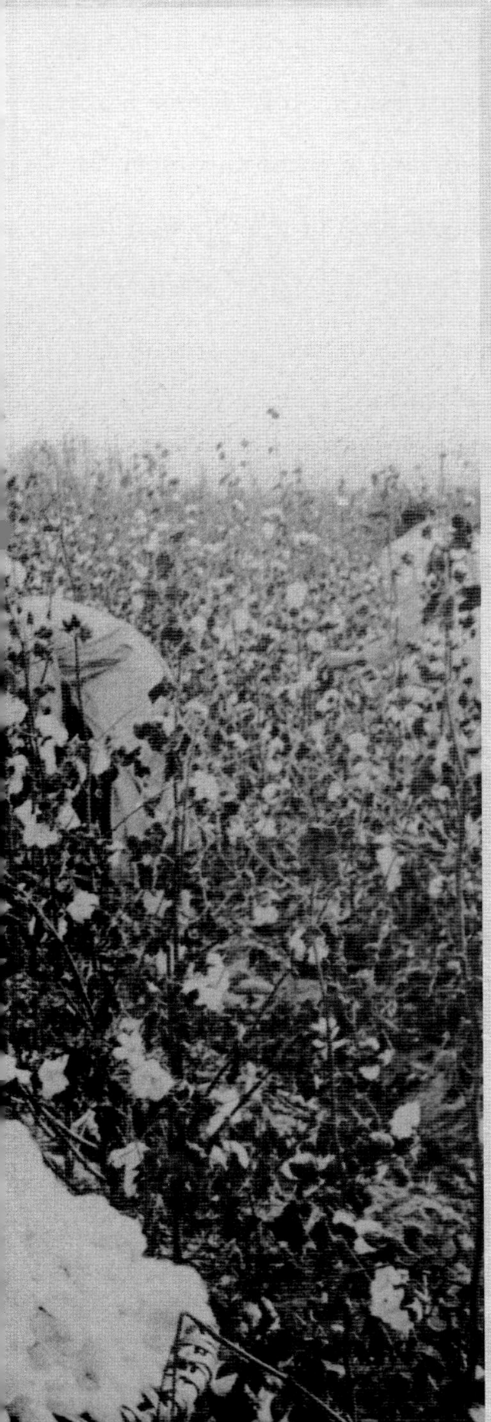

1820–1905

1820 *Shelby County Government*

1851 *Catholic Schools of the Diocese of Memphis*

1851 *St. Agnes Academy-St. Dominic School*

1859 *Oak Hall*

1869 *Union Planters Bank*

1871 *Christian Brothers University/Christian Brothers High School*

1873 *National Bank of Commerce*

1883 *The Kroger Company*

1883 *BellSouth*

1891 *Mednikow Jewelers*

1893 *Memphis University School*

1899 *FaxonGillis Homes, Inc.*

1902 *Hutchison School*

orking for You in Ways You Never Imagined is more than the motto for Shelby County Government. It is also the reality. That is because county government is the only umbrella government that serves every citizen within its borders, regardless of whether they live in Memphis, Germantown, Lakeland, Millington, Collierville, Arlington, Bartlett, or unincorporated areas in this Tennessee county. This responsibility provides elected officers

with the challenge not only of providing services for such diverse needs, but also of educating citizens about the role and responsibilities of county government and its impact on the future of Memphis and its surrounding areas. Shelby County Government is a constitutional government, created by the Tennessee Constitution, and the elected offices of Shelby County are also created by the state constitution, which make them independent and autonomous within the county structure.

The Scope of Services

When citizens of Shelby County drive on county roads, walk into safe buildings, eat in clean restaurants, or send their children to public schools, they are witnessing the county government as it plays a role in all aspects of their lives.

Core services of the county government include education for both Memphis and Shelby County schools; the criminal justice system, including the sheriff, juvenile court, jail, and prisons; libraries; the massive Shelby Farms recreational area; advocacy programs for senior citizens, veterans, and victims of crime; health services, including clinics, nursing homes, and The Med, with its world-class burn, trauma, and newborn centers; land use and zoning; economic development; roads and bridges; human services, including HeadStart, housing, pretrial services, public defenders, and family planning; and emergency services,

including 911, ambulances, and fire department services.

The full-time elected officers who implement these services are Mayor Jim Rout, elected as the county's third mayor in 1994; Sheriff A.C. Gilless; Rita Clark, assessor of property; Bob Patterson, trustee; Tom Leatherwood, register; Jayne Creson, county clerk; and Chris Turner, Jimmy Moore, Bill Key, and Chris Thomas, court clerks for General Sessions, Circuit, Criminal, and Probate courts, respectively.

The 13 members of the Board of Commissioners, part-time elected officials, serve as the county legislative body. Commissioners include Walter Bailey Jr., Julian Bolton, Marilyn Loeffel, Bridget Chisholm, Tommy Hart, Morris Fair, Clair Vander Schaaf, Chairman James Ford, Michael Hooks, Cleo Kirk, Linda Rendtorff, Buckner Wellford, and Tom Moss.

When created on May 1, 1820, Shelby County was named for Revolutionary War hero Isaac Shelby, and the county has weathered the trials and tribulations associated with the nation through its history. The structure of today's county government was established in 1976 to improve efficiency and modernize services.

The Power of Education

In 1870, the quarterly court addressed the education needs of Shelby County youngsters, opening the first county-funded school in January 1871. Today, the commitment to educating the county's children is still the first priority of county government.

Every penny of sales tax and half of every property tax dollar are spent on schools in both the county and the city systems, with funding divided proportionately based on the number of students in each system. In the past decade, county government has invested about

FRONT ROW FROM LEFT: MARILYN LOEFFEL, LINDA RENDTORFF, MORRIS FAIR, WALTER BAILEY JR., AND JULIAN BOLTON. MIDDLE ROW FROM LEFT: BRIDGET CHISHOLM, CHAIRMAN JAMES FORD, AND MICHAEL HOOKS. BOTTOM ROW FROM LEFT: CLEO KIRK, CLAIR VANDER SCHAAF, TOM MOSS, TOMMY HART, AND BUCKNER WELLFORD.

$1.1 billion in funding for operations of the two public school systems and about $500 million for construction.

There are more than 160,800 youngsters in grades kindergarten through 12 in the two public school systems, but funding is the same for every school student, regardless of which system that child is in. Rout introduced the first master plan for the city and county schools' capital needs, a $655 million investment in schools over eight years.

The Importance of the Arts

Shelby County has been the single largest contributor to the Memphis Arts Council for some 20 years, and has inspired a number of new programs in the cultural arts. The UrbanArt Commission was created to improve urban design and to add public art to construction projects and neighborhoods. Play It Again Memphis is an award-winning initiative that refurbishes used musical instruments and recycles them into the hands of student musicians in the public schools. Shelby County also created the new Music Commission and the Film and Tape Commission.

A funding partnership with Memphis resulted in a $1 million loan to construct the Smithsonian Institution's only permanent exhibit outside the Northeast, the Rock 'n' Soul Museum housed in the Gibson Guitar plant, which pays tribute to Memphis' rich musical heritage. The county also provides grants to such projects as the Germantown Arts Alliance, Memphis Arts Festival, Memphis Blues Foundation, and Playhouse on the Square.

The Regional Framework

Rout's second term as mayor has been spent working toward the development of a regional blueprint to set priorities for the Memphis region for the 21st century, particularly in the area of jobs growth, which has been a focus of his administration. Since taking office, Rout has led record growth in economic development with $7 billion in business investment in five years.

This growth has resulted in Shelby County's average per capita income not only reaching the state and national income averages for the first time, but surpassing them. Numerous national magazines have hailed the economic progress that has been recorded, citing milestones such as the FedEx World Headquarters, FedEx Technology Center, UPS Regional Center, International Paper Operations Center, St. Jude Children's Research Hospital, Northwest Airlines expansion, and KLM's direct route to Europe.

Economic development is the centerpiece of two consensus-building programs that Rout developed with the City of Memphis and the Memphis Area Chamber of Commerce: Alliance for Regional Excellence and Memphis 2005. The alliance is a historic effort to develop the first blueprint for the three-state (Tennessee, Arkansas, and Mississippi) region. It was built on the foundation of Memphis 2005, a 10-year, strategic plan for economic development that set targets for private business investment, workforce development, minority business, and international business.

As part of this philosophy, Rout and the Board of Commissioners have made important investments in the regional quality of life, including the Mike Rose Soccer Complex; award-winning AutoZone Park; the Memphis Zoo and Lichterman Nature Center expansion; Soulsville; and a new performing arts center.

All of these accomplishments and initiatives have earned Shelby County the well-deserved reputation as one of the nation's most entrepreneurial governments, and clearly it is working for county citizens in ways they never imagined.

ith the world changing rapidly around Memphis' families, education has had to change as well. There are new discoveries to be taught and new technologies to implement. But as schools reengineer themselves to meet these new demands, many are making a special effort not to lose sight of the traditional foundations that have ensured a strong education for centuries. Catholic Schools of the Diocese of Memphis are shining examples of this twofold approach.

"Since the 1800s, the Catholic schools in West Tennessee have been embracing the latest in academic standards in a decidedly traditional setting," says Dr. Mary McDonald, the system's superintendent. "Our mission is to prepare students for a strong role in their church and their society. Today, Catholic schools make a difference because they educate students who graduate with an excellent academic background, as well as a strong foundation in the perennial truths of the Catholic faith."

A Strong Foundation

In the Diocese of Memphis, there are 17 elementary schools, three combined middle and high schools, one high school, two unit schools, and one special school. These schools are a mix of diocesan, parochial, and private entities.

The elementary school curriculum in the Catholic system includes the core subjects necessary to help students build a firm foundation on which to base their further studies. The elementary schools also provide enrichment opportunities such as drama, forensics,

MORE THAN 500 TEACHERS IN THE CATHOLIC SCHOOLS OF THE DIOCESE OF MEMPHIS DEDICATE THEMSELVES TO "A QUALITY EDUCATION WITH A CATHOLIC HEART."

DR. MARY MCDONALD, SUPERINTENDENT OF CATHOLIC SCHOOLS, MAKES REGULAR VISITS TO ALL THE SCHOOLS. THE CATHOLIC SCHOOLS OFFICE PROVIDES A FRAMEWORK OF SUPPORT THAT ASSISTS IN THE DELIVERY OF OUTSTANDING ACADEMIC PROGRAMS.

choral music, and band. Most importantly, the schools strive to provide a climate in which the students can develop to their full potential. Many of the elementary schools even include preschool programs, which serve three- and four-year-olds. All of the system's elementary schools have kindergarten programs.

The middle school program endeavors to meet the needs of preadolescents. In addition to the core subjects, the curriculum includes exploratory subjects, which provide the students with opportunities to explore areas of interest and develop their talents. The middle school students also learn life skills through the adviser-advisee program. Also, middle school students are encouraged to develop their talents and skills in an environment that nurtures them and allows them to take risks.

A college preparatory curriculum is the basic program of study in Catholic high schools. The students in the high schools in the Diocese of Memphis take more courses in math, science, and social studies than their public school counterparts. All of the high schools integrate computer technology into the curriculum so that the students will be prepared for the changing workplace demands of the 21st century.

Today, the school system even offers a Web site at www.cdom.org for the benefit of parents, students, and those interested.

The graduation rate in Memphis' Catholic high schools is an impressive 99.9 percent, and these students are accepted into colleges and universities across the nation. Graduates typically receive a combined $8 million in college scholarships each year. In all, the Catholic Schools of the Diocese of Memphis educate more than 7,200 students in prekindergarten through 12th grade.

A Cornerstone of Faith

In the Catholic Schools system, we believe that imparting a strong Catholic foundation is one of the greatest gifts we can give a young person," McDonald says. To that end, the Catholic Schools of the Diocese of Memphis has institutionalized a number of practices and programs designed to strengthen faith in its students' daily lives.

Students, for example, are required to complete community service hours. In fact, more than 140 local, national, and international organizations are served by Memphis Catholic Schools students through service outreach.

The Diocese of Memphis hosts the annual All Schools Mass, and the individual schools conduct retreats, liturgies, prayer services, and other occasions for spiritual growth. In addition, the schools feature dedicated study of church history and of Catholicism, active observance of holy days, and a learning environment framed in prayer.

A Miracle in Memphis

As Catholic families across the county move to the suburbs, many downtown areas find themselves short of resources. That 40-year migration has taken a toll on Memphis' inner-city Catholic schools. But in July 1999, the bishop of the Diocese of Memphis, the Most Reverend J. Terry Steib, S.V.D., announced a plan that has been referred to as "nothing short of a miracle."

Several donors, who chose to remain anonymous, gave a multimillion-dollar donation as seed money to secure the reopening of six long-closed Catholic parish schools in Memphis' inner city. Bishop Steib dubbed them Jubilee Schools, honoring the Old Testament tradition of a year of mercy to the poor, as well as the Jubilee Year 2000.

"These schools are for all children," McDonald says. "We teach the children, not because they are Catholic, but because we are. That is our vocation. Catholic education is a mission in our church, and the teachers in the Catholic schools are the missionaries of the new millennium."

At first, the biggest challenge appeared to be finding strong, caring, and faithful teachers to fill the classrooms. But the diocese had faith. "Because God has already provided us with the miracle of reopening these schools, I trusted him to call those who were needed to serve in them," McDonald recalls. "I was not disappointed."

The next miracle for the Jubilee

Schools came when the Christian Brothers became the first religious order to partner with the diocese in this initiative. The brothers agreed to participate in the unique partnership and to operate a renovated school, now called De La Salle at Blessed Sacrament School. Shortly after the brothers' announcement, the Sisters of the Holy Family, an African-American congregation of pontifical status from New Orleans, answered the call to staff St. Augustine Jubilee School.

The Jubilee Schools are continuing their rebirth. Buildings are being renovated, teachers are answering the call, schools are being reopened, students are enrolling, and additional funds are being raised for even more impact.

"From our traditional schools to the Jubilee Schools, the Catholic Schools of the Diocese of Memphis are working to make sure that this time of change brings change for the best, and does so for the honor and glory of God," McDonald says.

A CATHOLIC SCHOOLS MARCHING BAND PERFORMS PRIOR TO THE ANNUAL ALL SCHOOLS MASS FOR MORE THAN 7,200 CATHOLIC SCHOOLS STUDENTS.

hen the Campus Voice—the quarterly newsletter for St. Agnes Academy-St. Dominic School—is opened, it looks and reads like a family album. Along with updates on events, people, and projects, there are various news items and photographs of students and alumni alike. Notes about career moves, obituaries, reunions, marriages, and births keep members of the school's family up to date with each other, enhancing the close-knit

community even more. Built on family values such as respect, honesty, and reaching one's full potential, the institution offers Memphians a strong educational alternative.

Having served the Memphis community since 1851, St. Agnes is the oldest continuously run school in Memphis. Founded by the Dominican Sisters of Saint Catharine, Kentucky, St. Agnes occupied the same downtown location for 100 years before moving to its present site on Walnut Grove. The Sisters played an important role in Memphis' history, caring for the sick during the yellow fever epidemic, operating an orphanage, and supporting the civil rights movement.

St. Dominic School was established on the campus of St. Agnes in 1956 by a group of parents seeking private education for their sons. Boys are enrolled as day students in prekindergarten through eighth grade, with coeducational preschool programs between the two schools. Grades seven and eight are coordinated for both boys and girls, while college preparatory classes for grades nine through 12 are for girls only. The boys then go on to other college preparatory schools in the area.

A Roman Catholic day school with an ecumenical charter, St. Agnes Academy-St. Dominic School seeks to provide a values-based education that is both grounding and liberating, preparing students for higher academic learning

THROUGHOUT ITS HISTORY, ST. AGNES ACADEMY-ST. DOMINIC SCHOOL HAS APPLIED HIGH STANDARDS OF EXCELLENCE TO ACADEMICS, LEADERSHIP SKILLS, SOCIAL RESPONSIBILITY, AND MULTICULTURAL AWARENESS, EMPHASIZED IN PROGRAMS MARKED BY CHALLENGE, DIVERSITY, AND RESPECT.

while deepening their faith and relationship with God. The school's students come from Memphis and surrounding communities, giving representation to a wide range of backgrounds.

Academic and Spiritual Strength

Accredited by the Southern Association of Colleges and Schools, St. Agnes Academy-St. Dominic School holds membership in the Tennessee Association of Independent Schools, as well as several other professional organizations. The 17-member board of trustees is comprised of religious members and laypeople, and the Parents Club and Alumnae Association support the school through fundraising, recruitment, and special events all year long.

The Lower School incorporates traditional methods of learning with hands-on experiences to both develop and reinforce basic skills. Students in prekindergarten through third grade are taught French, while Spanish is taught in the fourth through sixth grades. The seventh and eighth grade curriculum is adapted to meet the

developmental and academic challenges of early adolescence, and the ninth through 12th grade curriculum is college preparatory.

Computer science classes are introduced to prekindergarten students, and all grades are taught religious studies, as well as the basic and necessary skills of math, reading, language arts, science, and social studies. This curriculum is combined with the appropriate enrichments for each grade, such as newspapers, photography, forensics, computers, and community service. There is only one class per grade, with a low student-teacher ratio. Student activities are vast, with academic, athletic, and religious clubs and teams to meet student needs and interests.

Throughout its history, St. Agnes Academy-St. Dominic School has applied high standards of excellence to academics, leadership skills, social responsibility, and multicultural awareness, emphasized in programs marked by challenge, diversity, and respect. As it has always done, the school continues to enrich the Memphis community with its presence.

These days, it is increasingly hard to find old-world clothing shops that offer the finest-quality men's and women's clothing in an atmosphere of rich tradition and uncompromising service. But for nearly 150 years, Oak Hall has offered Memphians just that. ▲ Oak Hall was founded in 1859 by Solomon Halle, and it has been sustained by five generations of his descendants. President Bill Levy, the founder's great-great-grandson,

remembers working for his grandfather in the three-story building as a very young man.

A Tradition of Quality

In those days, our store was in the center of the trade district, and also convenient to the residential areas," explains Levy. "Our moves to the east have virtually duplicated that situation, during this time when the core of Memphis is moving east." Located downtown at 55 North Main for more than 100 years, Oak Hall moved to the Oak Court area near Poplar Avenue and Perkins Extended in the 1960s, and followed the city's population eastward again in 1996, when the store moved into its spacious and elegant location in the Regalia shopping area at Poplar Avenue and Ridgeway Road.

Oak Hall's selection of high-quality clothing ranges in style from updated traditional to the finest Italian fashions. The store features apparel from the finest designers, universally recognized by discerning shoppers. Oak Hall's collection includes the latest designs from noted international designers such as Ermenegildo Zegna, Canali, and Zanella. The high-quality selection also features such classics as Oxxford, Hickey-Freeman, Jack Victor, Hart Schaffner & Marx, Bradford, Southwick, and Samuelsohn.

Oak Hall is home to the only complete Ermenegildo Zegna shop in the Memphis area. This shop-within-a-shop offers the line's full collection of exquisite Italian sport coats, suits, and trousers.

Oak Hall also offers a Hermes boutique that carries a wide selection of the designer's scarves, neckwear, fragrances, and other accessories. Other familiar names in sportswear and furnishings include Robert Talbott, Gitman Brothers, Polo, Scott Barber, and Lacoste.

Oak Hall prides itself on the issue of

sizing. While many stores stock only the most popular sizes, Oak Hall carries a full selection of shorts, longs, and extra-longs. Another valued service is Oak Hall's in-house tailoring shop, which keeps 15 to 20 expert tailors and seamstresses occupied full time.

The store's complete selection of menswear is complemented by a ladies department that emphasizes style and fashion for occasions ranging from casual to more dressy.

Giving to the Community

Oak Hall is happy to give back to the community it serves by contributing to a variety of deserving organizations in Memphis. For example, the store places a special emphasis on its Oak Hall Run for St. Jude, an annual affair that celebrates its 25th consecutive year in 2002. The event draws as many as 5,000 people annually and, through the years, it has

raised more than $2 million for St. Jude Children's Research Hospital, where no child has ever been turned away. In 1994, Oak Hall received the Volunteer Support Group Award of the Year from the fund-raising segment of the hospital.

Oak Hall's clientele is served by longtime employees who know their customers and merchandise well. Oak Hall employs some 55 people—many of whom have been with the store for several decades—who are much appreciated by the owners. Says Bob Levy, vice president, of his employees, "Our people are, without doubt, our greatest strength." The store's excellent customer service has ensured continued customer loyalty through the years.

With its commitment to quality and excellence, Oak Hall will continue to bring the finest in men's and women's clothing to future generations of Memphians.

SINCE 1859, OAK HALL HAS OFFERED MEMPHIANS THE FINEST IN CLOTHING FOR MEN AND WOMEN WITHIN AN ATMOSPHERE OF RICH TRADITION AND UNCOMPROMISING SERVICE.

hen visitors walk into any bank today, they pretty much find the same environment—similar products, similar rates, and similar delivery channels. "The only thing that differentiates us from the competition today is the quality of our employees and the services we provide," says John V. White Jr., president and CEO of Union Planters Bank Memphis. "We're intensely focused on three things—our employees, our customers, and our shareholders.

Because our frontline people are our greatest strength, everything we do is really centered around empowering our employees to help—and even obsess over—our customers, one at a time."

A Rich Tradition of Service

Union Planters Bank's commitment to customer service goes back to 1869, when the bank was founded. Memphis was recovering from the devastation wrought by the Civil War, and banks were needed to help in the rebuilding process. The 15 individuals on the bank's first board of directors were locals who represented every important line of business in the city—from cotton and railroads to steamboats and saloons. The founders decided to call the new entity the Union and Planters Bank of Memphis, indicating the bank's intent to serve both national and local interests.

Building on the needs of customers paid off, and by 1907, Union and Planters had the second-largest amount of deposits among all the banks in Memphis. By 1919, it was the largest bank in the city, with deposits of nearly

$20 million and a workforce of some 160 employees. During the late 1920s, the bank opened an installment-lending department, which was one of the first such services in the South.

The drive to build and adjust services around the needs of customers continued throughout the bank's history. One of the most recognizable of its innovations was ANNIE, the first automatic teller machine (ATM) in the region and a welcome time-saver for increasingly busy families.

The Super Community Bank

Today, Union Planters is spreading its tradition of service across the South and Midwest. Union Planters Corporation has banks in 12 states, and seeks to inspire them all with a renewed passion for service. "The customers of today are unlike banking customers of even a decade ago," White says. "They have more sophisticated needs and a greater expectation of service. Customers demand the broad array of products and services that a large bank can provide with the heart and soul of a community bank, one that genuinely cares about its customers and its community."

That, in essence, is the motivation behind Union Planters' concept of the super community bank. To complement its nationally recognized strength and diversity of offerings, Union Planters is building excitement about service to customers that far exceeds their expectations. "Excellent service is a culture, and we're building a new passion here for exceeding customers' expectations," White says. That commitment to providing outstanding customer service can best be summarized by the banner hanging in the bank's lobby headquarters: Our Pledge—Our Best Every Day.

"THE ONLY THING THAT DIFFERENTIATES US FROM THE COMPETITION TODAY IS THE QUALITY OF OUR EMPLOYEES AND THE SERVICES WE PROVIDE," SAYS JOHN V. WHITE JR., PRESIDENT AND CEO OF UNION PLANTERS BANK MEMPHIS.

TO COMPLEMENT ITS NATIONALLY RECOGNIZED STRENGTH AND DIVERSITY OF OFFERINGS, UNION PLANTERS IS BUILDING EXCITEMENT ABOUT SERVICE TO CUSTOMERS THAT FAR EXCEEDS THEIR EXPECTATIONS. PICTURED ARE THREE OF THE BANK'S DIVISIONS—CORPORATE BANKING (TOP), PRIVATE BANKING (LEFT), AND RETAIL BANKING (RIGHT).

O n any American campus or classroom, the first Christian Brother, John Baptist de la Salle, a native of France, likely inspired the educational model at work. De la Salle's 17th-century innovations—including group instruction, segmented grade levels, and practical coursework in the native language rather than in Latin—made education, previously reserved for the wealthy upper classes, accessible to thousands of children. ▲ De la Salle also

founded a religious teaching order dedicated to preserving his spiritual and widely inclusive educational philosophy. Today, 7,000 Christian Brothers and 66,000 Lasallian educators live out this commitment in 82 countries across the globe, in 950 educational institutions, serving nearly 1 million students. In Memphis, 32 Christian Brothers form the heart of Christian Brothers University (CBU), while 12 Christian Brothers uphold the Lasallian philosophy at Christian Brothers High School (CBHS).

Serving the Whole Student

In November of 1871, Brother Maurelian Sheel and a small group of Christian Brothers dedicated a new, combined college and high school at 612 Adams Avenue for a group of 26 enrolled students. Earning the nickname Temple of Tolerance, the school quickly grew as the brothers taught Catholic, Jewish, and Protestant boys.

Today, CBU is housed on a sprawling campus in Midtown and serves 2,100 full-time students—both male and female—from 40 countries. The university offers 31 undergraduate and graduate programs, including master's programs in engineering, business, and education. CBHS currently serves more than 860 students at a state-of-the-art campus at Walnut Grove Road

and I-240, where the student-teacher ratio is 24-to-1.

According to the schools' leadership, the Lasallian influence makes CBU and CBHS attractive to many students. "A Christian Brothers education is a whole education," says Brother Chris Englert, principal of CBHS. "We pride ourselves on an extremely rigorous curriculum for the mind, which empowers our students' academic and professional success. But as a Catholic and Lasallian institution, it is equally important to us to enrich the student's soul and spirit."

Brother Stan Sobczyk, president of CBU, agrees. "For more than 130 years, our predecessors have done a remarkable job of building this values-based, interfaith community that prepares students for success in their communities, their families, their church lives, and their professions."

Access and Inclusion

The Christian Brothers believe that attention to the individual student within a values-based atmosphere is the hallmark of the Lasallian heritage. Both the high school and the university follow De la Salle's philosophy of offering an education to anyone who desires it, and actively raise funds to provide a strong financial aid program. The two schools welcome a student body that is diverse with respect

▲ PAUL TALLEY

to faith, ethnicity, and economic background. While CBHS remains all male, CBU has been coed since 1970.

In 2000, CBU and CBHS further extended their commitment to education in the Lasallian tradition. Taking a leadership role in the Catholic Diocese of Memphis' plan to reopen inner-city schools, also known as the Jubilee schools project, the Christian Brothers are responsible for the educational mission and operation of De La Salle School at Blessed Sacrament.

The Jubilee schools project is one more chapter in the Lasallian story that began more than 300 years ago across the globe. In Memphis, the Christian Brothers continue to deliver the rigorous and multifaceted education that prepares students for successful, moral, and rewarding lives.

BOTH CHRISTIAN BROTHERS UNIVERSITY AND CHRISTIAN BROTHERS HIGH SCHOOL CONTINUE TO DELIVER EDUCATION IN THE LASALLIAN TRADITION THAT PREPARES STUDENTS FOR SUCCESSFUL, MORAL, AND REWARDING LIVES.

ince the late 1800s, The Kroger Company has been an integral part of life for people throughout the eastern United States and beyond. In Memphis, the Kroger Delta Marketing Area operates some 110 stores throughout a five-state region—western Tennessee, Arkansas, Mississippi, southern Missouri, and southwest Kentucky. Today, the Kroger Delta Marketing Area has approximately 17,000 associates and serves more than 1.5 million guests each week.

The Kroger Delta Marketing Area is a region of The Kroger Company, established in 1883 and headquartered in Cincinnati. One of the nation's largest food retailers, The Kroger Company operates more than 1,300 food stores, 800 convenience stores, and 36 food manufacturing and processing plants in 28 states across the nation.

Serving Memphis

The Kroger Delta Marketing Area offers customers some 33 convenient Memphis-area locations, including West Memphis, Arkansas; Olive Branch, Southaven, Horn Lake, and Hernando, Mississippi; and Covington and Millington, Tennessee. From the freshest produce in the Kroger Garden to providing the best quality and variety of goods available, as well as being the people's choice in meat and seafood, Memphis-area Kroger stores offer a wide range of products and services to their guests.

In addition, Memphis-area Kroger stores offer an array of special conveniences for its guests. Twenty-five of

Kroger's 33 Memphis-area locations have full-service pharmacies, with five of those offering drive-through convenience and one even offering a walk-up window. This attention to service and convenience has not gone unnoticed. In fact, in independent consumer research, The Kroger Company has been voted the number one supermarket pharmacy.

Convenience

Fifty-five Kroger stores have the latest U-SCAN technology.

This system allows guests in a hurry to scan their own express orders. This very popular system accepts cash, checks, credit/debit cards, and food stamps. The innovative checkout device is user friendly and access is bilingual.

WHEN MEMPHIS SHOPPERS THINK ABOUT THE KROGER COMPANY, MANY EQUATE THE SUPERMARKETS WITH THE LATEST IN FRESHNESS AND CONVENIENCE.

In 2000, the Kroger Delta Marketing Area began making one-stop shopping easier. Kroger Fuel Centers are now located at the Kroger Hickory Hill location, Highway 70 (Bartlett location), and at the newest area locations in Collierville, Tennessee and Hernando, Mississippi. Plans are to add many more Fuel Centers in the future.

Six Memphis-area Kroger stores are particularly appealing for children to visit. Since 1999, the Kroger Delta Marketing Area has added facilities in which kids can play while mom or dad shops. Children are registered by parents in the play center, and the parent can watch his or her child on closed-circuit monitors throughout the store. Play-center staff is specially trained in CPR and first aid.

Moving beyond just groceries and household necessities, most Kroger stores offer floral shops staffed by highly trained Master Florists. In fact, The Kroger Company is the world's largest floral retailer.

Part of the Community

The Kroger Delta Marketing Area is committed to the communities and the people of the communities it serves. Continually supporting charitable organizations that benefit the health, well-being, and education of children, and combating such challenges as hunger are just two ways the Kroger Delta Marketing Area gives back to these communities.

During Kroger's nine years as the title sponsor for the Kroger St. Jude Tennis Tournament, more than $2 million has been raised for the children of St. Jude Children's Hospital in Memphis. The tennis tournament funds support the ever necessary research conducted by the hospital in its efforts to combat—and one day eliminate—multiple types of childhood cancer.

The Kroger Delta Marketing Area proudly supports other children's charities and educational facilities such as the WONDERS cultural series, the Returning Baseball to the Inner City (RBI) summer program, and the Children's Museum of Memphis—where Kroger's

Kids' Market exhibit is a consistent favorite of the children who visit.

Each year, Kroger associates and guests raise funds and food for the Mid-South Food Bank. During Feed the Need month, special events are held to raise not only funds, but also awareness of the hunger problems that plague society. Since 1994, the Kroger Delta Marketing Area stores and associates have raised in excess of $500,000 to benefit the Mid-South Food Bank.

The Kroger Delta Marketing Area is committed to being the number one grocery store in the Memphis area. The Kroger Company not only offers its guests shopping convenience and value with the Kroger Plus Shopper's Card, but also believes in superior value and services for its guests, an obligation to work within the community to support continued economic growth, and the continued education of the children in the communities it serves.

hen tourists call to make reservations for Memphis' many attractions, BellSouth is there. When cotton brokers call to check prices on international markets, BellSouth is there. When thousands of truck drivers call to check in with their Memphis depots, BellSouth is there. ▲ *Few companies can claim such a big role in the growing success of the Mid-South, but BellSouth has been doing it, under a variety of names, since 1883. With an*

impressive, advanced infrastructure and a commitment to customer service, the company is hard at work fueling area progress.

And BellSouth plays a big role in the community in other ways that many people don't know about. From its state-of-the-art network to its community investment programs to its educational contributions, the company has truly become one of the area's most important corporate citizens.

An Infrastructure for Tomorrow

Memphis has always been a leader in telecommunications technology. With BellSouth's ongoing commitment and investment in modernization and expansion averaging $350 million every year in Tennessee, and with Memphis' position as a key market, the area maintains its lead on the technological edge. At the end of 2000, BellSouth's West Tennessee network included more than 116,000 miles of fiber-optic cable—with more than 400,000 miles installed throughout the state.

BellSouth's synchronous optical network technologies (SONET) ring design assures reliable, continuous communication for business communications, enabling calls to be rerouted in a split second in the event of a service interruption at some spot in the network. The network is monitored and tested 24 hours a day. The self-healing system sends messages to local serving locations to warn of pending troubles, often before the customer detects trouble. This advanced feature has been very successful in attracting

high-tech operations to the area.

Consistently recognized for customer satisfaction, BellSouth provides a full array of broadband data and E-commerce solutions to business customers, including Web hosting and other Internet services in Memphis. BellSouth's digital subscriber line (DSL) high-speed Internet access service is very popular. Other value-added services that keep Memphians in touch with their family and business associates include wireless E-mail and advanced voice and messaging services.

A True Mid-South Neighbor

For this regional powerhouse, serving its home communities is about more than phones and fiber. Investing in the future of each community means supporting a long list of educational, cultural, and human services organizations. BellSouth delivers $3 million in annual charitable contributions into Tennessee, and its employees give more than 1 million hours of service to the state's nonprofit organizations each year.

BellSouth, for example, has been the exclusive corporate sponsor of Dream Mission, in partnership with the Jackson Foundation, since 1998. The program was designed to get kids interested in math, science, and technology. Dream Mission is a half-size scale model

BELLSOUTH'S SPONSORSHIP OF DREAM MISSION GAVE HUNDREDS OF MEMPHIS AND SHELBY COUNTY SCHOOL STUDENTS, AT PUBLIC AND PRIVATE SCHOOLS, AN OPPORTUNITY TO PARTICIPATE IN SIMULATED SHUTTLE MISSIONS AS A WAY TO PEAK THEIR INTEREST IN MATH, SCIENCE, AND TECHNOLOGY.

BELLSOUTH POURS $3 MILLION IN ANNUAL CHARITABLE CONTRIBUTIONS INTO TENNESSEE, AND ITS EMPLOYEES, THE BELLSOUTH PIONEER VOLUNTEERS, GIVE MORE THAN A MILLION HOURS OF SERVICE TO THE STATE'S NONPROFITS EACH YEAR.

▲ SHIRLEY BURFORD / BELLSOUTH

▲ SHIRLEY BURFORD / BELLSOUTH

BELLSOUTH
Community Matters℠

▲ EARL STANBACK

@ BELLSOUTH   March 26, 19 99

PAY TO THE ORDER OF *National Civil Rights Museum* $350,000

Three hundred fifty-thousand dollars   Dollars

For *Power of the Dream Campaign*   *BellSouth*

BellSouth's gift of $350,000 to the National Civil Rights Museum helps to make the Power of the Dream campaign a reality. The fundraiser supports renovation and expansion of the museum and boarding house where the fatal shot was fired in the assassination of Dr. Martin Luther King.

replica of the NASA space shuttle. Sixth-grade students participate in simulated shuttle missions to spark interest in these subjects and future careers in technology.

The company and the BellSouth Pioneers also brought the Reach for the Stars project to local students. A BellSouth pilot project, Reach for the Stars is a first-of-its-kind science and technology program that allows students to take part in ongoing protein crystallization research being conducted by the University of California-Irvine and by the University of Alabama-Huntsville in conjunction with its NASA Flight Program. A team of Germantown High School students, who created protein crystals as chemistry and biology experiments, traveled to NASA to see their projects developed and flown into space for scientific research.

BellSouth has committed $350,000 to the National Civil Rights Museum's Power of the Dream campaign, a fundraising effort to expand the museum's educational facilities and programs. The expansion will include a complete renovation of the boarding house from which the fatal shot was fired in the assassination of Dr. Martin Luther King, and will depict post-King progress in human rights.

BellSouth also plays a major role in *The Commercial Appeal*'s Newspaper in Education Program, which teaches more than 25,000 students every week reading, writing, social studies, and other critical skills such as building self-esteem, learning how to be kind to others, and developing conflict resolution skills. The company offers grants to Memphis teachers and

underwrites an international student exchange program, and its BellSouth Pioneer Volunteers paint giant maps of the United States onto playing surfaces at school playgrounds.

BellSouth is the title sponsor of the Colors of Memphis/Let the Games Begin corporate races and festival to benefit the Memphis Boys and Girls Clubs. The festival offers Memphians a chance to learn more about the clubs while raising much-needed operating funds. BellSouth also donated its 10 South McNeil building outright to the Boys and Girls Clubs. Valued at $375,000, the building was sold to benefit the organization.

In Memphis, BellSouth's community outreach runs deep through its partnership with Hands on Memphis. BellSouth partners with Hands on Memphis as the title sponsor of the BellSouth Day of Community Healing. The communitywide day of volunteering draws hundreds of volunteers each

year to spruce up neighborhoods throughout the city.

The company's support of Hands on Memphis has helped the nonprofit organization touch countless people and neighborhoods throughout the city. BellSouth donated office space for the Hands on Memphis headquarters that can accommodate the organization's meeting and training needs, as well as a company van to transport tools and supplies to project work sites.

It's difficult to catalog the countless ways BellSouth fuels success in Memphis and across Tennessee. Governor Don Sundquist may have said it best when he helped BellSouth celebrate a recent birthday. "Over the years, BellSouth has proven itself as a community leader and a good corporate citizen," Sundquist said. "We salute BellSouth for its continued, positive economic impact on the state and for its part in making Tennessee a great place to work and live."

BellSouth's sponsorship of the Colors of Memphis/Let the Games Begin corporate races and festival raises awareness of the Boys and Girls Clubs and helps to raise funds for the organization.

▲ SHIRLEY BURFORD/ BELLSOUTH

Nobody knows the neighbor's kids like BellSouth.

*M*ednikow Jewelers is a rare gem—a family-owned firm that carries on a tradition originating with European immigrants in the late 1800s. Few like it remain. ▲ The jewelry tradition in the Mednikow family goes back many generations. In Russian, the name Mednikow can be translated to "coppersmith," indicative of the family's profession centuries ago. Eventually, coppersmithing led to goldsmithing and then to jewelry making.

Mednikow Jewelers in Memphis owes its creation to Jacob Mednikow, who learned jewelry making from his father in Russia, sought a new life in the United States, and established a wholesale jewelry business in 1891. With a base in Memphis, Mednikow had branches throughout the country. "At that time, a branch was located wherever a family member was willing to live and sell jewelry," says Robert Mednikow. "Several family members had come to the United States, and we had branches in New York, Milwaukee, Oklahoma City, Chicago, and New Orleans."

A retail store for Mednikow soon followed, originally located on the south side of Union Avenue between Main and Front streets, and later moving to 83 South Second Street across from the Peabody Hotel. At Jacob's death in 1935, his younger brother John took over the business and moved it to 5 South Main Street.

By the early 1950s, "Mr. M.," as John became known, was approaching his 70th birthday with hopes that his son Robert would return to the family business. In 1955, Lt. Bob Mednikow returned home from the Korean War and began putting his personal touch on the business by expanding services and merchandise. It was during this period that Rolex, Mikimoto, and Patek Philippe began their long associations with Mednikow.

Another meaningful change occurred in December 1959, when Bob met his future bride, and Bob and Betty Mednikow began planning for the future of the business. By the time their children were born—Jay in 1964 and Molly in 1968—Bob and Betty were sensing the trend toward suburban growth, and they opened the East Memphis location of Mednikow in 1968. Rapid growth created a need for Bob to acquire advanced management skills, and he enrolled in the Owner/President Management Program at Harvard Business School in the 1970s.

Today, Mednikow is still run by Bob and Betty, along with Jay and Molly, who have joined the business and bring modern ideas to a traditional family business, but still continue the traditions of quality,

MEDNIKOW CONSIDERS ITS EMPLOYEES
"AMONG OUR MOST TREASURED RESOURCES."

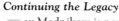

service, and integrity that began more than 100 years ago.

The Employee Family

Since the first nonfamily members joined Mednikow in the 1910s, employees have played a major supporting role in the firm's success. "Our employees are among our most treasured resources. Many have given us a lifetime," says Bob Mednikow. "Several have started to work here, thinking it was a stop in the road, and have stayed."

There are three traits employees of Mednikow must possess: integrity, enthusiasm, and a love of fine jewelry. Continuing education is also a stipulation. "Every person here is required to take professional courses of study through the Gemological Institute of America. All members of the sales staff are trained gemologists," notes Bob Mednikow.

In accordance with the standards of operation specified by the American Gem Society's statement of purpose, employees of Mednikow are "genuinely interested in the establishment of a high level of business ethics for the jewelry industry."

Made by Mednikow

Although Mednikow represents the finest designers and watch brands in the world, the firm has never lost sight of the individual designs that distinguish it from other jewelry stores. More than half of Mednikow's jewelry is made in the firm's own workshops.

"We believe that our customers are entitled to fine quality, immediate delivery, and proper service. The only way to provide that is to make the jewelry ourselves," says Bob Mednikow. "There are still some fine jewelers from whom we buy. The man who makes our wedding rings makes rings for Tiffany & Co., and another craftsman does special order work for Cartier. But by establishing our own manufacturing arm, we have assured our customers a continuing emphasis on quality as my son leads the firm into the next century."

Continuing the Legacy

Jay Mednikow is now president of Mednikow. Continuing the tradition of excellence in business management, Jay received a degree in economics from Harvard University and a master of business administration degree from Duke University's Fuqua School of Business, and worked outside the jewelry industry before returning to manage the Memphis store. Since Jay has returned to Memphis, Mednikow has added several designer jewelry lines, such as those of David Yurman, Michael Bondanza, Penny Preville, Seiden Gang, Steven Lagos, Charles Krypell, and Michael Good, as well as new watch lines by Cartier and Jaeger-LeCoultre.

Molly graduated from the University of Georgia and entered politics before returning to school to get her master of business administration degree from Georgia State University. She currently manages the new Mednikow store in Atlanta. Having opened in 1995, the Atlanta location is the first expansion of Mednikow outside the Memphis market since it was a wholesale jeweler at the turn of the past century. This offers proof positive that Mednikow is still operating under the location philosophy of its founder—"wherever a family member is willing to live and sell jewelry"—and that Mednikow wants its quality jewelry to sparkle throughout the South.

emphis' National Bank of Commerce (NBC) was founded on the banks of the Mississippi River in 1873 to serve the financial needs of the city's cotton industry. The region was rebuilding in the wake of the Civil War and a yellow fever epidemic, and even the help provided by the tiny, new bank was vital. ▲ *Today, NBC looks a lot different than it did then. NBC and its sister banks in the $16 billion-plus National Commerce Financial*

Corporation family cover eight states, and are known for their service-driven branches and financial strength.

But NBC's core mission has not changed. After more than 125 years in Memphis, the bank is still passionately dedicated to fueling the strength and success of the city's businesses and families.

Pioneers in Convenience

According to Thomas M. Garrott, chairman of the board for National Commerce Financial, serving today's bank customer is all about convenience. Garrott came to National Commerce Financial from the supermarket industry, where he experienced firsthand the needs and demands of modern customers. "People today are busier than ever," he says. So Garrott began to implement a focus on convenience at National Commerce Financial that gained national attention. "We've found that nothing brings customers to the bank like a belief that you truly understand their needs," says Garrott. "You don't convince them of that with catchy slogans. You do it by offering innovative programs and

products that serve them like no one ever has before."

To that end, NBC soon became an international pioneer in opening extended-hours bank branches in grocery stores. For many years, NBC had more in-store branches than any bank in the world. The bank's expertise in convenience is so well known that National Commerce Financial operates a consulting subsidiary that helps other banks launch in-store branches and teaches them how to maximize the in-store branches' convenience.

"It's the same way we look at account structures, branch locations,

credit programs, Internet banking, and every other aspect of our business," Garrott says. "We know that service and convenience make the difference for today's busy customers."

Strong for Tomorrow

In addition to doing whatever it takes to make customer relationships convenient, NBC is also committed to continuing the strength and stability that have been the hallmark of its century in Memphis. Decades of foresight and careful management have built the bank into one of the nation's strongest financial institutions.

The hard work has paid off. For more than 20 years, National Commerce Financial has annually outperformed the S&P 500 in total returns. And National Commerce Financial recently was ranked the nation's top-performing banking company by *U.S. Banker*, a major financial trade publication. It was the bank's second time to earn the honor in recent years.

National Bank of Commerce and its parent company are growing and changing—a situation that will likely continue. According to Garrott, "We will continue to do whatever it takes to safeguard our customer relationships and financial strength."

With strength and a steadfast commitment to service, NBC will grow and prosper for generations to come.

SINCE 1873, NATIONAL BANK OF COMMERCE HAS BEEN DEDICATED TO FUELING THE STRENGTH AND SUCCESS OF THE CITY'S BUSINESSES AND FAMILIES.

Memphis University School (MUS), a day school for boys in grades seven through 12, provides students a vigorous, college-preparatory education. Founded as a proprietary venture in 1893 by E.S. Werts and J.W.S. Rhea, MUS provided classical education for the city's leading families until the ravages of the Great Depression forced the school to close in 1936. Following World War II, MUS' alumni and other local leaders re-created the spirit

and excellence of the city's legendary prep school on a 94-acre campus then east of Memphis.

Opening its doors to 90 students in September 1955, MUS has grown to an enrollment of 600 students and must wait-list some qualified applicants. Nondenominational and nondiscriminatory, MUS grants more than $535,000 of need-based aid to approximately 15 percent of its student body. As with its predecessor, MUS emphasizes striving for excellence and the building of character through its strong academic curriculum, honor system, opportunities in the arts, and dynamic athletic program, as well as a plethora of other student activities.

Building Minds

MUS works hard to inspire each student to demand the best of himself. The school's well-trained, experienced, and dedicated faculty—averaging 18 years of teaching, with 80 percent holding advanced degrees—is committed to this goal. A 12-to-1 student to faculty ratio means teachers give students a great deal of personal attention. MUS offers a largely traditional curriculum, while also providing college-caliber access to technology, library facilities and services, and laboratories.

Not surprisingly, MUS students excel on standardized tests and in Advanced Placement programs. Because of their performances and the school's excellent college advisory program, 100 percent of MUS graduates are accepted for college work, many of them qualifying for admission to the most competitive universities in the nation. In recent years, MUS students have gone to 102 institutions of higher learning in 38 states, the District of Columbia, Britain, and Japan. From the class of 2000 alone, more than 40 percent of the seniors were offered academic, leadership, or athletic scholarships.

Building Values

The school's motto is *Veritas Honorque* (truth and honor). The moral heart of MUS is its student-operated honor system, which permits no lying, cheating, or stealing. Each student assumes responsibility for his own actions and for respecting the rights of others. Failure to abide by the honor code results in expulsion.

Extracurricular activities also aid students in their character building and growth. MUS offers participation in 11 interscholastic sports, student government, publications, dramatics, civic service, government club, and more

than 30 other clubs. Along with the other daily interactions on campus, these diverse pursuits help students internalize life's numerous informal lessons. Such experiences teach them to respect their peers, set priorities, budget time, plan ahead, accept constructive criticism, and make long-range choices.

Building Leaders

The MUS academic- and values-focused program prepares its young men for college, corporate, and community leadership roles. MUS alumni, including the approximately 70 percent who return to live in Memphis, frequently become leaders in their communities. These men demonstrate excellence, and provide guidance in business, the professions, and public service. Exemplars of such MUS community builders include AutoZone's "Pitt" Hyde, Class of 1961, and FedEx's Fred Smith, Class of 1962, who have helped shape their city and their respective industries in significant ways.

More than 100 years after first opening its doors, Memphis University School today provides its students with doors to numerous opportunities to grow academically, physically, morally, and socially. MUS produces men who will shape Memphis, and other communities, for generations to come.

MORE THAN 100 YEARS AFTER FIRST OPENING ITS DOORS, MEMPHIS UNIVERSITY SCHOOL TODAY PROVIDES ITS STUDENTS WITH DOORS TO NUMEROUS OPPORTUNITIES TO GROW ACADEMICALLY, PHYSICALLY, MORALLY, AND SOCIALLY.

FaxonGillis Homes, Inc.

axonGillis Homes, Inc. entered the Memphis real estate arena as Faxon Homes in 1899. F.W. Faxon, a local builder, saw a growing need for high-quality homes that were affordable for working families in the region. Faxon Homes built thousands of homes in the area and developed some of the city's largest neighborhoods. ▲ In 1974, Gillis & Company was founded by Jerry Gillis. Like Faxon Homes, Gillis & Company was

determined to build high-quality starter homes that were affordable for families with lower and moderate incomes. Gillis & Company perfected the formula with more than 1,000 homes in 15 years, including industry-leading zero-lot line town homes in Charlestown Place, Huntington Place, Heather Ridge, and Kings Mill.

Faxon Homes and Gillis & Company merged in 1988 and became FaxonGillis Homes, Inc. Owned and operated by Leader Federal Bank, the company grew to the point that it was building 350 homes every year. In 1991, Gillis and his wife, Bobbi, purchased the company and maintain 100 percent ownership today.

"It takes a lot of expertise to build affordable homes that don't cut corners," Jerry Gillis says. "Our hands-on, personalized approach makes it possible to ensure an exceptional level of quality and customer satisfaction in every home we build."

An Unwavering Commitment to Satisfaction

FaxonGillis retains its century-old commitment to the needs of the home buyer. Complete customer satisfaction is the goal of everyone at the company, and there is a long list of procedures in place that ensure buyers are happy with the process from beginning to end. "We're a little obsessed with complete customer satisfaction," Gillis says. "We drill it into our team. We demand it of our partners. We measure it after every sale. And we don't accept anything less."

FaxonGillis' sales representatives, licensed real estate professionals equipped with volumes of information, work out of organized and friendly sales centers in furnished model homes. They offer a number of airy, modern floor plans that are the result of extensive research into modern family life and the best uses of space. If, after the no-pressure sales process, the customer decides FaxonGillis is a match for his or her needs, he or she is introduced to the FaxonGillis construction manager who will oversee the construction of the new home. The manager is always available to answer questions, offering customers a new-home orientation when the house is completed and addressing any concerns or requests before the move-in.

As further evidence of the company's commitment to complete customer satisfaction, FaxonGillis has contracted with the National Research Service to survey customers' satisfaction and

response. Ninety days after move-in, the third-party company completes an unbiased survey of the family's satisfaction with the home and the level of service the family received.

"And when a customer indicates anything less than an eagerness to refer FaxonGillis to a friend or relative, I take it personally," Gillis says. "I call those people and offer to visit the home personally. I embrace every opportunity to listen to customers' concerns and solve their problems."

This personalized commitment to complete customer satisfaction is at the heart of FaxonGillis Homes, Inc.'s success, and there is little doubt that this approach will fuel the company's continued popularity.

FAXONGILLIS HOMES, INC., OWNED BY BOBBI AND JERRY GILLIS, HAS BEEN PROVIDING AFFORDABLE, HIGH-QUALITY HOMES THROUGHOUT THE MID-SOUTH FOR MORE THAN A CENTURY.

▼ MIKE BOATMAN

▼ MIKE BOATMAN

utchison School, one of the top college-preparatory schools in the southeast, is preparing young women for rewarding careers and lives of integrity while developing the strength to excel and the courage of independence. Entering its second century of educating females, Hutchison maintains its long-standing reputation for supporting academic, athletic, and creative talents. ▲ First established as Miss Hutchison's School in 1902, Hutchison has always

been dedicated to academic excellence and to the development of mind, body, and spirit. Hutchison focuses on helping girls grow into young women prepared to succeed not only in college, but also in life as responsible citizens.

Commitment to Academic Excellence

Few places are better equipped than Hutchison to prepare young women to find their places in the world. The school has always recognized the importance of advanced programs and facilities, and it continues that tradition today with a new athletic center and an impressive new learning and technology complex complete with NASA satellite feed, interactive media, wireless technology, and an e-classroom.

Hutchison teaches foreign language as early as age three and provides hands-on science labs as early as first grade. Forward-thinking classes such as electronic music and robotics are available. Girls are provided ample opportunity for research and for student-directed presentations. The upper school offers a strong liberal arts education with a complete array of Advanced Placement and honors courses. As Hutchison is a college-preparatory school, students learn study skills in preparation for the demands of academics on a college level.

Opportunities for Balance

In addition to its challenging academic program, Hutchison is also known for the variety and quality of its extracurricular activities. Students benefit from a variety of choices in arts, athletics, organizations, and service. Through the school's visual and performing arts programs, girls are encouraged to explore avenues of self-expression and to experiment with their creative sides. Hutchison's athletic program promotes teamwork, sports-

manship, self-discipline, confidence, and physical fitness. Numerous organizations expand leadership opportunities and tap students' creative and organizational sides, while service to the school community and the larger community emphasizes civic responsibility.

Focus on the Individual

With an approximate enrollment of 820 students ranging from three-year-olds to 12th-graders, Hutchison School maintains a commitment to personal attention. The student-to-faculty ratio of 10-to-1 provides a nurturing environment for young students and a supportive environment for older students. The rapport between teachers and students is believed to be one of the reasons for the success of Hutchison's

challenging academic program. That environment is paying off. Every year, roughly 25 percent of Hutchison's students are recognized as National Merit Scholars.

As the young women move into adulthood, they remember their Hutchison years as a time of self-discovery and as a time of building lifelong friendships. Hutchison is where they acquire knowledge, discipline, extraordinary confidence, and a sense of their responsibility in the world.

"Hutchison is a very special place," says Annette C. Smith, Hutchison's head of school. "We teach students to think and feel, not just read and act. That's what makes a strong woman who leads a workplace or a community. That's what makes a Hutchison graduate."

FROM ITS ATHLETIC PROGRAMS TO ITS STRONG LIBERAL ARTS CURRICULUM, HUTCHISON SCHOOL PREPARES YOUNG WOMEN FOR FULFILLING CAREERS AND REWARDING LIVES.

FIRST ESTABLISHED AS MISS HUTCHISON'S SCHOOL IN 1902, HUTCHISON HAS ALWAYS BEEN DEDICATED TO ACADEMIC EXCELLENCE AND TO THE DEVELOPMENT OF MIND, BODY, AND SPIRIT.

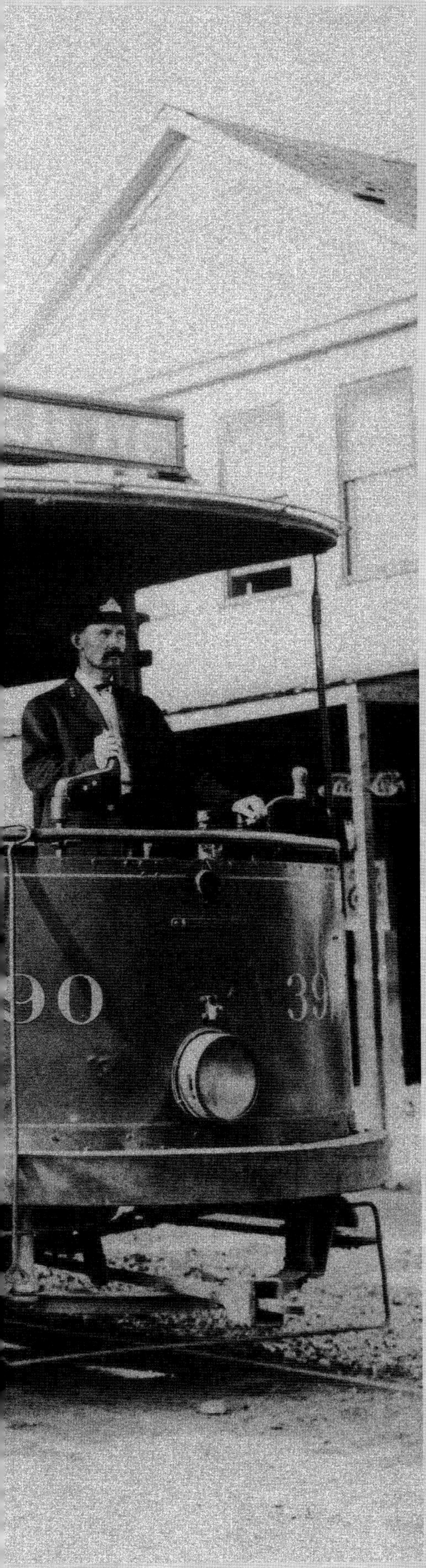

1906

1908 Schering-Plough HealthCare Products

1911 Baker, Donelson, Bearman & Caldwell

1911 University of Tennessee Health Science Center

1912 Baptist Memorial Health Care

1919 Grafco, Inc.

1921 Buckeye Technologies Inc.

1922 Clear Channel Communications

1924 Methodist Healthcare

1924 Clark & Clark

1925 Rhodes College

1925 The Mallory Group Inc.

1925

ith deep roots in Memphis, Schering-Plough is a worldwide pharmaceutical company committed to discovering, developing, and marketing new therapies and treatment programs that can improve people's health and save lives. The company is a recognized leader in biotechnology, genomics, and gene therapy, offering a long list of pharmaceutical products. The company has a global animal health business, as well, but is perhaps best known for its

consumer health care products that are shipped across the world from right here in Memphis.

Though Schering-Plough Corporation today has facilities on six continents, its origins are in a tiny downtown Memphis office where Abe Plough started a pharmaceutical business in 1908 when he was only 16 years old. Passionate about both science and sales, he created a homemade antiseptic and borrowed $125 from his father to begin marketing his remedy. The money went to purchase a horse and wagon, and Plough began selling the product—and others that he invented—to people on the farms and in the small towns surrounding Memphis.

By the 1920s, the Plough Company was growing strong, and it incorporated as the Plough Chemical Company in 1922. Plough Chemical soon acquired the St. Joseph line of children's aspirin, and Abe Plough used his marketing savvy to establish the brand as a

national leader. Over the next half-century, Plough repeated the pattern and slowly became a world leader in consumer health care products. In 1957, for example, Plough acquired the Coppertone sun care lines, which soon became the market leader.

Even though the Plough Chemical Company primarily focused on the drug industry, diversification was a company objective. By the early 1970s, Plough had acquired 28 companies. In 1971, Plough, Inc., merged with another national leader—the Schering Corporation—to become Schering-Plough. Abe Plough served as the first chairman of the board.

A Century of Trusted Brands

A trip to almost any supermarket or drugstore will likely turn up a number of products that reflect this Memphis heritage. There are the successful Dr. Scholl's, Tinactin, and Lotrimin foot care products, as well

as the constantly evolving Coppertone and Bain de Soleil lines of sun care products. And medicines such as Afrin, Corcidian HBP, Chlor-Trimeton, and Drixoral have become staple over-the-counter remedies.

All products of the HealthCare Products division of Schering-Plough, these lines, and their brand teams continue to lead the way in the over-the-counter pharmaceutical and health care products industry. As today's knowledgeable and on-the-go consumers demand effective products that fit their lifestyles, the Schering-Plough HealthCare Products division focuses on delivering innovative and effective products.

Though headquartered in New Jersey, the division is true to its founder's legacy and develops and distributes its high-quality products from West Tennessee at their National Center for Logistics and Research on Jackson Avenue. More than 600 employees in Memphis and 450 in Cleveland,

Tennessee, manufacture and deliver the global supply of these trusted products.

A Premier Memphis Employer

While the company's commitment to leadership and innovation draws many of its employees, Schering-Plough recruits and retains team members with one of the most employee-friendly environments in the city. In fact, Schering-Plough Corporation was recently named one of the 100 Best Companies for Working Mothers by *Working Mother* magazine. Schering-Plough has made the list four times.

"At Schering-Plough, we believe that our continued success is directly tied to the well-being of our diverse workforce," says John P. Ryan, senior vice president of human resources.

Schering-Plough's initiatives include a first-class, nationally accredited on-site child-care center for working parents in its Memphis facility and subsidized childcare in some other company locations. The company offers Enhanced Family Leave, which gives new mothers up to 28 weeks of job-guaranteed time off and gives new fathers a 16-week benefit. The company even offers an Adoption Assistance Program that reimburses employees up to $3,000 of adoption expenses.

There are on-site medical services, medical screening, immunizations, and wellness lectures by full-time physicians and nurses, as well as a highly competitive benefits program that includes profit sharing and a traditional indemnity medical plan for employees and their families.

Schering-Plough was also recently honored as one of America's Best Companies for Minorities by *Fortune* magazine and ranked among the World's 100 Best-Managed Companies by *Industry Week* magazine for the fifth consecutive year.

A Heritage of Philanthropy

Abe Plough was, by many accounts, Memphis' leading philanthropist. He believed that if a business prospers, it has an obligation to do its part to help the greatest number of people in the community. Plough personally contributed millions to local and national organi-zations. His efforts earned him the Human Relations Award from the National Conference of Christians and Jews and the first-ever individual award from the U.S. Consumer Product Safety Commission for his pioneering efforts to assure safe products for children.

In the spirit of its Memphis founder, Schering-Plough's HealthCare Products division contributes more than $50,000 each year to health related causes, including the Council on Family Health and St. Jude Children's Research Hospital. The company gives about $20,000 each year to education charities and more than $60,000 to community initiatives such as the Boy Scouts of America, the Memphis Area Chamber of Commerce, Memphis in May, and the NAACP. And the division and its employees together contribute a staggering $250,000 each year to United Way. The Schering-Plough Foundation contributed to three major local expansion projects recently, including $50,000 for a wilderness trail at the Lichterman Nature Center, $125,000 to the National Civil Rights Museum, and $250,000 to St. Jude Children's Research Hospital for Phase 2 of the Target House.

Due to its contributions to the community and the industry, it is hard to find a company that can match Schering-Plough's connection to Memphis. Its heritage in the city and its commitment to its employees make Schering-Plough one of the city's most revered corporate citizens.

AS TODAY'S KNOWLEDGEABLE AND ON-THE-GO CONSUMERS DEMAND EFFECTIVE PRODUCTS THAT FIT THEIR LIFE-STYLES, THE SCHERING-PLOUGH HEALTHCARE PRODUCTS DIVISION FOCUSES ON DELIVERING INNOVATIVE AND EFFECTIVE PRODUCTS.

SCHERING-PLOUGH RECRUITS AND RETAINS TEAM MEMBERS WITH ONE OF THE MOST EMPLOYEE-FRIENDLY ENVIRONMENTS IN THE CITY.

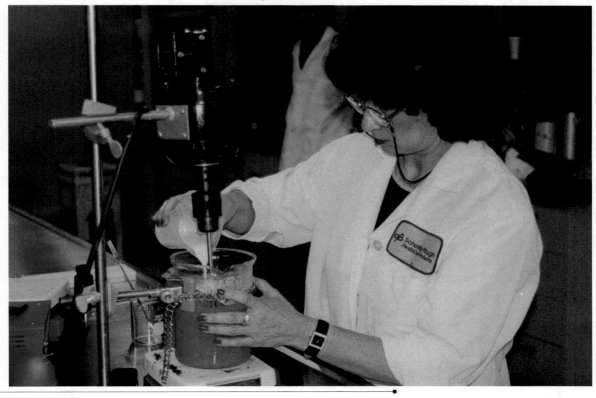

aker, Donelson, Bearman & Caldwell was established in 1911 as the Shepherd Heiskell firm. In 1994, Heiskell, Donelson, Bearman, Adams, Williams & Caldwell combined with Baker, Worthington, Crossley & Stansberry to form what is now known as Baker, Donelson, Bearman & Caldwell. The firm, headquartered in Memphis, is the largest Tennessee-based law firm and one of the 200 largest law firms in the United States.

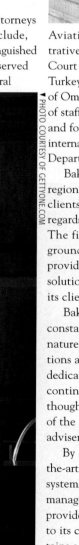

Through strategic acquisitions and mergers, Baker, Donelson, Bearman & Caldwell has grown to include more than 240 attorneys and public policy advisers in nine offices across the southeastern United States, as well as a representative office in Beijing. In the United States, Baker Donelson has offices in Memphis, Nashville, Knoxville, Chattanooga, Huntsville, and Johnson City, Tennessee, as well as in Jackson, Mississippi; Washington, D.C.; and Atlanta, Georgia.

Current Baker Donelson attorneys and public policy advisers include, among many other highly distinguished individuals, people who have served as U.S. secretary of state; Federal Aviation administrator; administrative assistant to a U.S. Supreme Court chief justice; ambassador to Turkey; ambassador to the sultanate of Oman; deputy governor and chief of staff for a governor of Tennessee; and former deputy undersecretary for international trade for the U.S. Department of Commerce.

Baker Donelson represents local, regional, national, and international clients across numerous industries in regards to a myriad of complex issues. The firm's service philosophy is grounded in the commitment to provide innovative, results-oriented solutions, while placing the needs of its clients first.

Baker Donelson understands the constantly evolving and changing nature of the law and political conditions around the world, and is highly dedicated to providing the necessary continuing education to maintain the thought leadership and sophistication of the attorneys and public policy advisers within the firm.

By investing in and using state-of-the-art Web technologies, collaborative systems, and the latest knowledge management tools, Baker Donelson provides efficient, streamlined service to its clients, and, in so doing, maintains a competitive advantage in the legal services industry.

For decades, Baker Donelson's seasoned corporate attorneys have provided services to clients in all phases of the business life cycle. Clients, including corporations, general and limited partnerships, and limited liability companies, are provided strategic counsel regarding purchase and sale agreements, mergers, acquisitions, corporate conflicts, venture capital financing, private placements, and public offerings. Baker Donelson adds value to its clients' businesses by anticipating and adapting to the ever changing market conditions that affect their industries, and by providing critical support and knowledge to efficiently complete business transactions, from start to finish.

The Baker Donelson e*Business practice is comprised of a multidisciplinary group of more than 30 lawyers who help clients navigate the complex issues of e-business. Due to its speed, limitless geographic boundaries, and technology, e-business has stretched traditional legal principles to a breaking point.

Baker Donelson's e*Business attorneys have experience in diverse and wide-ranging areas of the law, such as securities; mergers and acquisitions; and corporate, international, high-technology, tax, intellectual property, and litigation law. These attorneys have

BAKER, DONELSON, BEARMAN & CALDWELL, HEADQUARTERED IN MEMPHIS, IS THE LARGEST TENNESSEE-BASED LAW FIRM AND ONE OF THE 200 LARGEST LAW FIRMS IN THE UNITED STATES.
THE INDIVIDUALS PICTURED ARE MODELS AND ARE USED FOR ILLUSTRATIVE PURPOSES ONLY.

the requisite e-business knowledge and diversity of backgrounds to provide comprehensive solutions to the e-business issues faced by traditional and emerging companies in a wide variety of industries.

The attorneys of Baker Donelson's Litigation department are committed to achieving client goals while compressing the life cycle of the dispute. In following this approach, the firm's goals are to minimize the cost to the client and the interference to the client's day-to-day business operations. In complex litigation, the firm has been very successful in both reducing the time frame of cases and achieving positive results.

Baker Donelson's International group provides practical and cost-effective strategic advice on legal, commercial, and political aspects of global business activities. The firm's strength lies in its depth of resources and knowledge of the international affairs and the cultural differences that have a powerful impact on companies operating abroad. While currently the firm's focus is on Pacific Rim and Middle East countries, it will continue to aggressively expand into other global markets in response to the needs of its client base.

Baker Donelson's Public Policy group has proved to be a critical ally in the monitoring and shaping of federal and state legislation. The firm provides long-term, strategic counsel to clients, as well as day-to-day representation before Congress and the executive branch. The group has proved very effective, and was recently cited by *Fortune* magazine as one of the top 10 lobbying organizations in Washington, D.C.

Baker Donelson's Health Care group consists of a flexible, multidisciplinary team of attorneys who fully understand the vast array of regulations governing health care delivery. Given their resources, their depth of knowledge, and the diversity of the clients they serve, these attorneys provide strategic business techniques and advice to health care companies. *Healthcare Business Review* recently identified Baker Donelson as the largest health care practice in the Southeast.

In addition to the above practices, Baker Donelson has a growing reputation for its skills in the areas of high technology, intellectual property, white-collar defense, environment, labor and employment, and immigration law.

In recognition of the global economy that exists today and the complexities this economy presents, Baker, Donelson, Bearman & Caldwell will continue to strategically grow its firm with the underlying goal of providing maximum benefits to its clients.

I n 1911, the University of Tennessee established a new campus in downtown Memphis devoted exclusively to education and research in the health sciences. Today, that campus is known as the University of Tennessee Health Science Center (UTHSC), which is part of the new University of Tennessee, comprised of campuses in Knoxville and Memphis; the Space Institute in Tullahoma, Tennessee; and the institutes of Agriculture and Public Service.

THE UNIVERSITY OF TENNESSEE HEALTH SCIENCE CENTER (UTHSC) CAMPUS IS ONE OF THE LARGEST ACADEMIC HEALTH SCIENCE CENTERS IN THE UNITED STATES WITH FACILITIES TOTALING MORE THAN 2.9 MILLION SQUARE FEET ON APPROXIMATELY 75 ACRES IN THE HEART OF THE MEDICAL CENTER DISTRICT.

THE UTHSC GRADUATES APPROXIMATELY 600 STUDENTS PER YEAR. A BROAD RANGE OF POSTGRADUATE TRAINING ATTRACTS MORE THAN 1,000 CLINICAL RESIDENTS AND OTHER POST-DOCTORAL STUDENTS ANNUALLY.

Beginning with programs in medicine, dentistry, and pharmacy, UT's Memphis campus grew over the years, adding programs in graduate health sciences, nursing, allied health sciences, and biomedical engineering. UTHSC now includes the Graduate School of Medicine in Knoxville, as well as graduate medical education programs in Knoxville, Chattanooga, and Nashville; Family Medicine centers in Knoxville, Jackson, and Memphis; public and continuing education programs across the state; and the UT Bowld Hospital in Memphis.

UTHSC is accredited by the Southern Association of Colleges and Schools to award baccalaureate, master's, and doctoral degrees, and currently offers seven undergraduate and 10 graduate/professional degrees. Each of the professional colleges or programs is accredited by the appropriate agency for the profession or program. The campus has 43 endowed professorships, of which 19 are Chairs of Excellence. UTHSC is home to seven Centers of Excellence: Neurosciences; Molecular Resources; Pediatric Pharmacokinetics and Therapeutics;

Vascular Biology; Diseases of Connective Tissue; Neurobiology and Imaging of Brain Disease; and Genomics and Bioinformatics. The endowment has increased from $1 million in 1970 to an excess of $167 million today.

A Great Impact

Because of its size and scope of activities, UTHSC has a significant impact on the economy of Memphis and the Mid-South region. It is one of the largest academic health science centers in the United States. UTHSC is the ninth-largest employer in Memphis, with approximately 4,000 faculty and staff employees.

The UT Medical Group, the private practice arm of the Health Science Center faculty, is the Mid-South's largest multispecialty physician group practice. UTHSC contributes approximately $1.7 billion to the Memphis metropolitan area's economy each year, including the direct and indirect contributions of purchases of goods and services, patient care, and research activities.

This economic impact accounts for more than 5 percent of the total personal income earned in the Memphis area, making the university a major contributor to the local economy. For

every dollar of state appropriation, UTHSC and its related operations generate $20 of economic contribution to the local economy.

An Essential Part

UTHSC isn't just making history around the world in the fields of health science. The center is also an essential part of the Memphis community, helping to meet community and statewide needs with a number of programs that serve the dual purpose of furthering the education of students and providing valuable services.

UT's resident physicians directly impact the health care of a substantial number of people needing hospital services in the Mid-South area. These resident physicians are at the core of care at the Regional Medical Center at Memphis (The Med), and serve at a number of other teaching hospitals in the city and across the state.

Other UTHSC programs include a regional newborn center; a rehabilitation engineering program; the Boling Center for Developmental Disabilities; the Drug Information Center; the Southern Poison Center; the University Dental Practice; the Organ Disease Management Center; a recently

▼ API PHOTOGRAPHERS

established eye disease institute; the Center for Health Services Research; summer programs for students exploring the possibilities in health science careers; a HealthWorks (Families First) program to educate single mothers who depend on government assistance to qualify for a career in health care; the Center for Women's Health; and the Longitudinal Community Program.

Hands-on training is a crucial element in the process of education excellence for future health care professionals. Traditionally, most clinical learning for a typical medical student occurred in a hospital environment, and students didn't see their first patient until the third year of their four-year program. Now they get exposure at the very beginning of medical school.

UTHSC has implemented a new Longitudinal Community Program, a mentor-based curriculum where medical students receive practical experience by working alongside local physicians in their offices. By the time a student graduates, he or she will have 13 weeks

of firsthand training with mentors in various medical specialties. At the end of the year, students are tested and graded on everything from bedside manner to accuracy of diagnosis.

The Key to Health Care's Future

Administrators at UTHSC are promoting initiatives to make UT a top-25-ranked research institution in the United States through a commitment to promoting the university's health science and biomedical research missions. The quality of health care tomorrow relies on research being conducted today, and research efforts at UTHSC hold great promise for the future.

In March 2001, the National Institutes of Health (NIH) released a listing of awards made to public medical schools in fiscal year 2000. The UT College of Medicine now ranks 34th in NIH funding of public medical schools, which improves the college's ranking to 63rd from its previous ranking of 68th for all medical schools nationwide. The UT College

of Medicine increased its total NIH awards from $24 million in fiscal year 1999 to $37.6 million in fiscal year 2000, marking a 57 percent increase in a single year.

The University of Tennessee provides a comprehensive postsecondary educational experience of the highest quality to a wide and varied constituency. As the University of Tennessee's academic health science center, UTHSC's mission is to improve human health through education, research, and public service, with an emphasis on improving the health of Tennesseans.

RESEARCH IS A KEY COMPONENT IN UTHSC's TRIPARTITE MISSION.

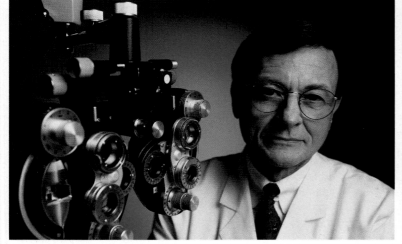

PLANS FOR THE NEAR FUTURE AT UTHSC INCLUDE THE ESTABLISHMENT OF A WORLD-CLASS EYE INSTITUTE (LEFT).

LIBRARY RESEARCH, ALONGSIDE CLINICAL AND LABORATORY TRAINING, HELPS TO FORM THE UTHSC STUDENT'S ACADEMIC PROWESS (RIGHT).

ince it began tending to the health needs of the Memphis area almost a century ago, Baptist Memorial Hospital has grown into a vital health care system that includes 17 hospitals in three states, numerous minor medical clinics, and the Baptist College of Health Sciences. At the same time, the system has become nationally renowned for its cardiovascular, oncology, neurology, and obstetric services, as well as its Sleep Disorders Center. ▲ *The Baptist*

Hospital that opened in 1912 is today Baptist Memorial Health Care Corporation (BMHCC), one of the largest not-for-profit health care systems in the United States. The system features a network of more than 2,500 physicians in virtually every medical specialty.

With hospitals in Arkansas, Mississippi, and Tennessee, including five hospitals in the metro Memphis area and more than 14,000 employees total, Baptist continues to be an important community partner.

FOR NEARLY A CENTURY, BAPTIST MEMORIAL HEALTH CARE HAS BEEN TENDING TO THE HEALTH NEEDS OF THE PEOPLE OF THE MID-SOUTH.

Nationally Recognized Expertise

Long recognized for its quality of care, BMHCC continues to gain national and international attention and recognition. *U.S. News & World Report* recently named Baptist one of the nation's top 50 hospitals for neurology services. With additional services such as home, hospice, and psychiatric care, as well as a system of surgery, rehabilitation, and other outpatient centers, Baptist is one of the top-rated integrated health care delivery systems in the nation, according to the American Hospital Association.

The Baptist Cancer Institute, which provides adult cancer treatment, research, education, and support services such as genetic counseling and testing, is one of only about 50 programs in the nation to be selected by the National Cancer Institute to be a Community Clinical Oncology Program (CCOP). As a CCOP, the Baptist Cancer Institute conducts National Cancer Institute-supported clinical trials in which local patients can participate without having to travel great distances.

"Top quality care with compassion is our number one goal," says Stephen C. Reynolds, president and CEO. "Baptist has a long tradition of service to this community. We have delivered generations of babies in the same families and cared for thousands of people throughout their entire lives. We're very proud of this."

Teaching, Preaching, and Healing

While exceptional quality and dedication to offering the latest in medical science to patients have long been hallmarks of Baptist, compassion and a personal level of service to patients also helped form our reputation," says Reynolds. "With a mission that echoes the threefold ministry of Jesus Christ, Baptist is devoted to teaching, preaching, and healing. As a nonprofit health system, we exist only to care for the community."

Despite the challenging, changing times for the health care industry, Baptist continues to follow this goal. Baptist spends millions of dollars on charity care each year.

Baptist also continues its goal to place state-of-the-art, quality health care in the most rapidly growing communities of the Mid-South, through either expansion or new facilities. Funding for this growth will come from a $400 million expansion project known as Health Care for the 21st Century. One example of this commitment is the new Baptist Memorial Hospital for Women on Baptist's East Memphis campus.

Baptist, which delivers more than 13,000 babies a year and has long set the standard in labor and delivery, began work on this facility as the new millennium arrived. Specially designed by women for women, the new hospital provides comprehensive services for women in all stages of life and health. The freestanding women's hospital has 140 beds that include postpartum,

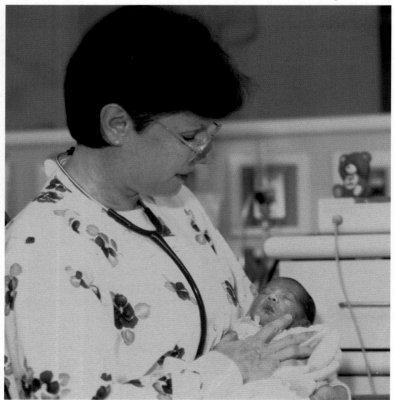

BAPTIST DELIVERS MORE THAN 13,000 BABIES EACH YEAR.

high-risk pregnancy, gynecology, and labor and delivery beds. Laboratory and diagnostic support, adult intensive care, and specially designed surgical suites to accommodate cesarean sections and other gynecologic procedures are included.

Baptist's East Memphis campus also made room for an expanded, 19-bed Helen & Jabie Hardin Pediatric Center, specifically designed to meet children's growth and developmental needs, as well as their medical needs. The hospital also features the Pediatric/Adolescent Emergency Department, which is separate from Baptist East's traditional emergency room and is exclusively for pediatric medical emergency cases.

Baptist is also expanding into another area: health information. With www.baptistonline.org, its Internet magazine, Baptist is setting the standard for health care informa-

tion to the public. Another Web site, www.pdparrot.org, even offers important health care information to youngsters.

"With services for every stage of life and health, Baptist Memorial Health Care is leading the way into the future of health care for the Mid-South," observes Reynolds. "As we

move into the 21st century, I think our patients will find that we're here to meet all their needs—not only with the best that medical care has to offer, but also with the most compassionate of care. That's what we've been doing for almost 100 years now, and what sets us apart."

BAPTIST CONTINUES TO EXPAND, PLACING STATE-OF-THE-ART, QUALITY HEALTH CARE IN THE MOST RAPIDLY GROWING COMMUNITIES OF THE MID-SOUTH.

WITH HOSPITALS IN ARKANSAS, MISSISSIPPI, AND TENNESSEE, INCLUDING FIVE HOSPITALS IN THE METRO MEMPHIS AREA AND MORE THAN 14,000 EMPLOYEES TOTAL, BAPTIST CONTINUES TO BE AN IMPORTANT COMMUNITY PARTNER.

Founded in 1919, Grafco, Inc. has grown alongside Memphis—the city it calls home. Just as Memphis has developed into a world logistics hub, Grafco has grown from a small automotive parts distributor into a full-service provider of materials-handling solutions. ▲ "Many of the largest and most respected companies in North America run distribution operations out of Memphis," notes Fred Graflund, president. "As a result, Memphis is home to some of the

most advanced and complex warehousing and logistics systems you'll find anywhere."

Smarter Space

As Grafco has served Memphis' prestigious roster of distribution operations through the years, the company's expertise has grown. Today, the firm delivers solutions—consisting of materials-handling products and systems—with the aim of helping customers store products and materials in a way that maximizes space utilization and allows employees to work as efficiently as possible.

The company's solutions may incorporate a variety of conveyor and storage systems, each tailored to meet the goals and needs of its clients. Systems include sortation conveyors, horizontal and vertical carousels, and pick modules, which incorporate carton flow racks and pallet racks. Sometimes, structures such as work platforms or mezzanines are utilized.

THE GRAFCO, INC. SHOWROOM AND SALES OFFICES ARE LOCATED ON GETWELL ROAD NEAR WINCHESTER.

Grafco also offers a wide range of handling equipment such as steel shelving, bulk racks, parts bins, modular drawers, workbenches, shop carts, hand trucks, pallet jacks, and tote boxes. Grafco—and its customers—can utilize these numerous products to help lift, move, or store any requirement.

"A big part of our reputation for strength is our years and years of experience in supporting customers with a complete line of durable and reputable products," Graflund says.

Full-Service Solutions

But Grafco sees itself as more than an off-the-shelf provider of materials-handling products. "Many of our customers come to us with complex needs, and they count on us for efficiently designed and well-built solutions," Graflund says.

To better serve its customers, the company has for years offered additional services, including consulting, engineering, computer-aided design, installation, and assistance with building permits and inspection. "As a result, our solutions are really custom solutions," says Graflund. "We discuss many options on the front end, and this helps customers plan solutions that will move their businesses forward."

Grafco has helped companies develop solutions for warehousing a wide range of products with very specific needs. For example, the company helped one customer develop a warehousing solution for full-sized automotive engines, and helped another develop a pick-and-ship infrastructure for a compact disc music distributor. "We were even hired to complete a custom project for a company that distributes contact lenses," Graflund says.

GRAFCO PRESIDENT FRED GRAFLUND HAS SEEN THE COMPANY GROW FROM A SMALL AUTOMOTIVE PARTS DISTRIBUTOR INTO A FULL-SERVICE PROVIDER OF MATERIALS-HANDLING SOLUTIONS.

Experience is the key to approaching such varied situations. Experience in diverse industries and locations has given the company the ability to design and implement solutions efficiently. That experience also helps Grafco cut through the "permitting" red tape that might take customers months if they attempted it on their own.

In Memphis, for example, the building code requires permits for shelving, pallet racks, and conveyors. In addition, the seismic code requires a certain stress tolerance for structures more than eight feet tall. "Our expertise as a licensed contractor allows us to assist our customers with all aspects of engineering documentation, permit approval, and inspection," Graflund says.

Emphasis on Partnership

If asked to distill the Grafco difference, Greg Graflund, vice president, insists that it is the company's emphasis on the partnership rather than the products. Customers do not need a new shelving system as much as they need the efficiency that an advanced shelving system will provide. And since customers are buying efficiency, Grafco believes its job is to provide the solution that will offer the best performance in the customer's specific environment.

Grafco has extensive experience with integrating products into a system so that they work flawlessly in conjunction with the machinery and operations in the customer's facilities. This systems approach reduces the chance of misapplications, lost time, and inefficiencies that can cost the customer profits. The planning process also takes into account future needs, and makes allowances for expansion if projections indicate it may be necessary.

"When customers allow us to analyze and review their requirements, it's not uncommon for Grafco to get the job based on price and value," Greg Graflund says. "Even if our bid is a little higher, customers see the value we provide and know what it will mean to their businesses. Most customers know that any purchase—no matter the price—is only a bargain if it works."

Grafco's thorough, customer-focused approach has meant a steady stream of referrals and repeat business, and this will surely continue to fuel growth. "Our reputation for accountability, dependability, and delivery of positive results is one of our most valuable assets," Graflund says. "We're not about to stop now."

CLOCKWISE FROM TOP:
GREG GRAFLUND (RIGHT) AND WIL HUTCHERSON (LEFT) USE THE "TEAM APPROACH" WHILE REVIEWING PLANS FOR A RECENT CUSTOMER INSTALLATION.

THE GRAFCO SHOWROOM GIVES CUSTOMERS AN OPPORTUNITY TO SEE FIRSTHAND THE WIDE RANGE OF EQUIPMENT OFFERED.

GRAFCO'S SOLUTIONS MAY INCORPORATE A VARIETY OF CONVEYOR AND STORAGE SYSTEMS, EACH TAILORED TO MEET THE GOALS AND NEEDS OF ITS CLIENTS. SYSTEMS INCLUDE SORTATION CONVEYORS, HORIZONTAL AND VERTICAL CAROUSELS, AND PICK MODULES, WHICH INCORPORATE CARTON FLOW RACKS AND PALLET RACKS.

B uckeye Technologies Inc. has been a leading manufacturer and worldwide marketer of high-quality, value-added specialty cellulose and absorbent products for almost a century, but there's a lot more to this global leader than the simple manufacture and distribution of its products. ▲ *"Our secret ingredient is not cellulose—it's innovation,"* says Robert E. Cannon, chairman and CEO. Buckeye's leadership, Cannon adds, is a

result of two major strengths: the company's ongoing ability to introduce new products and its ability to engineer solutions to specific customer problems. "And both of those strengths depend heavily on research and development," Cannon says. "Innovation is the lifeblood of our business."

Customers in a long list of fields depend on Buckeye's expertise in polymer chemistry, as well as on the company's state-of-the-art, global manufacturing facilities. And the company's superior product line is supported by a strong, long-term management view. "What has characterized our management is an ongoing focus on the company's future," says David Ferraro, president and COO. "Just look at our commitment to research and development, our dedication to our employees, and our stewardship of the environment. These are all very real indicators of our dedication

to a strong Buckeye, both today and decades from now."

A History of Innovation

E stablished in the early 1900s as Buckeye Cottonseed Oil Company, a division of Procter & Gamble, Buckeye was originally founded to produce vegetable oil for manufacturing and resale markets. Seeking to expand its scope beyond cottonseed oil, Buckeye began to explore the potential of producing cellulose from cotton linters, short fibers attached to the cottonseed. Cellulose, which contains the basic organic compounds found in plants, can be extracted and purified to produce materials with a wide range of uses. One of the first customers to benefit from Buckeye's growing cellulose expertise was the U.S. government, which purchased Buckeye's cotton-based cellulose for munitions.

During the 1950s, Buckeye expanded into wood-based cellulose to supply the chemical and specialty fiber industries. The company was soon renamed Buckeye Cellulose to reflect its new expertise worldwide.

By the early 1990s, it had become clear to both Procter & Gamble and Buckeye's management that the company had changed significantly. The cellulose business had become increasingly specialized, and Buckeye had grown into one of the industry's world leaders. In 1993, corporate and divisional leaders organized a management buyout that launched Buckeye as an independent company. Just two years later, Buckeye held a successful initial public stock offering.

The company has grown significantly since then, through both internal development and acquisitions. Buckeye's acquisitions include cotton-cellulose manufacturing facilities

BUCKEYE TECHNOLOGIES INC. HAS BEEN A LEADING MANUFACTURER AND WORLDWIDE MARKETER OF HIGH-QUALITY, VALUE-ADDED SPECIALTY CELLULOSE AND ABSORBENT PRODUCTS FOR ALMOST A CENTURY.

Ireland; and Americana, Brazil, Buckeye has progressed a long way from its roots as a tiny cottonseed oil subsidiary almost a century ago.

Industry-Leading Fibers for Industry-Leading Clients

Starting with the natural cellulose molecules from wood and cotton, Buckeye turns renewable resources into innovative products that meet the technologically demanding requirements of its customers around the world. Today, the company's products are hard at work in a number of diverse applications.

Eyeglasses and other optical products, for example, are manufactured with acetate plastics made from Buckeye's chemical cellulose. Thanks to Buckeye, these plastics have exceptional clarity, purity, and uniformity. In addition, the currencies of numerous nations are printed on Buckeye's paper cellulose. The specialty fibers enhance the life span of currency by delivering enhanced color permanence and tear resistance.

A large percentage of the disposable diapers made each year rely upon Buckeye's products for their rapid absorption of fluid and their protection against leakage. Buckeye continues to lead the way in innovations that give these materials both increased absorbency and lighter weights.

Buckeye also contributes its expertise to food—hot dogs, sausages, and other comestibles are often made with Buckeye chemical cellulose casings. These Buckeye products provide the

AERIAL VIEW OF BUCKEYE'S MEMPHIS COTTON CELLULOSE FACILITY

located both in the United States and abroad. Buckeye has also acquired air-laid nonwovens manufacturing facilities in the United States, Canada, Germany, and Ireland.

"In the late 1990s, we recognized that we had entered a new chapter in our history," Cannon recalls. "Our focus was no longer the simple manufacture of cellulose. We had grown to depend on the advanced technology and expertise required to use polymer chemistry to solve problems. It was this approach that really differentiated us from our competitors."

To officially recognize the company's refined strength and purpose, the company changed its name to Buckeye Technologies in 1997.

Today, Buckeye Technologies is a global business and the world's only manufacturer to offer specialty cellulose products made from both wood and cotton, utilizing both wetlaid and air-laid processes. The company has leading positions in most of the high-end niche markets in which it competes.

Buckeye now has 10 manufacturing plants in strategic locations around the globe. Operating in Memphis; Perry, Florida; Lumberton, King, and Mount Holly, North Carolina; Glückstadt and Steinfurt, Germany; Vancouver, British Columbia; Cork,

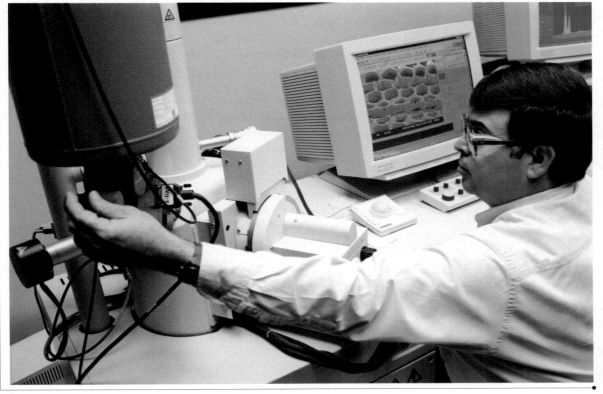

RESEARCH SCIENTIST BOB LINDSEY ADJUSTS A SCANNING ELECTRON MICROSCOPE TO VIEW INSIDE THE CELL WALLS OF COTTON AND WOOD, BUCKEYE'S RAW MATERIAL SOURCES FOR THE PRODUCTION OF SPECIALTY CELLULOSE AND ABSORBENT PRODUCTS.

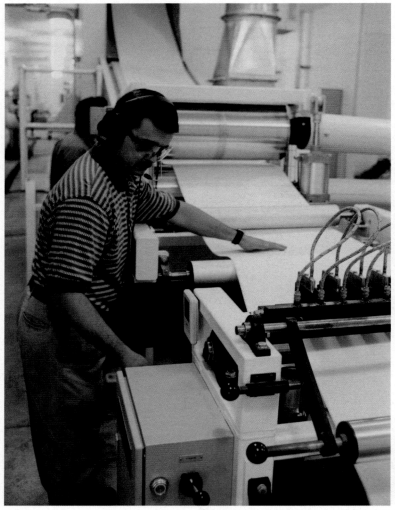

Operations engineers Bill Howell (top) and Jim Wilcutt (bottom) produce pilot scale samples of Buckeye's proprietary cellulose fibers for the expanding absorbent products market.

consistent purity and strength required by meat processors worldwide.

The examples go on and on. Many time-release medications are made with Buckeye cellulosic materials that aid in absorption. A large number of rayon and acetate fabrics derive their silklike appearances from Buckeye cellulose. High-performance automotive tires draw on the superior heat resistance and exceptional strength of tire cord made from Buckeye specialty cellulose.

Expanding Technology

At Buckeye, technology is the driving focus. "Technology makes innovation possible," Ferraro says. "Technology makes customer solutions possible. Technology makes it possible to offer proprietary new products that serve the market like no one else can. We've been able to use technology to fuel the success of this company because, from the early days, we have refused to view our products as a mere commodity."

Toward that end, Buckeye spends close to $12 million on research each year. With nearly 100 research and development (R&D) employees, the company is committed to helping customers lead in their market segments with the newest, best-performing products. The firm succeeds by delivering powerful product upgrades, innovative breakthroughs, and results-driven customer service. In the diaper and feminine hygiene markets, for example, there is a constant pressure on Buckeye's customers to deliver higher absorbency with lower fiber mass.

Buckeye focused its seasoned, high-tech R&D team on the problem, and the company recently developed a new, complex fiber with multiple structures that give it a special "wicking" property. The material has an unprecedented ability to move moisture from a layer of fibers next to the skin—where dryness is important—to the back fibers, which are capable of storing a large volume of liquid. "The new wicking fiber is a great example of the power of R&D," Ferraro says.

"The product cements our role as this market's preferred, high-end provider."

And that's just the beginning. Buckeye R&D helps customers in a variety of ways, from the molecular analysis of manufacturing by-products to the enhancement of raw materials.

Powered by People

It is important to Buckeye management, though, that the focus on technology not be viewed as a focus on machinery. "R&D expertise isn't equipment," Cannon explains. "Computers and microscopes don't invent anything. R&D is knowledge. It's people."

When a customer recently sent Buckeye's laboratories an unidentified fiber, the firm's people delivered the answer. The fiber was examined with a high-power electron microscope, and was broken down to its most basic elements in the lab. But the analysis couldn't be made until Buckeye's experienced scientists looked at the pictures and recognized the patterns.

"Equipment comes and goes," Cannon says. "But if you can retain, maximize, and empower your people, you've got an amazing advantage that no one will be able to match."

So Buckeye makes a strong effort to acknowledge and reward its employees. Employee teams are rewarded for success with incentive bonuses, which include payments of company stock to their retirement plans. "Buckeye is more than 40 percent owned by its employees," Cannon says. "That gives everyone a very real stake in the success of this company."

That stake is an effective one. Cannon, who started at Buckeye in

1954 as a mechanical engineer, and Ferraro, who started with Procter & Gamble in 1964, are just two examples of the company's hundreds of career-long employees. "That longevity gives us amazing efficiency," Cannon says. "We've managed to stay incredibly focused, because we haven't had in-and-out management teams like so many other companies."

Managing for Tomorrow

Buckeye also places top priority on the protection of the environment. This, once again, stems from the company's focus on the long-term future of its operations, its employees, and the communities

in which it operates. In fact, Buckeye remains one of the few companies, if not the only company, in the cellulose industry to operate with a penalty-free record in the environmental arena.

"We're proud of our record as one of the best environmental performers in our industry," Cannon says. "But we never want to let up in our passion for finding new ways to protect the land and the communities that have made our success possible."

That diligence is evident in a long list of programs and innovations. Buckeye scientists, for example, have developed a way to recycle the cotton cellulose fibers in old, denim blue jeans into premium-quality, custom-

ized cellulose for currency papers. It's one of the many ways Buckeye is putting its concern for the environment into action.

"It's all part of that constancy of purpose," Cannon says. "Financial stability, an impeccable environmental record, an unflinching drive to develop tomorrow's leading products—all these traits are part of a disciplined focus on the future. This company has done an amazing job of staying true to that vision.

"And that's how you build strength," Cannon adds. "You constantly build on your foundation, turning past success into even greater success in the future."

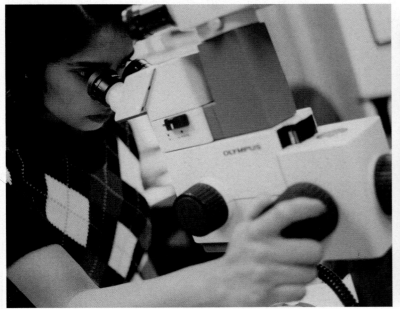

As one of the world's foremost media companies, Clear Channel Communications provides Memphis and Mid-South businesses unparalleled reach for their advertising messages. On a larger scale, the company—headquartered in San Antonio—owns or operates approximately 1,170 radio and 19 television stations across the United States, and has equity interests in more than 240 radio stations internationally. Clear Channel

also operates more than 700,000 outdoor advertising displays, including billboards, street furniture, and transit panels around the world. And, in 2000, Clear Channel produced more than 25,000 shows and events.

Locally, Clear Channel owns and operates seven radio stations, two television stations, and hundreds of prime outdoor media sites. The synergy of having so many media options available through one unified source makes for a powerful voice for Memphis-area merchants who want to reach a diverse target audience, and the company serves local audiences with popular, diverse, and cutting-edge programming.

Equally important to the success of these outlets is Clear Channel's vision to

allow its media to maintain the voice and presence that made them viable in the first place. Even after joining the Clear Channel family, the various entities have stayed rooted in their histories and continue their vital, trusted roles within and around the community.

Clear Channel Radio: Popular Programming for a Variety of Tastes

The radio arm of Clear Channel Communications is as rich in history and diversity as the city it calls home. The Clear Channel family of media outlets can trace its beginning in Memphis to 1922, when AM radio station WREC first hung its shingle, signaling to all that the initial broadcaster in the Mid-South was open

for business. Memphians able to tune in that day had no idea how the media would one day help shape and promote their city.

The station struggled through the Great Depression, but managed to remain on the air and even began to grow as the country emerged from the depths of despair in the mid to late 1930s. WREC would indelibly prove its worth to the entire area when, in 1937, a gigantic rush of water down the Ohio and Mississippi rivers flooded millions of acres in 12 states—darkening cities, contaminating water systems, crippling transportation, and imperiling hundreds of thousands of families. To rescue and rehabilitate the more than 1 million refugees required the prodigious,

RADIO PERSONALITY JANEEN GORDON OF WHRK-FM K-97 IS JUST ONE OF THE MULTITUDE OF TALENTED INDIVIDUALS THAT MAKE UP THE CLEAR CHANNEL COMMUNICATIONS FAMILY.

in the area. Additionally, this group of beloved Memphis icons supports the local economy by employing dozens of local residents in a variety of positions. They have also been longtime proponents of the rebirth of downtown Memphis, having been stationed there long before the area was considered fashionable.

"I couldn't imagine being anywhere else," says Sherri Sawyer, general manager. "Radio has always been such an important part of this community—not just for entertainment, but also culturally and spiritually. To me, downtown is the heart of any great city. So this is where we had to be."

Rock 103 consistently leads the Memphis ratings with a popular mix of classic rock and roll and some of the city's best-known radio personalities. Rock 103's Tim, Bev, and Bad Dog dominate morning drive time, and Drake and Zeke command the afternoon airwaves. The recipe makes for one of the most popular mixes in the city, especially with Memphis' elusive 30- and 40-something males. Also, it doesn't hurt that those same men spent high school years glued to Rock 103. Heritage and humor go a long way with those guys.

WOTO-FM Oldies 95.7 is the Memphis oldies station. The station's popular *Top 5 at 5* revisits the hits of a particular year, and the station's overall programming is popular in workplaces and with women. Oldies 95.7 also operates www.memphisoldies.com, where surfers can log in for music news, test their knowledge of music trivia, play an interactive oldies Name that Tune, or even review *Top 5 at 5* lists from the past.

WREC-AM 600 is the leader in Memphis talk radio. From the local morning-drive *Memphis Today* to the long list of leading syndicated programs to the popular weekend do-it-yourself lineup, WREC offers some of the best programming that talk radio has to offer. The station is Memphis' home for Michael Reagan, Dr. Laura Schlessinger, financial guru Dave Ramsey, Paul Harvey, and ratings dominator Rush Limbaugh. During afternoon drive time, Memphis news-and-sports veteran Mike Fleming takes calls on local issues.

Bev Hart is part of the Wake-Up Crew, WEGR-FM Rock 103's immensely popular morning drive-time show.

cooperative efforts of the Red Cross, the army, and the Coast Guard, as well as numerous federal, state, and local agencies.

The key to the success of this effort was communications. In the flood-ravaged Mid-South, Memphis sat high and comparatively dry on the Chickasaw Bluffs. From its studios, then located in the Peabody Hotel, WREC remained on the air for more than 23 days—a total of 572 consecutive hours—linking the Red Cross and other rescue agencies with the public and, via 30 to 40 ham radio operators, with areas isolated by the rising waters. People all over the United States heard WREC's flood reports through CBS, and others around the world heard accounts beamed by the station directly to the BBC in London.

As the 1930s drew to a close, WREC would once again bring Memphis into the national spotlight with its network broadcasts from the Peabody Skyway of performances from the day's most popular orchestras. Appearing regularly would be Les Brown and his Duke Blue Devils; Clyde McCoy; Rudolph Friml Jr.; Ted Fio Rito; Buddy Rogers; Ted Weems, whose vocalists were Perry Como and Marilyn Maxwell; Jan Garber; Freddy Martin; and Ozzie Nelson, with a pretty, young vocalist named Harriet Hilliard.

Today, there are seven Clear Channel radio stations in Memphis. Three of those are urban- or African-American-targeted stations—WHRK-FM K-97, KJMS-FM V101, and the historic WDIA-AM 1070—and are run from offices located downtown on Union Avenue, just a few blocks from the banks of the mighty Mississippi River. The other stations include WEGR-FM Rock 103, WOTO-FM Oldies 95.7, and all-talk WREC-AM 600, which have their operations in an office overlooking Beale Street—the rock, soul, and blues mecca of the world.

Together, these two clusters of stations reach a significant percentage of the Memphis radio audience, and have among them the top-rated stations

Radio for the Heart of the City

Only a few short years after WREC began its Peabody Skyway broadcasts, another station now in the Clear Channel family made its historic debut. In 1948, WDIA became the first African-

American-formatted radio station in the nation. And since its inception, the station has been nothing less than a Memphis institution and historical landmark.

WDIA first hit the airwaves with a country-and-western format. However, that approach failed to draw a significant audience, so the station tried various other formats, including classical music and even more country, which also failed. Advertisers began pulling out, and the station was put up for sale. None of the offers the station received were feasible, showing that no one seemed interested in a station with such a poor track record.

It was then that Bert Ferguson and Chris Spindel, program director—feeling the pressure of having to do something to salvage the fledgling station—first developed the idea of the all-African-American format that would make them a hit. Shortly afterward, the station hired Nat D. Williams—a well-known local educator, showman, and emcee—as the first African-American disc jockey south of the Mason-Dixon Line. Soon, the station would again make history, as it became the first station in America with an all-African-American on-air announcing staff.

"I'm not sure if they were trying to start such a social revolution," says Bruce Demps, general manager. "They probably were trying to save their jobs. But what a difference it made. Working here, you feel like you are a part of something a little bigger—something a little more important."

From that point forward, the landscape of broadcasting was never the same. Drawing from talent throughout the Mid-South, WDIA became the opportunity that the then unknown performers had been praying for.

Local stars like Rufus Thomas, who was a fixture at WDIA for more than 45 years; Dwight "Gatemouth" Moore; and Maurice "Hot Rod" Hulbert began as disc jockeys at WDIA. B.B. King and Bobby Blue Bland began the road to fame, plugging their gigs on the station's airwaves.

But WDIA was more than a star-maker station. It was the voice of the African-American community,

TIM SPENCER (TOP) AND "BAD DOG" MCCORMACK (BOTTOM) ROUND OUT THE TRIO OF PERSONALITIES THAT COMPRISE ROCK 103'S WAKE-UP CREW.

James Davis (top) and Jay Michael Davis (bottom)—The Davis Brothers—host the weekday afternoon program on WDIA.

providing a forum to reveal and discuss their particular problems of the day. In so doing, WDIA became a powerful catalyst that resurrected the esteem of its listeners, and forever changed the familial and economic relationships of the Mid-South. This distinction earned the station the title of the Goodwill Station. In later years, WDIA became the first African-American station to go to 50,000 watts and the first to gross $1 million in one year.

But the story of WDIA is more about the present than about the past. The station is a vital part of the community, and today offers some of the most popular radio personalities in the city. Bev Johnson, Bobby O'Jay, and W.C. Brown, for example, start weekdays off with the *Fun Morning Show*, a mixture of music, comedy, news, and community interests that keeps morning-drive listeners informed and entertained. Johnson, a WDIA fixture with near-celebrity status, stays in the studio each weekday for a talk show that breaks the rules. There are in-studio guests, discussions of contemporary issues, call-in topics, and plenty of good music. Janis Fullilove tackles controversial topics on her afternoon show, and the Davis Brothers mix classic soul music with calls from the What's on Your Mind Line. With a powerful and unique blend of community interest and music programming, WDIA continues as a strong player on the Memphis radio landscape.

Clear Channel knows how to cater to the tastes of its unique home markets, and nowhere is that more obvious than at KJMS V101.1. Offering Today's R&B and Jammin'

Old School, the station plays the music that Memphis was built on. Added to the mix is *The Tom Joyner Morning Show*, a live, nationally syndicated, urban morning program that treats listeners to an entertaining on-air team, drop-in celebrity guests, on-site remotes, and an audience-tested urban play list. Joyner is the four-time winner

of *Billboard Magazine*'s Best Urban Contemporary Air Personality Award. Popular music programs like *Old School Party Mix* on Friday and Saturday nights also help keep V101's big audience tuned in.

WHRK-FM K-97 is one of Memphis' top-rated stations. From *Mike Evans & the Early Morning Team*

to the *Commercial Free Crunk Lunch* to afternoons with Stan Bell to the nightly *Phat Jams at 8*, the station delivers a mix of the nation's most popular urban contemporary music. And K-97 doesn't neglect the issues. The station's new *On Point* program is one of the few talk shows in Memphis and the Mid-South for youth.

Rounding out the Clear Channel Radio family is AM 990 KWAM The Light. Billed as the Mid-South's first and only 10,000-watt, all-music-inspirational-song station, The Light offers listeners a modern blend of contemporary and traditional gospel music, performed by artists such as Kirk Franklin, BeBe and CeCe Winans, Yolanda Adams, Whitney Houston,

Shirley Caesar, Al Green, the Mississippi Mass Choir, and Stephanie Mills.

Better Communication through Television

Over the past half century, television has emerged as the nation's, if not the world's, most dominant medium. In Memphis, Clear Channel Communications owns and operates two stations that live up to their commitments to entertain and inform.

More than 25 years ago, WPTY Channel 24 became the first UHF station to be broadcast in the Memphis market, breaking new ground that was previously dominated by the old guard. Growing slowly but steadily, the station

hit the big time when it became one of the original Fox network affiliates. Employing a strong lineup of national programming, combined with innovative, local-based shows, WPTY took another major leap forward in the mid-1990s when it became an ABC affiliate. In addition to featuring ABC heavyweights such as *Who Wants To Be A Millionaire*, *NYPD Blue*, *Monday Night Football*, *Nightline*, and others, WPTY, under its new name as ABC 24 WPTY, also launched a full-scale news department.

"WPTY has run the full cycle of local television, beginning in the 1970s as a pure independent TV station featuring mostly network reruns, to joining the new Fox Network in the 1980s,

THIRTY-SHEET POSTERS CAN TARGET AUDIENCES DEMOGRAPHICALLY AND GEOGRAPHICALLY. THEY CREATE RAPID CONSUMER TOP-OF-MIND AWARENESS. POSTERS ARE WIDELY DISTRIBUTED THROUGHOUT THE MARKET, REFLECTING CONSUMER TRAFFIC PATTERNS.

and then moving on to ABC in the 1990s. And, thanks to the power of Clear Channel, we're ready to meet the technical challenges of the new century, beginning this year with digital television," says Jack Peck, general manager of ABC 24 WPTY and UPN 30 WLMT.

In addition to rising in the ranks with a powerful local news operation and quality ABC programming, WPTY has become the Memphis affiliate for Warner Brothers' WB Network. Designed for the rapidly changing and cutting-edge tastes of young people, WB already has a number of hit offerings, including *7th Heaven*, *Dawson's Creek*, *Gilmore Girls*, *Jamie Foxx*, and *Steve Harvey*.

During the 1980s, it became clear that there was still room for yet another local television station in the Memphis area, and WLMT Channel 30 was created. With its roots planted firmly in the independent tradition of sister station WPTY, WLMT also focused its initial programming efforts on a local level. This dedication to Memphis led

to the broadcast rights for the University of Memphis Tiger basketball games, the gem of local on-air sports opportunities.

Taking its lead once again from WPTY, the newer station took a chance on a new network known as UPN. Its programming targeted an enormously underserved portion of the Memphis community—the African-American population. The network was a perfect fit. Combined with syndicated programming and a focused, targeted promotion machine, WLMT soon became one of the flagship affiliates of UPN, garnering some of the network's highest ratings in the country.

This two-pronged stalwart of local stations gives both advertisers and the viewing public exactly what they need. For advertisers, having one source to reach the two major segments of Memphis' viewing audience is unprecedented. For the customer, national programming with a dash of local flavor has proved to be a winning combination.

"We're very pleased with our current position in the market," says Peck.

"Having such strong ties with both the ABC and the UPN networks, in addition to the WB Network, brings a wide, diverse range of national and local programming to the Mid-South area. Additionally, being a key member of the Memphis Clear Channel family allows us to serve the community in ways that could not be possible without the support of our sister stations."

Clear Channel's Memphis television presence is a remarkable operation. Like the company's radio operation, its television stations balance a commitment to information, entertainment, and community advocacy. It's a compelling combination for viewers, and a powerful mix for advertisers.

Unparalleled Reach: Clear Channel Outdoor

Clear Channel Outdoor's out-of-home media is the final piece of Clear Channel's Memphis network. Worldwide, Clear Channel Outdoor owns more than 500,000 outdoor displays. Having the dominant inventory in the markets

the company serves provides Clear Channel Outdoor's customers unparalleled locations. In fact, the company's national network gives customers the ability to reach more than half of the entire U.S. population and some 75 percent of the entire U.S. Hispanic population. That's a lot of people, and with that reach comes a tremendous amount of advertising power.

Clear Channel Outdoor can help customers plan a true outdoor strategy to focus their advertisements on target customers as they travel throughout their daily lives. Clear Channel Outdoor's outdoor advertising products put ads in front of the people that customers want to reach, whether they're commuting on the freeway to work, riding the bus, going to the grocery store, or simply picking up the kids after soccer practice.

Outdoor advertising is more than just billboards, as evidenced by the extraordinary variety of products that Clear Channel Outdoor offers its customers. Bulletins, posters, benches, airport displays, convenience store posters, mall displays, mass transit displays, and mobile ads are all products that Clear Channel Outdoor has developed with customer needs in mind.

"Outdoor is great because you can't turn it off, throw it away, or click on the next page," says Tony Dailey, president and general manager of Clear Channel Outdoor's Memphis office. "That means your message is reaching consumers everywhere—all the time, every day."

By utilizing this powerful medium, along with the other entities of the Clear Channel network, advertisers can have tremendous consistency and synergy for their messages to the public. They can easily extend their reach

beyond the borders of Memphis to reach a regional or national target audience, and can do it all from their home base.

There are other considerations for an outdoor company, and few are stewards of their surroundings like Clear Channel Outdoor. The company is extremely conscious of the impact its medium has on its environment. In Memphis, the only five-time winner of the nation's cleanest city award, the attention to that particular detail is quite acute.

"We go to great lengths to make sure there is a balance between the impact a board has on the target audience and the impact it has on the environment," says Dailey. "We strive to make sure our media fits in—like using the sides of buildings on Beale Street. In that case, the advertising actually adds to the flavor of the area."

Historically speaking, the billboard as it is currently known has been around since the 1830s, starting with the classic American large-format circus poster. As the targeting of narrower demographic markets has improved, new applications have been uncovered. It's not at all

unusual to spot wrapped buses, mall posters, taxi tops, phone kiosks, and truck panels as advertising platforms. Digital printing techniques have brought down the cost of duplication, improved image resolution, and shortened the time required for the development and rollout of ad campaigns.

As Clear Channel Outdoor celebrated its 100-year history in 2001, the history of the company says a lot about who it is and why it's still in business today. As one of the oldest outdoor advertising companies in the world, Clear Channel Outdoor has earned its success. The company knows what works and what doesn't, appreciates its customers, and knows how to assist them with their outdoor needs.

As part of the Clear Channel family of media outlets, Clear Channel Outdoor's strength and impact have grown by leaps and bounds. And while Memphis takes giant leaps forward in development, Clear Channel Outdoor will be right there, helping to promote the products and services that make the city run.

In a further commitment to the communities it serves, Clear Channel

Outdoor donates millions of dollars worth of public service advertising space each year to nonprofit organizations throughout the country. On a national level in 2000, Clear Channel Outdoor led the industry by assisting the Outdoor Advertising Association of America (OAAA) with the creative executions and space donations for the National Highway Traffic Safety Administration's (NHTSA) Drive Nice campaign. Clear Channel Outdoor also donated space to support the Hispanic Scholarship Fund, an organization that aims to develop the next generation of Hispanic business leaders in America by awarding scholarships to deserving Hispanic students.

This integration into the communities the company serves is part of the Clear Channel philosophy. With the leading television, radio, and outdoor outlets in Memphis to its name, Clear Channel takes its responsibility to the city seriously. Whether providing high-quality programming for citizens, targeted advertising for businesses, or generous support for communities, Clear Channel Communications stands as a media leader in the Memphis area.

FLEXIBILITY IS THE MAIN ADVANTAGE OF THIS MOBILE BILLBOARD. THE PRODUCT CAN BE USED TO REACH CONSUMERS IN AREAS WHERE TRADITIONAL OUTDOOR ADVERTISING IS RESTRICTED OR IT CAN BE STRATEGICALLY PARKED AT SPECIAL EVENTS OR IN SPECIFIC AREAS WHERE CONSUMERS ARE LOCATED.

ith what has become one of the Mid-South's most recognized tag lines, Methodist Healthcare continually reassures the area's citizens that "We know what a miracle you are." It is likely that people in Tennessee, Mississippi, and Arkansas remember the tag line because so many of them have been touched by Methodist's expansive and compassionate network. ▲ Chartered by the Methodist Church to provide high-quality, affordable health care that

reflects the church's mission and principles, Methodist opened in Memphis in 1924. The original building was located on Union Avenue, at the same site where Methodist Healthcare-Central Hospital is currently located. In those days, the four-story building housed 125 beds. During the first year, there were 3,148 patients admitted and 297 babies born.

Some 80 years later, Methodist Healthcare is the largest hospital in the city, serving more people than any other network in the Mid-South. With close to 2,500 beds and a medical staff of more than 2,500, Methodist extends its special brand of care to a growing number of patients.

In fact, more than 70,000 inpatients and 325,000 outpatients are treated annually. Each year, open-heart surgery

is performed on more than 1,500 people in Methodist's facilities, and, at the same time, its hospitals welcome more than 9,000 babies to the world.

"I'm at a loss for words when it comes to how proud we are of what the system has become," says Maurice Elliott, Methodist's CEO. "We are really blessed to be able to offer the Methodist brand of personalized health care to so many people each year."

The Whole Person, the Whole Family

In every discipline and department at Methodist, patients benefit from advanced equipment and the expertise of leading physicians. They also benefit from Methodist's affiliation with several colleges within the University of Tennessee Health Sciences Center. Many physicians practicing at Methodist Hospitals are faculty members at the University of Tennessee, which gives them access to the latest research and procedures.

But Methodist's strength is its commitment to cohesion and compassion as an integrated health care network. A growing national trend among leading health care organizations, the goal of integrated health care delivery is to

offer a wide range of services in addition to hospital care, including home health care, clinics, outpatient surgery, and diagnostic centers. The entire Methodist team approaches this broad spectrum of services with an unwavering commitment to compassion and excellence in every field.

Methodist's Heart Institute is a perfect example. In terms of volume of cases, the institute's cardiac program is the largest in Memphis and one of the largest in the country. In addition, Methodist offers chest-pain emergency centers at all four of its Memphis general hospital locations, complemented by a heart emergency network with locations throughout the region.

Methodist's heart patients have access to the latest in technology, including a computed tomography (CT) scanner with innovative software that can detect early calcium or plaque buildup in the coronary arteries of the heart. This revolutionary, noninvasive procedure is called Cardioscan℠, and can detect even small amounts of plaque in the coronary arteries. In less than a minute, Cardioscan can take about 350 pictures of the coronary arteries for a closer look at plaque buildup. The earlier the detection, the better the

chances of slowing and even reversing this condition.

Methodist Healthcare's Cancer Center is a self-contained facility with a specialized team of doctors, nurses, and support personnel. The center provides an outpatient chemotherapy unit, radiation therapy, a stem cell transplant program, overnight guest rooms, a cancer information library, and the services of a resource coordinator, chaplain, medical social worker, home hospice coordinator, and clinical dietitian. The center is also home to a nationally recognized, multidisciplinary breast cancer program, which focuses on breast conserving, as well as lifesaving solutions.

Women's services are a major emphasis at Methodist as well, and among the services offered are several subspecialties, available conveniently at several locations. Among the services included are gynecological surgery suites, the Radiology and Mammography Center, and family-oriented Methodist maternity centers.

These centers comprise the largest maternity service in Memphis, with state-of-the-art equipment, board-certified neonatologists, and nurses who are certified for advanced pediatric life support at all Memphis hospital locations. From maternity to breast cancer to urology, Methodist has the equipment and skilled professionals necessary to make a difference in the lives of area women.

Dedicated to the advanced research and treatment of neurological disorders and diseases, Methodist's Memphis Neurosciences Center was the first of its kind in the city. Applying an interdisciplinary approach to neurological care, physicians and staff perform a variety of specialized procedures. The center's 125 beds include a neuro-intensive care unit, supported by more than 100 specially trained nurses who use the latest in technical diagnostic, monitoring, and treatment equipment.

In 1995, Methodist established a partnership with the renowned Semmes-Murphey Clinic to form the Medical Education and Research Institute (MERI), a world-class surgical teaching and research facility. With the introduction of the Memphis Regional Gamma Knife Center, patients in a seven-state area can now benefit from gamma knife therapy, one of the most advanced neuroradiological treatment options available.

"It's not easy to deliver such a broad level of service and still maintain the strength and compassion the region expects from Methodist," Elliott says. "But our team of physicians and associates has done a miraculous job."

Elliott isn't the only one who has taken note of Methodist's successes. The system is turning heads nationally.

Methodist's leadership in the delivery of integrated health care services was recently honored with a ranking in *Modern Healthcare* magazine's prestigious Top 100 Integrated Healthcare Networks. The highest-ranking Mid-South health care system on the list, Methodist was ranked for its level of technology integration, hospital utilization, financial stability, services and access, contracts, physicians, overall system integration, and outpatient utilization.

Special Care for the Smallest Patients

I f you ask any Mid-Southerner why Methodist is so special, you won't have to wait long before most mention Le Bonheur Children's Medical Center. Founded in 1952 through funding raised by the committed women of the Le Bonheur Club, who still lend significant support, this 225-bed premier pediatric hospital provides service to 95 counties in a six-state area, as well as to children from around the country who come for specialized treatment and surgical procedures.

Le Bonheur receives national attention for its breakthroughs in research and its commitment to treating critically injured and ill children. But Le Bonheur's real success comes from a simple, underlying philosophy about pediatric medicine.

"Children aren't miniature adults," says Jim Shmerling, senior vice president of Methodist Healthcare. "Their

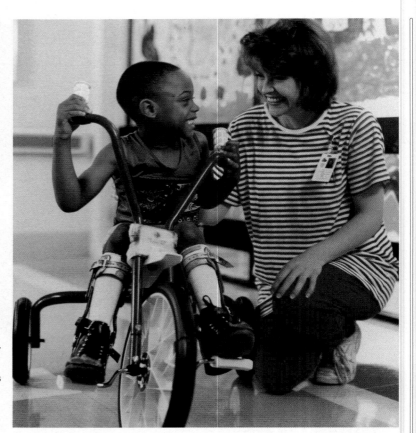

growing bodies need specialized equipment and expertise. And equally important, they have unique fears and questions about their conditions that need to be addressed by people who are trained in medical counseling for children."

With those specialized needs in mind, Le Bonheur has built one of the most comprehensive and respected children's medical centers in the nation. The center operates the region's only dedicated pediatric emergency department and its only pediatric intensive care unit.

Recently, Le Bonheur dedicated a new unit called the Le Bonheur Special Care Unit. The unit serves infants who are awaiting, or have just returned from, surgery; who need to be monitored closely; who are undergoing genetic testing and diagnosis; or who have heart and lung problems. The 20-bed unit contains 12 isolation rooms, and has an overhead sound system that plays music to help soothe the tiny patients. Each patient bed is a self-contained unit with individual heart and lung monitors. The machines read all vital signs at any time without disturbing a baby. Other features include parent sleeping rooms and a parent teaching room.

As the principal pediatric teaching hospital for the University of Tennessee-Memphis, Le Bonheur conducts clinical research and has a medical staff with 42 pediatric subspecialties represented. Among these programs are cardiovascular medicine, critical care, surgery, transplantation, rehabilitation, epilepsy, brain tumors, allergy and immunology, nephrology, pulmonology, and urology—all staffed by physicians and associates with expertise in pediatric medicine.

The Mid-South Sickle Cell Center provides comprehensive treatment to more than 1,000 infants, children, and adolescents each year in a joint effort with St. Jude Children's Research Hospital and the University of Tennessee. Le Bonheur also operates a

Transitional Care Program, which is the first of its kind in the state. The program provides care for technology-dependent children, and helps to train family members how to operate medical equipment in their homes.

Le Bonheur supports and operates the Center for Children and Parents, a treatment center for abused and neglected children and their families, and serves as the headquarters for the Mid-South SAFE KIDS Coalition, part of a national, long-term effort to prevent childhood injury. Le Bonheur also supports the Southern Poison Center, which provides a 24-hour poison prevention hot line.

Miracles Where People Live

In addition to the expansive range of health needs met by the system, Methodist Healthcare has an equally long list of constituent neighborhoods and communities.

Methodist operates 14 hospitals in Memphis and West Tennessee, as well as clinics, physician practices, and home health care. Methodist hospitals can be found in the Tennessee cities of Memphis, Germantown, Jackson, Dyersburg, Somerville, Brownsville, Selmer, Martin, Lexington, and McKenzie.

Methodist Healthcare-Memphis Hospitals—consisting of four general hospital locations, the Methodist Extended Care Hospital, and Le Bonheur Children's Medical Center—serves more people than any other hos-

pital in the Mid-South. "As an anchor of the medical-center area of Memphis for more than 75 years, Methodist is committed to patients in the heart of the city," says Cam Welton, president of Methodist Healthcare-Memphis Hospitals. The system prides itself on accepting patients without regard to their ability to pay, and is the largest acute care Medicare provider in the area. Methodist is also one of the largest TennCare providers in Tennessee.

A Pioneer in Efficiency

Methodist's success through the years has come from its exceptional care combined with a remarkable system for maintaining and enhancing efficiency. With its commitment to caring for the entire community, Methodist has emerged as the system of choice for area families and their managed care providers.

Methodist's remarkable distribution of care has been accomplished, in large part, through the involvement of medical staff in all aspects of system management and strategic planning—from board membership to managed care governance, strategic planning, and continuous-improvement-process team participation.

Methodist's medical staff has collaborated to analyze practice patterns and develop consistent practice parameters, which has measurably increased the quality of care while reducing length of hospital stay and, accordingly,

costs. A volunteer board of directors gives oversight to a very effective process for developing strategic planning, the operating budget, and capital budgeting. The quality management committee of the board of directors gives oversight to the system's efforts in clinical quality, service quality, and patient satisfaction standards. The system's employees, called associates, are encouraged to submit new ideas through participation in the system's continuous-improvement process.

Methodist Healthcare has been named a Top 100 Hospital in the United States, and has received both the Greater Memphis Quality Award and the Tennessee Quality Achievement Award, while consistently receiving full accreditation from the Joint Commission on Accreditation of Healthcare Organizations.

"As long as we continue to focus on delivering the latest in individualized care to the entire community, I'm confident we'll continue to be the choice for area families," Elliott says. "And that's what we plan to do. We're going to continue to focus all of our expertise and resources on treating the area's adults and children like the miracles we know they are."

METHODIST HEALTHCARE WAS THE FIRST IN THE MID-SOUTH TO OFFER A REVOLUTIONARY CARDIAC SCORING PROCEDURE. CARDIOSCAN^{SM} IS A FAST, PAINLESS WAY TO DETECT EARLY PLAQUE BUILD-UP IN THE CORONARY ARTERIES. EARLY DETECTION CAN HELP PATIENTS SLOW DOWN, STOP OR EVEN REVERSE THIS POTENTIALLY SERIOUS SITUATION.

METHODIST'S SERVICES INCLUDE LEADING-EDGE SURGICAL PROCEDURES.

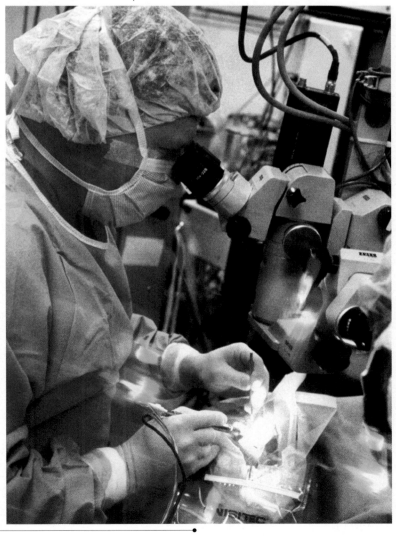

or more than a century, Memphis has steadily grown eastward from the banks of the Mississippi River. And for most of that time, the development firm Clark & Clark has been at the forefront of encouraging and developing the city's growth. Founded in the 1920s, Clark & Clark is today a leader in the industry, and finds itself at the helm of some of Memphis' most progressive and farsighted new developments.

THREE GENERATIONS AT WORK: BILL CLARK (SECOND FROM LEFT) WATCHES NICK, BEN, AND DIANA CLARK BREAK GROUND FOR CLARK TOWER AS FATHER BUCK CLARK TAKES THE PICTURE (TOP).

FOUNDED IN THE 1920S, CLARK & CLARK IS TODAY A LEADER IN THE DEVELOPMENT INDUSTRY, AND FINDS ITSELF AT THE HELM OF SOME OF MEMPHIS' MOST PROGRESSIVE AND FARSIGHTED NEW DEVELOPMENTS (BOTTOM).

In 1924, William B. Clark developed the family plot of land on Mitchell Road. Clark's father had been urging him for some time to subdivide the land into residential lots. Clark enjoyed the business and went on to develop property in some of the city's most historically significant neighborhoods, including Vollentine-Evergreen.

Following the Great Depression, Clark noticed that more people were asking about homes on the quiet eastern edge of town, at that time the area near Poplar Avenue and Goodlett Street. In what was to become a hallmark of his style, Clark cashed out of an existing project and focused entirely on the neighborhoods that have become Galloway Terrace, Belle Meade, and the Village, some of Memphis' finest and oldest neighborhoods.

In the 1940s, Clark was confident that the city's growth would continue its steady progress eastward, so he bought a part of the 9,000-acre White Plantation on the outermost edge of the city. In 1958, he purchased the adjoining land for what would become the future site of the White Station Tower at a cost of $11,300 per acre. Here, he planned to construct Memphis' first office tower outside the downtown area. People thought he was nuts, employees would later recall, but that did not stop Clark from breaking ground on the 24-story, 278,000-square-foot building at 5050 Poplar in 1965. He projected it might take five years to lease, but surprised everyone with a fully occupied building just after its completion. The family sold the building in 1998 for $18.4 million.

The White Station Tower project proved so successful that, in the early 1970s, Clark and his son William B. "Buck" Clark Jr. began construction on a 34-story adjacent building. Many of the city's civic leaders opposed the project because of the business it would drain from downtown. Clark had purchased the land for this build-

ing in 1947 for $15,000, and then subdivided the land to sell 26 homes. Clark & Clark's reacquisition of the Harvey Acres subdivision in 1969 cost the company $1.3 million. The 670,000-square-foot building was opened in 1972 at a cost of $21.3 million, and eventually sold in 1984 for $44.7 million.

"My grandfather had amazing vision, and he never hesitated to pursue it," says Nick Clark, partner in Clark & Clark and grandson of the company's founding patriarch. "I don't think any of us will ever appreciate the widespread opposition and ridicule he faced in planning for these projects. Today, they are East Memphis' defining landmarks."

Clark & Clark also operated as a general contractor from 1967 until the late 1970s. The company completed a long list of key Memphis development and construction projects during that time, including Central Church and the control tower at the Memphis International Airport.

New Technology Corridor

In the 1960s, William B. Clark told a newspaper reporter that development in East Memphis was only just beginning. "Growth feeds on itself," Clark predicted. "I think it will build all the way up to Collierville,

and East Memphis will be in the center of what is now metropolitan Memphis." With the completion of the Nonconnah/385 Parkway to Collierville in 2000, Clark was proved correct.

"Downtown was Memphis' first generation of office space, and East Memphis was the clear second generation," says Ben Clark, partner in Clark & Clark and grandson of the company's founder. "My father and I inherited my grandfather's vision, and saw the potential for the third generation of office development in southeast Shelby County." The city was growing in that direction as the East Memphis Class A office market was beginning to fill up, and the Clarks took notice.

In the summer of 1995, Clark & Clark began work on Lenox Park, the first speculative Class A office building in the Nonconnah corridor. Today, seven of the eight planned buildings have been completed, and the Clarks once again find themselves at the helm of some of the city's most desirable office space. The $100 million park is Memphis' largest Class A integrated-technology office park.

As technology-reliant companies increasingly dominate the economy, Clark & Clark predicts a surge in demand for high-tech, Class A speculative office space. "The economy moves so fast these days, many of these companies find themselves in an unplanned growth mode and have no space wait-

ing," says Nick Clark. Lenox Park provides not only office space, but also the technological infrastructure to support the initial and future needs of its tenants. The park is already home to a number of Fortune 500 divisions, including those of FedEx, International Paper, WorldCom, and Monsanto.

After more than 75 years, Clark & Clark remains committed to building for the city's future. The company has played a remarkable—and often quiet— role in Memphis' emergence as a regional business center. "And that's probably the way my grandfather would have wanted it," Ben Clark says. "He knew the projects spoke for themselves. That's a standard we strive to live up to every day."

I n 1925, the City of Memphis earmarked $500,000 to help a small, private, coeducational liberal arts college— founded in 1848 and affiliated with the Presbyterian Church— move from Clarksville, Tennessee, to a beautiful, 100-acre site in a residential area now known as Midtown. Few guessed that some 75 years after the move, the little college would have earned a reputation as one of the strongest liberal arts colleges in the nation.

From the beginning of its history in Memphis, Rhodes College's growth has been interwoven with the city's. In those days, the college was looking for a larger population to support the institution. At the same time, Memphis wanted—and needed—a good liberal arts and sciences college. Fortunately, the two found each other. As Memphis has grown into the 18th-largest city in the nation, Rhodes has become one of the finest liberal arts colleges in the United States.

For Southwestern—as it was named before becoming Rhodes College in the mid-1980s—the move to Memphis signaled a new start for the school and its president, Dr. Charles Diehl.

"It was a chance to start afresh in every way—a new campus and a new approach to education," says Dr. William E. Troutt, who became president of Rhodes in July, 1999. Not only did Dr. Diehl bring to Memphis all the physical property of the college, but, more important, he brought a clear and compelling vision of the type of quality education a liberal arts college ought to provide.

"Dr. Diehl was proposing a liberal arts education far more ambitious than

SINCE MOVING TO MEMPHIS IN 1925, RHODES COLLEGE HAS GROWN TO BECOME ONE OF THE FINEST LIBERAL ARTS COLLEGES IN THE UNITED STATES.

TREY CLARK

most other church-related colleges could even imagine," Troutt adds. "It would be an education that was, in his words, 'challenging, engaging, and connecting.'"

By being located in a large, diverse city, Rhodes benefits from a wide range of available cultural and recreational offerings. The college's students are also able to take advantage of research opportunities and internships made possible by Memphis' role as a major regional medical and business center.

Rhodes' student population of some 1,500 comes from some 40 states and numerous countries. More than 75 percent of the students live on the beautiful campus—with its stately old trees; large expanses of lush, green lawns; and classic Gothic stone and slate buildings, some of which were

designed by architect Henry Hibbs— a student of Charles Z. Klauder's— whose creations can also be found at Princeton and Wellesley. Indeed, no fewer than 13 of the original buildings at the Rhodes campus in Memphis are listed on the National Register of Historic Places—and, yes, many of the buildings are covered with ivy.

A Strong Purpose

A s it grew into one of the nation's premier liberal arts colleges, Rhodes was able to bring together three core strengths, which remain at the heart of the college's success. First, the college fosters intellectual growth, sustained by intensive interaction between students and faculty. Second, the college's focus on preparing graduates for professional

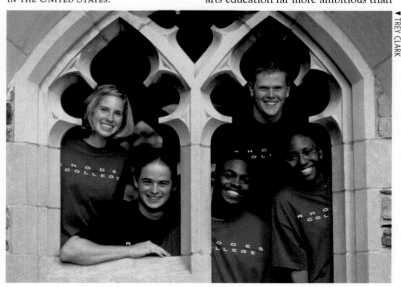

life is supported by a strong internship program that draws on Memphis' diverse resources. And third, the Rhodes community is built on a set of values that serve as a strong foundation for the student body, which adheres to a student-run honor code.

The extraordinary results of Diehl's vision have been well documented. Rhodes is one of a mere 40 schools included in Loren Pope's *Colleges That Change Lives*, and is also listed in *Choosing the Right College: The Whole Truth about America's Top 100 Schools*. Rhodes is named one of the best buys in *The Fiske Guide to Colleges*, and is ranked 35th in *Kiplinger's Personal Finance Magazine*'s Top 100 Best Values in Private Colleges and Universities. In 2000, *U.S. News & World Report* ranked Rhodes among the top 40 liberal arts colleges in the nation.

According to Troutt, the recognition comes from the college's approach to education. "Our campus, our faculty, our city—they all give us a wonderfully unique opportunity to integrate living and learning in ways that strengthen social and academic connections," Troutt says.

Rhodes' students can choose from 24 departmental and 11 interdisciplinary majors leading to BA or BS degrees—and, during the course of their education, students also benefit from the college's 12-to-1 student-faculty ratio. The college's active and varied campus life was further enhanced in 1998 when the $22.5 million Bryan Campus Life Center was completed. Rhodes' wide-ranging extracurricular activities offer everything from the internationally touring Rhodes Singers to the mock trial team that finished second nationally in 1999. In spring 2000, Rhodes' College Bowl team took second place in the National Academic Quiz Tournament in Boston, losing only to Harvard in the final round. The four-member Rhodes team defeated a number of the most prestigious private and public colleges and universities in the nation, including Princeton, Yale, Stanford, Massachusetts Institute of Technology, and Virginia. Rhodes sponsors more than 80 activities, clubs, and organizations; more than 250 annual events; campus publications; and NCAA Division III men's and women's sports.

Rhodes' students govern themselves on campus through the Student Government Association and the Honor Council. The honor system succeeds to such a degree that professors often feel comfortable leaving their classrooms during tests.

"The Rhodes campus offers an uncommon level of intellectual intensity," observes Troutt. "This has been brought about by a number of factors, including an extraordinary faculty, staff, and student body; a full and diverse campus life; and world-class speakers and scholars-in-residence. Additionally, we are one of the few highly competitive liberal arts colleges located in a metropolitan area."

Obviously, the union that began in 1925 continues to pay handsome rewards. "We have been on a remarkable journey since 1925," says Troutt. "We have a great heritage—a past, I believe, that is but a prologue to an even greater future."

For more than 75 years, The Mallory Group Inc. has been providing special expertise in transporting such valuables as white gold, priceless artifacts, expensive electronics, and delicate flowers. Originally warehousing and shipping cotton, The Mallory Group now operates as two separate subsidiaries—Alexander International and Mallory Distribution Centers—and lends its expertise to customers in a variety of industries. ▲ Today, The

Mallory Group enjoys a reputation as one of the country's leading logistics companies. Headquartered in Memphis, the company operates an extensive network of public and contract warehousing facilities, freight forwarding and import/export services, and intermodal trucking and transportation systems. The Mallory Group is among the top container exporters in the country, and the firm continues to use its expertise to solve the time-sensitive logistics needs of its many customers.

A Vital Role in Memphis Industry

Founded in 1925, The Mallory Group is a fourth-generation company with more than 350 employees and operations throughout the United States. Originally called Memphis Compress and Storage Company, the operation met the storage and handling needs of area cotton merchants and producers. The company diversified to serve more industries, and in the early 1960s, Memphis Compress established Chickasaw Warehouse Company to store and handle general merchandise. In the late 1960s, the company expanded its services with a new subsidiary called Shelby Delivery Service, which provided local truck

delivery. In the mid-1970s, the company entered the contract warehousing business under the name of Trans-International Warehouse, and soon had major facilities in New Orleans, Houston, Seattle, and Oakland.

In 1971, The Mallory Group acquired the export division of V. Alexander & Company, an established international freight forwarder specializing in air and ocean shipping. The firm continued to add state-of-the-art services, including customs brokerage and domestic air freight. During the 1980s, The Mallory Group organized itself into three operating divisions: cotton warehousing, general merchandise warehousing, and transportation services, which had the trade names of Memphis Compress and Storage Company, Mallory Distribution Centers,

and Alexander International, respectively. The cotton operations were sold in 1996.

"There have been a lot of changes over the years," says B. Lee Mallory, president of Mallory Distribution Centers and grandson of the founder. "But one thing hasn't changed. This company has continued as a leader in the industries that fuel our region."

Alexander International

Today, Alexander International is a total transportation company that offers freight forwarding, customs clearance, domestic and international air, and ocean forwarding services. With offices throughout the United States, Alexander International has a diverse customer base ranging from the lumber and cotton industries to the hi-tech computer field to shippers of fine arts, including valuable paintings, sculpture, and artifacts. Alexander International's agency network extends worldwide with special emphasis on the European Common Market and the Pacific Rim areas.

The company is dedicated to providing domestic transportation customers with the right service at the best price, and offers next-flight-out, overnight, second-day, third-day, and deferred shipping services for time-sensitive shipments.

Alexander's offerings for international shipments are equally diverse, and they provide importers and

UNDER THE WATCHFUL EYES OF TWO GENERATIONS OF MALLORYS ON THE WALL, (FROM LEFT) NEELY MALLORY III, NEELY MALLORY JR., AND B. LEE MALLORY III GUIDE THE MALLORY GROUP INC.

▲ MATT McGOVERN

exporters with the flexibility they need to meet demand quickly and efficiently. The company's comprehensive range of international products is tailored to customers' specific needs, and Alexander International is known for its willingness to customize operations and information systems to provide transportation solutions that meet customer requirements.

"Our success is due to the outstanding quality of the staff and the loyalty of our customers," comments Neely Mallory III, president of Alexander International. "Combining these with an efficient and flexible information system has been our focus."

In short, Alexander International has positioned itself to be at the forefront of offering the international trading community the best in customer service and technology available.

Mallory Distribution Centers

Mallory Distribution Centers (MDC) is the logistics and warehousing arm of The Mallory Group. Operating more than 1.5 million square feet of public and contract distribution space for a variety of local, regional, and national accounts, MDC delivers a professional program of conventional and custom value-added services that meet clients' needs and budgets.

MDC's recipe of location and expertise is a popular one with customers. The company, for example, serves a 400-mile radius overnight, and can reach more than 65 percent of the nation's population on a next-day basis. MDC serves clients in a broad range of businesses, including automotive, paper, packaging, chemical, and consumer goods.

The most exciting development at MDC is its growing worldwide reputation for fast and smart logistics solutions. The company can combine inbound receiving, kitting, assembly, fulfillment, exporting, and a variety of other services to offer clients a turnkey distribution system that is noted for its speed and ability.

An Internet florist, for example, hired MDC to handle a part of its volume on Valentine's Day. In concert with the customs clearance services of Alexander International, the company imported flowers from various international origins, assembled the bulk flowers into individual arrangements, and shipped them to customers' doorsteps around the United States. It took 100 extra workers working all night just before Valentine's Day, and the project was completely successful.

In the electronics field, MDC provides warehouse logistics services, including kitting, inspection, and packaging for multinational companies like Nintendo and Nike. For the manufacturing industry, MDC coordinates and delivers transloading and cross-dock services for everything from large rolls of paper for International Paper to automotive parts for General Motors suppliers.

"Cotton was the foundation of this city's economy, and it was the foundation of our business," says W. Neely Mallory, president of The Mallory Group. "But—like Memphis—we've entered the new, high-speed, global economy. We've been committed to serving our global customers with the latest in distribution technology, and we look forward to another century of advanced and efficient partnerships."

1926

Radisson Hotel Memphis *1927*

Dunavant Enterprises, Inc. *1929*

Memphis Convention & Visitors Bureau *1929*

Baxter Healthcare Corporation *1931*

Boyle Investment Company *1933*

Smith & Nephew Orthopaedics *1934*

Memphis Light, Gas and Water *1939*

APAC Tennessee, Inc. Memphis Division *1945*

WALKER-J-WALKER, INC. *1945*

API Photographers/Film & Video *1946*

Belz Enterprises *1946*

Grace-St. Lukes Episcopal School *1947*

Wright Medical Group, Inc. *1950*

Towery Publishing, Inc. *1951*

Coleman-Etter, Fontaine Realtors *1951*

Allen & O'Hara, Inc. *1952*

Memphis Area Teachers' Credit Union *1957*

1960

Mid-South Specialties, Inc. *1959*

estled in the heart of downtown Memphis sits one of the city's oldest and greatest treasures. Today, the Radisson Hotel Memphis continues its tradition of serving as one of the city's leading hotel choices for tourists and businesspeople alike. Located in the historic Gayoso-Peabody District—a five-block area of approximately 50 buildings dating from 1880 to 1927— Radisson Memphis is gearing up for another century of serving Memphians and their guests.

Radisson Memphis, listed on the National Historic Register and one of Memphis' finest restorations, began as the Hotel Tennessee, which celebrated its grand opening on September 3, 1927. At that time, the latest conveniences included private baths, circulating cold water, and a foundation of steel and concrete—and rates were only $2 to $3 a night.

Making New History Downtown

Today, Radisson Memphis is still at the center of all that happens in downtown Memphis. The latest downtown renaissance–a $2.3 billion undertaking that is changing the face of downtown–is occurring all around the hotel. And because of that excitement, combined with Radisson Memphis' value and elegance, the historic hotel is still making its mark. There is genuine hospitality at every point of contact with customers.

While one of the most popular tourist hotels in the city, Radisson Memphis is also emerging as the top choice of business professionals and

LOCATED IN THE HISTORIC GAYOSO-PEABODY DISTRICT—A FIVE-BLOCK AREA OF APPROXIMATELY 50 BUILDINGS DATING FROM 1880 TO 1927—RADISSON HOTEL MEMPHIS IS GEARING UP FOR ANOTHER CENTURY OF SERVING MEMPHIANS AND THEIR GUESTS.

business functions. The full-service hotel includes a six-story atrium; a banquet facility; a complete sales and catering staff; 8,500 square feet of meeting space that can accommodate up to 500 people; a Gold Rewards program for frequent visitors; smoking, nonsmoking, and handicapped-accessible rooms; a number of recreational choices; room service; and T.G.I. Friday's food and beverage service. Amenities include seven suites and executive rooms, remote control cable television, in-room movies and games, coffeemakers, irons and ironing boards, work desks, telephones equipped with dataports, and artwork by local artists in every room.

A good location is essential for any hotel, and Radisson Memphis has one of the best possible locales—across the street from AutoZone Park and the Peabody Hotel, and within walking distance of world-famous Beale Street, as well as the Cook Convention Center, Main Street Mall, Mud Island, and the Mississippi River. The hotel is also close to other city attractions such as the Brooks Museum of Art, Overton Park, Children's Museum, Liberty

Bowl Stadium, Memphis Zoo and Aquarium, Civil Rights Museum, Mid-South Coliseum, and Elvis Presley's Graceland.

From historical value and great service, to a quality stay and a successful business function, the Radisson Hotel Memphis has a lot to offer visitors. This hotel truly embodies the unique spirit and history of Memphis.

Dunavant Enterprises, Inc., the largest private company in Memphis, is also well known as one of the largest cotton merchandisers in the world, handling 4 million bales of U.S. and foreign cotton per year. What started out as a small company on Front Street is now posting more than $1.5 billion in annual revenues. But it was a long road to becoming an important company in one of the city's most critical industries.

Front Street in downtown Memphis was the epicenter of the agricultural industry for cotton during the early part of the 20th century, and was hailed as the Cotton Capital of the World. W.B. Dunavant, was then a partner in T.J. White & Company, a company founded in 1929, which he helped run successfully for many years. His son, Billy Dunavant, knew from the age of 12 that he wanted to follow his father's footsteps into the cotton business, where he would start out at as a "squidge," a person who put farmers' cotton samples on trays to be classed and priced. Billy Dunavant joined the company in 1952 at age 19 and was promoted to full partner after just four years. In 1960, the firm became W.B. Dunavant & Company, with both Dunavants in charge. Soon after, the elder Dunavant died, leaving his son solely in charge at the age of 29.

In the late 1960s, Dunavant decided to move his company to its current location on Getwell, becoming the first cotton company to move off of Front Street. In the 1970s, Dunavant Enterprises emerged and today is one of the world's largest cotton merchants. However, despite its growth and diversification, the company is still a family business headquartered in Memphis. Dunavant's oldest sons, along with his son-in-law, are an integral part of the business, and more family members are coming on board, an aspect that remains important to Dunavant. "I wanted to build this for my children," he says. "It's truly a family company."

A Global Cotton Leader

Under Billy Dunavant's leadership, Dunavant Enterprises has grown in volume through remaining open to new marketing strategies, including forward contracting with farmers—a marketing option where farmers agree to prices for crops before planting begins; taking advantage of technological advances; and expanding into markets nationally and internationally. Dunavant Enterprises was part of the first international sale of U.S. cotton to China in 1972, and was a pioneer in vertical integration within the industry. Today, Dunavant Enterprises has numerous sites and offices around the world, and is involved with cotton warehousing and trucking, ginning operations, and trading both in the United States and in other countries. In addition, the company deals in Southern and Northern Hemisphere crops, making the business year-round rather than seasonal.

"Flexibility has been the key—changing not with, but ahead of, the times," Dunavant says proudly. This aggressive strategy of flexibility has been the backbone of Dunavant Enterprises, Inc.'s success, making it an important part of the cotton industry, as well as of Memphis' history.

THE MEN OF DUNAVANT ENTERPRISES, INC. (FROM LEFT), BUCHANAN D. DUNAVANT; WILLIAM B. DUNAVANT, JR.; WILLIAM B. DUNAVANT, III; AND JOHN D. DUNAVANT, HAVE SEEN THE COMPANY GROW FROM A SMALL FIRM TO ONE OF THE LARGEST COTTON MERCHANDISERS IN THE WORLD.

ight now, somewhere in the city of London, a taxicab is cruising the streets, spreading a message about Memphis. The message, placed there by the Memphis Convention & Visitors Bureau (MCVB), reminds London residents, as well as visitors to this European hub, that Memphis is a terrific tourist destination. ▲ MCVB estimates that about 9 million people see this London cab each month, and it transports more than 12,000

passengers each year. Tourist brochures are available inside the taxi, and the driver has been trained to answer Memphis-related questions.

Year-Round Entertainment

The London taxi is just one clever method of delivering the important message that there is always a lot to do in Memphis, Tennessee. Live music, family fun, historic landmarks, and regional cooking combine with dozens of one-of-a-kind attractions to make Memphis one of the fastest-growing tourist destinations in the United States.

Beale Street, for instance, is now ranked as the state's top tourist attraction—and one of the hottest amenities in the Southeast. The Memphis Zoo, newly expanded and remodeled, will soon feature a rare exhibition of pandas. The Memphis Brooks Museum of Art, the Dixon Gallery & Gardens, and the new Peabody Place Museum & Gallery all present some of the finest collections of art in the South.

Then, there are museums and displays with more of a local or regional flair: the C.H. Nash-Chucalissa Archaeological Museum, Mud Island River Park's Mississippi River Museum, the National Civil Rights Museum, the Pink Palace Museum, the National Ornamental Metal Museum, and the 19th-century homes of Victorian Village. And, for youngsters, there are the interactive, hands-on exhibitions of the Children's Museum of Memphis and the Memphis Fire Museum. The Memphis Queen Line's paddle wheelers appeal to all ages, combining entertainment and relaxation with an indisputably southern touch.

Another powerful draw for visitors to Memphis and Shelby County is the area's host of annual festivals and special events. Memphis in May, the Southern Heritage Classic, Africa in April, Arts in the Park, the Memphis Music and Heritage Festival, the Liberty Bowl, the Kroger St. Jude Indoor International Tennis Championships, and the FedEx St. Jude Golf Classic are just a few of the dozens of events that help put Memphis on the traveler's map.

The new Peabody Place development, connected via sky bridge to downtown's Peabody Hotel, is the largest entertainment and retail complex in the region. Under one roof visitors enjoy shopping; a 22-screen movie theater; a Jillian's entertainment center complete with restaurant and nightclub, bowling, and billiards; Tower Records; NASCAR Simulator; and Isaac Hayes' Music Food Passion. A brief stroll away is the new AutoZone Park, possibly the nicest little baseball stadium in the world, which serves as home to the AAA Redbirds.

THE MEMPHIS CONVENTION & VISITORS BUREAU (MCVB) IS DELIVERING THE IMPORTANT MESSAGE THAT THERE IS ALWAYS A LOT TO DO IN MEMPHIS, TENNESSEE. LIVE MUSIC, FAMILY FUN, HISTORIC LANDMARKS, AND REGIONAL COOKING COMBINE WITH DOZENS OF ONE-OF-A-KIND ATTRACTIONS TO MAKE MEMPHIS ONE OF THE FASTEST-GROWING TOURIST DESTINATIONS IN THE UNITED STATES.

Perhaps most important, Memphis is known as the Home of the Blues and Birthplace of Rock and Roll. This well-earned reputation centers around Graceland, Sun Studio, and the area's newest music-related attractions, the Gibson Guitar Factory and the prestigious Memphis Rock 'n' Soul Museum.

Little wonder that, in recent decades, Memphis has become a magnetic force within the hospitality industry, attracting more than 8 million visitors a year. Yet, as powerful and appealing as the city's many attractions are, much of the credit for expanding the tourism industry here—and for helping generate its tremendous boost to the economic well-being of the community—falls to MCVB's effective and far-reaching promotional programs.

Spreading the Word

MCVB is a nonprofit membership corporation responsible for marketing Memphis and Shelby County as a convention site and visitor destination. Tourism is the state's second-largest industry. Visitors to West Tennessee are responsible for $2.1 billion in expenditures, with an estimated economic impact of $139 million in local and state taxes. In other words, tourism is big business.

The taxi rumbling around London is an excellent example of the creative ways MCVB gets the word out about the Bluff City. "Our tourism development department initiated a similar taxi campaign a couple of years ago as a co-op with the State of Tennessee's Department of Tourist Development," explains Kevin Kane, MCVB president and CEO. "That effort was tremendously successful. That's why we decided Memphis deserved its own cab. In fact, now there are three: two in London and one in Manchester, England."

MCVB's tourism development department employs several full-time sales representatives who attend trade shows and meet one-on-one with travel intermediaries like travel agents and tour operators. The department handles all consumer advertising, provides marketing assistance to MCVB's 600 members, comanages the Tennessee State Welcome Center on Riverside Drive, and directs an overseas sales and marketing force in Europe.

MCVB also has a convention development department. In addition to the national sales staff housed in Memphis and co-op assistance in select U.S. cities, the department recently placed a full-time representative in Washington, D.C., where more than 3,000 national associations have home offices.

"It is important for us to have close access to the key buyers who can generate so much economic impact for our city," says Kane. "Obviously, it is a huge plus to have someone there who can meet with prospective meeting groups."

MCVB's convention development department also provides special convention services to ensure the smooth-running success of meetings and conventions while they are in Memphis. This nationally recognized staff has won major service awards every year from 1995 to 2000.

There are many ways to build tourism business and revenues. MCVB not only promotes the Memphis destination to new markets, but it encourages repeat visits and the extension of their stays. Marketing, promotions, and public relations programs not only support the attractors, or tourist lures, but also draw attention to attractions and events that may be lesser known—activities that are worth adding an extra night or two to experience.

To this end, MCVB distributes official visitor guides, condensed travel guides and area maps, tour operator and convention planner guides, calendars of events, and other collateral that help sell all that Memphis has to offer. There are foreign-language versions, too, including French, German, Dutch, Spanish, and Japanese, among others.

Certainly, the most important new tool in marketing and promoting the Mid-South area is through the Internet. MCVB's Web site, www.memphistravel.com, is aimed at tourists, meeting planners, the media, travel intermediaries, and other travel industry businesses. Continuously updated, the site includes information about attractions, hotels, restaurants, and transportation—virtually everything a traveler needs to know for a pleasant and memorable experience.

Whether it is by London cab or on the Internet, by a sales call in Memphis or in Amsterdam, MCVB is getting the word out about Memphis. And while visitors are sure to have a great time, Memphians are the real beneficiaries, enjoying a higher quality of life made possible by increased revenues and, perhaps more important, developing a greater sense of pride in a hometown that is known and admired worldwide.

FROM THE NATIONAL CIVIL RIGHTS MUSEUM, TO THE MEMPHIS ZOO, TO ST. JUDE CHILDREN'S RESEARCH HOSPITAL, THE MCVB STRIVES TO PROMOTE ALL THE VARIOUS SITES AND ATTRACTIONS IN THE CITY.

PERHAPS MOST IMPORTANT, MEMPHIS IS KNOWN AS THE HOME OF THE BLUES AND BIRTHPLACE OF ROCK AND ROLL. THIS WELL-EARNED REPUTATION CENTERS AROUND GRACELAND, SUN STUDIO, AND THE AREA'S NEWEST MUSIC-RELATED ATTRACTIONS, THE GIBSON GUITAR FACTORY AND THE PRESTIGIOUS MEMPHIS ROCK 'N' SOUL MUSEUM.

*T*he year 2001 marked the 70th anniversary of Baxter Healthcare Corporation, a company with firmly established Memphis roots. Travenol Labs, a Memphis company founded back in 1931, was the foundation for Baxter. Today, Memphis plays a big role in Baxter's mission to deliver critical therapies for life-threatening conditions. ▲ Baxter's operating experience extends to nearly every type of health care system in the world, and its

CLOCKWISE FROM RIGHT:
MANY OF BAXTER HEALTHCARE CORPORATION'S EMPLOYEES HAVE BEEN WITH THE COMPANY SINCE THE FACILITY OPENED ON MENDENHALL MORE THAN 20 YEARS AGO.

THE BAXTER MEMPHIS GLOBAL LOGISTICS CENTER IS MORE THAN HALF A MILLION SQUARE FEET AND, AT ANY ONE TIME, CONTAINS THAT MANY CASES OF LIFE SAVING HEALTH CARE PRODUCTS.

BLOOD COLLECTION AND FILTERING DEVICES, ANESTHESIA TRAYS, AND PUMPS ARE JUST A FEW OF THE BAXTER PRODUCTS STOCKED AND DISTRIBUTED FROM THE MEMPHIS FACILITY.

▼ FRANK BRADEN PHOTOGRAPHY, INC.

▼ FRANK BRADEN PHOTOGRAPHY, INC.

▼ FRANK BRADEN PHOTOGRAPHY, INC.

products are sold in 112 countries. The company's medical breakthroughs have meant the difference between life and death for countless people. Baxter, for example, was responsible for the first commercially viable intravenous solutions, a market unheard of when it first began. The company also produced the first genetically engineered therapy for hemophiliacs.

All of Baxter's products relate to the blood and circulatory system. The firm's BioScience product line consists of products that collect, separate, and store blood, as well as therapeutic proteins derived from blood. The renal products cleanse the blood, and the intravenous (IV) products infuse drugs and other solutions into the blood.

Since Baxter's products are based on related technologies, each of its manufacturing plants produces a full range of the company's products. The expertise developed over years of leadership in producing critical health care products is utilized in every Baxter manufacturing plant around the world, including expertise in plastics extrusion, heat-sealing and filling, sterilization, and many other processes.

Baxter's some 40,000 employees worldwide are recruited on the basis of knowledge of business culture, customs, health care system and practices, and government policies in the markets where they work. The company has been recognized repeatedly by *Industry Week* as one of the 100 best-managed companies in the world. Baxter has 76 facilities worldwide, and its Memphis operation is a replenishment center that receives international bulk products and ships them to distribution centers. The company also delivers renal products directly to dialysis patients at home. Baxter's Anesthesia and Critical Care Business Unit, located in Bartlett, distributes injectable and inhaled anesthetics and pharmaceuticals to hospitals and wholesalers in the United States and abroad.

The nature of Baxter's work is very urgent in nature; it's not just supplies. People's lives depend on the products the company creates. "We don't just ship boxes; we save lives," says Alfred Green, group manager.

A Good Corporate Citizen

*B*axter is grateful for the role Memphis has played in its success, and reciprocates every chance it gets. The company participates in such important community projects as Race for the Cure, Junior Achievement Bowl-a-Thon, fund-

raisers for Ronald McDonald House, and RecycleFest for the Children's Museum. Thanks to a corporate culture that strongly supports a balance between the demands of work and family life, employees are rewarded for community involvement as a way to provide added value to their work environment. Policies such as this aided in Baxter's recognition in *BusinessWeek* magazine as one of the top 30 family-friendly companies in the United States. The Memphis facility has also won numerous internal environmental, health, and safety awards, as well as customer service awards.

In addition, the company established the Baxter International Foundation as its philanthropic arm to expand the quality and accessibility of health care for people domestically and abroad. The company's charitable giving has provided access to care for children, the uninsured, and the elderly; helped prevent child abuse and neglect; promoted health education; and expanded education opportunities for health care providers.

Baxter Healthcare Corporation, which has contributed to the local economy for decades, will continue to be an integral part of Memphis through business expansion, technology sharing, employment, and the introduction of medical products that benefit Memphians.

Roads and highways are a critical piece of America's success, and the APAC group of companies has contributed a significant portion of those roads and highways. In 1879, APAC laid the first commercial asphalt road in the country, and in 1900, the company received the patent for the material. Today, APAC's autonomous companies form one of the nation's largest highway construction groups and a leading materials supplier

to contractors. The dynamic group is focused on innovation, while the Memphis Division of APAC Tennessee delivers a high level of performance to transportation, corporate, commercial, and industrial customers across the region.

Offering Comprehensive Site Packages

The Memphis Division of APAC Tennessee specializes in asphalt production and laydown, asphalt and concrete cold milling, cement-treated base product and placement, stone base placement, grading, and cement, lime, and fly-ash soil stabilization. The division also sells cement-treated base material and hot-mix asphalt.

Clients get maximum value out of APAC's expertise, however, when they hire the company for a full-service site package. Companies preparing to build a facility, campus, or residential area call on APAC to design and engineer parking lots and roads, and then those companies rely on APAC to estimate the project, engineer an appropriate surface mix, test materials, install underground utilities, construct foundations, and lay surfaces.

"Clients tell us that our full-service management style is one of the most valuable parts of the relationship," says Victor Durkee, APAC Tennessee, Inc. Memphis Division president. "Every project gets a highly experienced management team with materials and installation expertise." That means APAC can help clients pick the best solution for their needs, and can stay on the job to make sure it is executed properly. "Our approach also offers accountability," Durkee adds. "Our clients know that it's APAC doing the work."

A long list of leading companies count on APAC for site packages. FedEx, for example, turned to APAC

Memphis for the soil stabilization, roads, and parking areas at its new World Technology Center. Wal-Mart has a regional relationship with APAC for the construction of its parking areas, and APAC has even designed and surfaced tracks for NASCAR speedways. The company did the surfacing work for the Pyramid arena, and has taken on massive runway, freight terminal, and interstate highway projects.

The Best Safety and Quality Practices

High-caliber employees distinguish APAC from the rest of its competition. They are committed to a best practices concept that instills exceptional value in their everyday activities. APAC has one of

the strongest safety records in the construction industry. With personal injuries 16 to 20 times lower than industry average, APAC companies employ specialized and National Safety Council-approved training programs, employee incentives, and awards. "We have accumulated almost 3 million man-hours without a single lost-time injury," Durkee says. "Our low accident and injury rates are unparalleled in the industry."

APAC employees have a commitment to safe and innovative practices that provide for greater productivity, higher morale, and greater overall quality. It is a philosophy that will likely ensure the company is laying the foundation for the nation's success for another century.

APAC TENNESSEE, INC. MEMPHIS DIVISION DID THE SURFACING WORK FOR THE PYRAMID ARENA, AND HAS TAKEN ON MASSIVE RUNWAY, FREIGHT TERMINAL, AND INTERSTATE HIGHWAY PROJECTS.

THE MEMPHIS DIVISION OF APAC TENNESSEE DELIVERS A HIGH LEVEL OF PERFORMANCE TO TRANSPORTATION, CORPORATE, COMMERCIAL, AND INDUSTRIAL CUSTOMERS ACROSS THE REGION.

*P*erusing any chapter in Memphis' rich history will lead to Boyle Investment Company's emergence as a key player that, over the years, has made the city what it is today.

A Boyle family ancestor, for example, was among the city's founders in 1819. The Boyle family developed stately Belvedere Boulevard in the early 1900s. Boyle paved the way for the city's growth eastward with its expansive, mixed-use Ridgeway Center in the 1970s.

And today, Boyle's innovative Schilling Farms development is heralded for its meticulous attention to design details and focus on quality of life.

While these projects and the multitude of others that bear the Boyle name are diverse in scope, Boyle Investment Company's developments all share a common trait. From the beginning, the company has demonstrated a commitment to quality that has given its projects long-term value.

Shaping the City's Growth

When Major General Andrew Jackson—a future president of the United States—founded the city of Memphis in 1819 and began to lay out the plans for the port city, he was joined by two cofounders: James Winchester and Boyle ancestor John Overton.

The Boyle family continued its critical role in the city's progression in the early 1900s, as real estate developer Edward Boyle began to develop prestigious subdivisions on the then-outskirts of the city. One such development—Belvedere Boulevard—is still home to some of the city's stateliest and most elegant Midtown homes.

In 1933, three of Edward Boyle's sons—Snowden Boyle, Charles Boyle, and J. Bayard Boyle Sr.—followed their father into the real estate business and founded Boyle Investment Company. Today, the company remains family owned and is headed by Chairman J. Bayard Boyle Jr., son of cofounder J. Bayard Boyle Sr., and his brother-in-law, President Henry Morgan.

The Boyle brothers' initial efforts focused on buying land and developing residential subdivisions and shopping centers. "My father had a remarkable ability to identify and acquire properties in areas that would soon become major growth corridors," J. Bayard Boyle Jr. says. "He was always researching, planning, and predicting."

In the 1950s, Boyle became a full-service real estate investment operation. The company's commitment to research

and planning paid off once again in the 1960s and 1970s, as Boyle began to develop a large property at Poplar and I-240, well to the east of the city's population center. The decades that followed proved the wisdom of the firm's decision. The offices, retail center, and homes in the development soon found themselves in the heart of Memphis' growth, and these sites remain some of the most desirable locations in the city.

Today, the company is once again proving the power of careful research and planning. Boyle's sizable Schilling Farms development is an innovative, $350 million entity in fast-growing Collierville that combines residential, retail, and office developments in one lush, pedestrian-friendly, self-contained community.

Landmarks for Living and Working

Boyle's notable Memphis achievements comprise a long list of projects. The company's River Oaks and Farmington subdivisions are some of the most prestigious in the city. Boyle's Ridgeway Center—known as one of Memphis' first office parks—houses the corporate headquarters

REGALIA, A 22-ACRE MIXED-USE DEVELOPMENT IN EAST MEMPHIS, OFFERS A WIDE VARIETY OF SPECIALTY SHOPS AND RESTAURANTS, AS WELL AS UNION PLANTERS BANK AND EMBASSY SUITES (RIGHT).

BOYLE DEVELOPED THIS 150,000-SQUARE-FOOT OFFICE BUILDING IN RIDGEWAY CENTER, WHERE ANCHOR TENANT MORGAN KEEGAN OCCUPIES 50,000 SQUARE FEET OF SPACE.

of many national and international companies. The firm's Class A Marsh Center and Morgan Keegan Center on the southern edge of Ridgeway Center have become East Memphis landmarks. Boyle also developed the upscale Humphreys Center, Regalia, and Village Shops of Forest Hill retail centers.

In addition, Boyle has developed office buildings for a number of major companies, including corporate headquarters for Thomas and Betts, an international manufacturer of electrical components and equipment, and the Southeast Regional Headquarters for the U.S. Postal Service.

The company's expertise has led to a growing list of projects outside of Memphis as well, including developments in Texas, Missouri, Illinois, Arkansas, Kentucky, and Mississippi. Boyle's expertise in planning retail centers is especially evident in the Dallas-Fort Worth area, where Boyle's Preston Shepard Place and Southwest Crossing power centers are popular shopping destinations.

Developing Property, Developing Value

There's no secret to Boyle's success. "We've built a strong company because the family, from the beginning, has been committed to developing for long-term value," says Morgan. "We operate on the belief that properties are long-term investments that should be meticulously planned, built, and maintained."

Boyle overlooks no detail, and often goes to great expense to ensure a property's aesthetics and longevity. "Thinking for the long term is in everyone's best interest," Morgan says. "Our buyers, partners, and tenants know they're part of a property that will be just as exquisite 20 years from now as it is today."

With excellent foresight and a tradition of quality development, Boyle Investment Company has been a boon to the Memphis area and beyond. The company will endure, through both its properties and its legendary expertise, for generations to come.

When T.J. Smith, a young pharmacist in Hull, England, opened a small chemist shop in 1856, he began his work of helping doctors help people. Smith turned to the wholesale trade, building the business from a small local shop into a hospital and pharmaceutical company that served most of the United Kingdom. His nephew, H.N. Smith, joined the company in 1896, making the company T.J. Smith & Nephew. World War I propelled the

expansion of the company in both product range and size, as it responded to the demand for wound dressings.

After the war, the company continued to expand and established operations in other countries, moving to the United States in the 1980s. It was then that Smith & Nephew was introduced to and acquired Richards Medical Company in Memphis. Founded in 1934 during the Great Depression by J. Don Richards, an orthopaedic product salesman from Indiana, Richards' early products included splints and rib belts, which were sold to local hospitals. Later, the company pioneered and gained an international reputation for innovation in orthopaedic trauma and joint reconstruction products. The coming together of Smith & Nephew and Richards in 1986 has transformed both businesses. Today, Smith & Nephew Orthopaedics has sales in excess of half a billion dol-

lars, and contributes a major share of the company's overall sales and profit.

Smith & Nephew Orthopaedics is headquartered in Memphis and is one of four core businesses for the London-based company. The other business units focus on the endoscopy, rehabilitation, and wound care segments of the medical device industry.

First Choice Performance

Smith & Nephew Orthopaedics has had a historic impact on the medical device industry. The company specializes in designing and developing replacement products for the hip, knee, and shoulder, as well as industry-defining trauma products such as nail systems that help bone fractures heal.

Smith & Nephew's vision is to become First Choice with its employees, customers, patients, and shareholders.

The behaviors of performance, innovation, and trust are what Smith & Nephew believes will help it reach that vision. The company will continue to develop and acquire innovative technologies that benefit the health care system by improving patient care, reducing health care costs, and educating and training health care professionals.

Industry-Leading Innovation

The development of industry-defining and clinically effective products is how Smith & Nephew stays ahead of the competition, and that is more critical now than ever before. Globally, life spans are increasing; in the United States, the baby boomers are graying. And that means a growing need for medical products that can help extend quality of life as longevity increases. Smith & Nephew's integrated teams are streamlining the

HEADQUARTERS FOR SMITH & NEPHEW ORTHOPAEDICS ARE LOCATED ON BROOKS ROAD, NEAR MEMPHIS INTERNATIONAL AIRPORT.

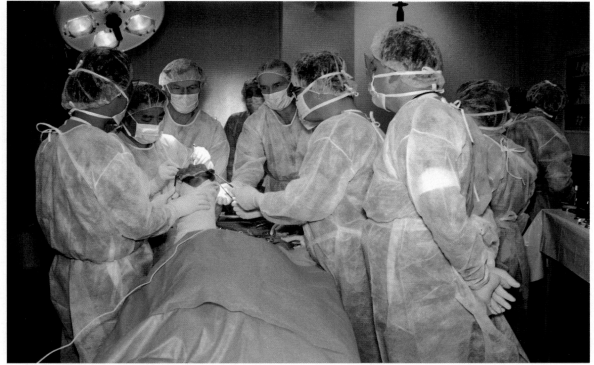

research and development process to get new and improved products on the market more quickly.

Smith & Nephew's cutting-edge approach is evidenced in areas like oxidized zirconium knee technology, a new implant material for orthopaedics, which the company believes will significantly reduce the amount of wear-debris generated throughout the life of an implant. The company has also acquired a winning product in Exogen, an ultrasound bone-growth stimulation device, as well as in developing cross-linked polyethylene technology.

SUPARTZ is a product that Smith & Nephew markets that relieves pain caused by osteoarthritis. eTrauma.com allows surgeons to view patient X-rays from the Internet. Through a number of partnerships such as those above, as well as the one Smith & Nephew has with Medtronic for image-guided surgery for orthopaedic applications, the company's products are making a profound impact on the lives of patients and health care systems around the world.

Building Trust

The heart of Smith & Nephew, though, comes through its employees, and social responsibility is a core value of the company. Smith & Nephew emphasizes the importance of giving back to the community to its employees, and their presence can be seen, heard, and felt all around Memphis. Smith & Nephew's employees have consistently supported, both individually and collectively, programs like the United Way, Memphis Arts Council, Junior Achievement, Adopt-

a-School, American Heart Association, Make-a-Wish Foundation, and Computers in the Community. The company was a founding member of the Memphis Model Partnership for a Prepared Workforce, which emphasizes cooperation among businesses, educational institutions, and civic leaders to ensure that students are prepared for and receive real work opportunities in the community after graduation.

Project Apollo was developed by Smith & Nephew's employees to sponsor surgeons donating their time on mission trips around the globe. The quality of the employees' participation is note-worthy, and is a tribute to the spirit and mission of helping and healing at Smith & Nephew.

Success and Continued Growth

A strong portfolio, a top-notch management team, and emerging markets that are demanding new and improved products are all fueling the continued growth and success of Smith & Nephew. Today's accomplishments are in line with the many firsts of the past. The company developed the first compression hip screw, the first American-designed total hip, and the first U.S. Food and Drug Administration-approved cementless total hip. Smith & Nephew Orthopaedics, quite simply, is continuing its tradition of significant contributions to the advancement of health care and getting closer to First Choice each step of the way.

emphians don't think about Memphis Light, Gas and Water (MLGW) too often, and that's the way the utility's employees prefer it. "For more than 60 years, our customers have enjoyed some of the most reliable and competitively priced services in the nation," says Herman Morris Jr., president and CEO of the utility. "If they take it for granted, it means our team is doing its job." ◢ As MLGW quietly serves the growing Memphis and Shelby

County area, it is earning a reputation as one of the most progressive utilities in the country. Today, MLGW is the largest three-service municipal utility system in the nation, and its nationally recognized programs provide service that is even more reliable, competitively priced, and beneficial to its hometown.

"MLGW's employees have exceeded all expectations," Morris says. "I think they deserve a lot of the credit for the success of their community."

A History of Service

MLGW was founded in 1939, when Memphis Mayor E.H. Crump combined all of the city's utility companies under one umbrella. Since those days,

the power needs of the region have radically changed.

What hasn't changed is MLGW's commitment to serving customers, whatever their needs might be. The utility provides reliable power to more than 400,000 residents of Memphis and Shelby County, and is also known for the exceptional service it provides

through programs such as Energy Solutions. This program, which was launched in 1999, helps businesses and other large organizations identify their true energy needs and maximize their usage.

"Providing for our community means we must remain strong for today and strong for tomorrow," Morris says. "There's no doubt that our employees and management have made MLGW one of the strongest and healthiest utilities in the country."

Strength and Endurance

From a fiscal standpoint, there are few utilities that can match MLGW's strength. The utility maintains a prestigious A1 rating from Moody's Investors Service, and remains the only utility in the nation to hold a AAA rating from Standard & Poor's.

MLGW also builds strength for tomorrow by working hand in hand with the Memphis Area Chamber of Commerce to lure major businesses to the community. With an office inside the chamber's headquarters, MLGW spends more than $500,000 each year on recruiting new business and encouraging expansion. MLGW's critical role in these economic development efforts earned it designations in 1999 and 2000 as one of the nation's top 10 utilities by *Site Selection* magazine.

Maintaining its information technology infrastructure, MLGW recently completed a $1.76 million upgrade to its System Control and Data Acquisition

MEMPHIS LIGHT, GAS AND WATER (MLGW) IS THE LARGEST THREE-SERVICE MUNICIPAL UTILITY SYSTEM IN THE NATION, AND ITS NATIONALLY RECOGNIZED PROGRAMS PROVIDE SERVICE THAT IS RELIABLE, COMPETITIVELY PRICED, AND BENEFICIAL TO ITS HOMETOWN.

master-control system. This upgrade complements a redesigned Web site and the ongoing development of the utility's e-commerce capabilities, as well as a comprehensive upgrade to its Customer Information System.

From service excellence to preparations for the future, MLGW's strong efforts were recently recognized with the Tennessee Quality Excellence Award. In 1999, the utility was one of only two organizations in the state to receive the award. The Tennessee Quality Excellence Award is presented by the Tennessee Quality Award organization, which is sponsored by the Tennessee Department of Economic and Community Development. The award's criteria mirror those of the national Malcolm Baldrige quality award. To qualify for the award, MLGW had to demonstrate quality awareness and best practices at progressive levels: quality interest, quality commitment, and quality achievement.

Extending Service into the Community

MLGW's commitment to service extends into the community in the form of the countless hours and resources its employees give to community projects. The long list of the utility's service programs includes the MLGW United Way Campaign, in which employees have broken city records with total contributions of $606,000; Plus-1, a program that spends $4 million each year to help pay the utility bills of members of the community in need; and Project MAX, an MLGW-organized

program that provides free weather-proofing and home repair assistance to elderly, low-income, and disabled area residents.

In addition, MLGW also supports LifeBlood drives, community leadership training sessions, MLGW Law Explorer Post, Special Olympics SportsFest, Junior Achievement Bowl-a-Thons, March of Dimes WalkAmerica, and many more.

MLGW employees' commitment to community service projects was recognized in 2000 by the Memphis Chapter of the National Society of Fund Raising

Executives (NSFRE), who presented MLGW with the Partners in Philanthropy Award. Only one other company has received this prestigious award.

MLGW's dedication to exceptional service is complemented by an equally strong commitment to great rates. That commitment was evident in late 1999, when the utility unveiled the first-ever rate decrease in its history. The decrease improves an average monthly residential utility bill that was already well below comparable cities such as Dallas, New Orleans, St. Louis, and Houston.

MLGW's commitment to service and cost efficiency is truly exceptional. In fact, J.D. Power and Associates—a research organization whose name is almost synonymous with customer satisfaction—recently named MLGW among the top utilities in the nation.

But awards are just the icing on the cake. To MLGW, what matters most is the utility's commitment to providing Memphians with quality service. "Total quality is more than a philosophy," Morris says. "It is something that the employees of MLGW practice every day. I can't thank these dedicated people enough for their unwavering commitment to quality and service."

ALKER-J-WALKER, INC. *was founded in Memphis in 1945 by Grover L. Walker Jr. and John P. Walker Sr. The company began as a small business that focused mainly on coal furnaces and has grown into quite a sizable entity. Today, the firm is a multimillion-dollar organization servicing and installing state-of-the-art HVAC systems.* ▲ *Lee Walker and John Walker Jr., second-generation owners, presently head the company.*

Lee Walker started with the company in 1970 after receiving a bachelor's degree in business administration from the University of Memphis. John Walker Jr. started with the company after receiving a bachelor of science degree in business administration from the University of Tennessee-Martin.

Having had an enduring presence in Memphis—a city known for muggy, intensely hot summers—the Walker family has witnessed the area's tremendous growth, and has worked behind the scenes to make sure that much of the city's development, old and new, is equipped with state-of-the-art HVAC systems for heating and cooling comfort.

WALKER-J-WALKER's customer base is strictly industrial and commercial, and the firm is one of the premier companies serving the tristate—Arkansas, Mississippi, and Tennessee—area. In its portfolio, WALKER-J-WALKER has such notable projects as the Hickory Ridge Mall, the Crescent Center, the International Paper twin towers, Lenox Business Park, the Williams-Sonoma distribution center, several Wal-Mart SuperCenters throughout the South and Southwest, Nike, and BMW in Mississippi. Most recently, the company added the Wolfchase Galleria shopping mall to that list.

WALKER-J-WALKER has some 170 highly skilled employees. "Many of our employees have been with us 20 to 30 years," says Lee Walker. "They have contributed an immeasurable amount to our success. We are very proud of the fact that we have several second- and third-generation employees working for us."

Comfort First

WALKER-J-WALKER is a company many people trust because of its Memphis roots and its excellent employees. But it is also a company with extensive capabilities. Areas of specialty include, but are not limited to, heating, air-conditioning, ventilation, sheet metal work, piping, controls, and energy management systems. These systems are run with the latest technology, and WALKER-J-WALKER's services apply to anything from new construction to maintenance.

The company runs a full sheet metal shop with 15 full-time shop mechanics and 65 field mechanics. The company's full-line service department has more than 40 service technicians, with someone on standby 24 hours a day to meet customer needs. Licensed in Arkansas, Mississippi, and Tennessee, the company also has an excellent safety program in place. WALKER-J-WALKER is now part of the Comfort Systems USA network of mechanical contractors, which numbers more than 85 companies and $1.5 billion in annual sales.

With the continued growth of Memphis and its surrounding areas, it is certain that demand for WALKER-J-WALKER, INC.'s expertise will continue to increase. And when the company's team of professionals do their jobs as well as they have in the past, consumers will notice only their pleasant environment instead of the sweltering Memphis heat.

FOUNDED IN 1945, WALKER-J-WALKER, INC. IS TODAY A MULTIMILLION-DOLLAR ORGANIZATION SERVICING AND INSTALLING STATE-OF-THE-ART HVAC SYSTEMS.

*N*estled since 1947 on a shady corner in the Central Gardens neighborhood of midtown Memphis, Grace-St. Luke's Episcopal School has spent some 50 years helping children explore and learn within a nurturing environment that emphasizes the development of a strong academic foundation, character, honor, and integrity. Today, the school serves children ranging from three-year-olds through eighth-graders. ▲ No matter the age, though,

Grace-St. Luke's addresses the whole child, and helps students develop a strong mind and a strong spirit. The special mix is made possible by the school's close relationship with its home parish, Grace-St. Luke's Episcopal Church. The school's Anglican roots give the program a loving approach, a strong sense of academic discipline, and a commitment to diversity that embraces a range of faiths and cultures.

Small Classes, Big Ideas

*W*e're a neighborhood school with a worldview," says Tom Beazley, Grace-St. Luke's headmaster. "Within a nurturing environment, we encourage the children to investigate, create, and explore."

That atmosphere starts in the classroom, where small class sizes ensure that students get the individualized attention they need. In fact, most classes have fewer than 18 students. The teachers who lead these small groups are truly exceptional, and more than 50 percent have master's degrees.

The curriculum is engaging. In preschool programs, Grace-St. Luke's students interact in small groups and in larger classes—all with the purpose of instilling the idea that learning is fun. In the lower school, academics are combined with activity to foster understanding. Children read their first book, then write and illustrate their own book. Children study Michelangelo and paint their own murals in the hallways. And in middle school, students exercise maturity in the selection of academic and extracurricular alternatives. By seventh grade, typically 50 percent or more of the school's students score in the 97th percentile or higher on their achievement tests, and are recognized for their scores by the Duke University Talent Search Program.

While the classroom plays a big role in a Grace-St. Luke's education, so

does the church's sanctuary. Regular chapel services and other faith-based activities encourage children to explore and develop spiritually.

But perhaps the most important piece of the Grace-St. Luke's puzzle is the family. Communication between school and home is important at Grace-St. Luke's, and the school partners with an active parents' association that provides a host of opportunities in which parents can get involved. In addition, parents are invited to worship with their children, to have lunch with them, or to join them on a special field trip. There are also times for families

to enjoy meeting other families, such as the preschool cookouts at Miss Lee's and the spaghetti supper on the main campus. Teachers throughout the school regularly communicate in writing and E-mail with parents, and parent-teacher conferences are periodically scheduled; teachers are also happy to schedule additional appointments.

A visit to Grace-St. Luke's Episcopal School's campus reveals that the approach is working. Students show a joy for learning, an enthusiasm for life, and a spirit of accomplishment. And that's a recipe for a strong, well-rounded, and happy foundation.

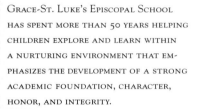

GRACE-ST. LUKE'S EPISCOPAL SCHOOL HAS SPENT MORE THAN 50 YEARS HELPING CHILDREN EXPLORE AND LEARN WITHIN A NURTURING ENVIRONMENT THAT EMPHASIZES THE DEVELOPMENT OF A STRONG ACADEMIC FOUNDATION, CHARACTER, HONOR, AND INTEGRITY.

illiam Carrier Jr., a Kentucky native, received honorary master's degrees in art and music while managing a dance band back in the 1930s. After serving with the U.S. Army as a photographer assigned to Intelligence during World War II, Carrier returned with a Bronze Star Medal for his efforts and a newfound passion for the power of photography. ▲ *After much research, Carrier and his wife, Flo, decided to move to Memphis. In 1946,*

he selected two other photographers and a technician, Joe Cianciola, and formed Allied Photographic Illustrators (API). The company was located at Main Street and Monroe Avenue, and Carrier often recalled that Abe Plough worked on the floor above—mixing up chemicals for Di-Gel. By the 1960s, the studio had relocated to Cooper Street and business was thriving, handling accounts such as Holiday Inn, Schering-Plough, Hunter Fans, and Cleo Wrap.

Through the years, Carrier and Bill Kingdon amassed hundreds of awards from the Professional Photographers of America, Kodak, Fuji, and others. Carrier, who also taught commercial photography at Winona School of Professional Photography in Illinois, began to establish a network of professional alliances through the Professional Photographers of America, an organization in which he would later serve as president in 1968.

PHOTOGRAPHERS JOE CIANCIOLA AND BILL KINGDON, WITH FOUNDER W. W. CARRIER, FORMED API. TODAY IT IS ONE OF THE TOP IMAGING COMPANIES IN THE SOUTH, PRODUCING EVERYTHING FROM CORPORATE VIDEOS AND TELEVISION COMMERCIALS TO FILM AND DIGITAL STILL IMAGES.

Made in Memphis

In 1983, API furthered its commitment to produce quality film and video in Memphis by building a soundstage and editing facility that brought its total production space to 15,000 square feet. Bill Carrier, son of the company founder, has followed in his father's footsteps to become active in national professional organizations such as Professional Photographers of America and Camera Craftsmen of America.

Bill Carrier believes that through teaching and sharing information among professionals everyone wins, and his participation creates an awareness of Memphis as well. Carrier is the only local director of photography sanctioned by the International Cinematographers Guild. He was instrumental in the planning of the Memphis & Shelby County Film & Tape Commission, and served on the original commission under Mayors Bill Morris and Dick Hackett. Carrier has also been active in the American Advertising Federation and the National Academy of Recording Arts and Sciences (NARAS).

Since its inception, API has promoted the development and hiring of local crews, artists, musicians, and theatrical talent. During the last some 50 years, API has served as a hotbed for developing talent. Some of the best local photographers and film/video professionals received their on-the-job training at API. Giving back to

WITH THE LARGEST SOUNDSTAGE IN THE REGION, API CAN MEET THE NEEDS OF PRACTICALLY ANYONE, FROM SHOOTING A ROOM FULL OF PIANOS FOR BALDWIN, TO INSTALLING AND PHOTOGRAPHING A WORKING AQUA GLASS WHIRLPOOL.

the community is still important to Carrier. His favorite projects are those that promote Memphis, public service, and local arts, including the Metropolitan Inter-Faith Association (MIFA), St. Jude, and the Wonders Series.

Carrier says, "As technology changes and the economy globalizes, our clients need to expand. Our digital capabilities, high definition, 16-by-9 format, DVD, editing, and special effects are state of the art. We've translated corporate videos into 14 languages. We've digitized our stock photography spanning more than 50 years. Today, we can service our clients with formats that are modular in nature, creating longevity of use and diversity of purpose, which are wise economic options."

API produces award-winning TV commercials and infomercials, point-of-purchase and product or presentation videos, print ads, Web site visuals, training or corporate image videos, multimedia, or CDs and DVDs—and all in still or motion formats.

Compelling Imagery, National Recognition

While API's still photography has continued to receive international recognition, the company's Film Division has also collected quite a few honors including winning numerous Telly, ADDY, and Council for Advancement and Support of Education (CASE) awards; gold and silver awards in the Houston and Chicago international film festivals; and several prestigious Cine Golden Eagle awards.

API and Carrier have been showcased in a number of national trade publications, and have completed projects for the likes of American Express, Burlington Northern Santa Fe Railroad, Wal-Mart, International Paper, FedEx Corporation, and Perkins

Restaurants. Carrier has served as director of photography, second unit, on feature films including *Silence of the Lambs*, *The Firm*, *A Family Thing*, and *Blind Vengeance*.

Aside from all the awards, Carrier insists that API's level of quality work comes from more than a half century of experience in the art of photography and client service. Diversity of style is yet another gift that a strong base has provided. Sometimes clients like to pigeonhole a particular style or specialty area—it helps them to select a photo or cinema professional. However, diversity takes more expertise. And, according to Carrier, longevity of uses should always outweigh trendy styles.

For example, when API produced a television commercial for a national ice-cream brand in the early 1980s, Carrier was committed to evoking human emotions that would transcend advertising fads and stand the

test of time. Little did API and Carrier know how successful they would be. More than 20 years later, the ice-cream company still uses that footage in its commercials.

Carrier spent his early years in the dark, learning the basics of processing film. Now, some 25 years later, API's new logo asks, "Have you seen the light?" Knowing how to shape, form, and orchestrate light is what API and Carrier do superbly. It is art, and that is one of the many things that makes API's work so unique. Carrier says, "There are technicians and there are artists. Technology has created a better medium, but documentation is not art, and trendy techniques are not likely to evoke emotion. Part of our artistic edge is to elicit an emotion or response from the viewer. Clients choose API's imagery because they know it has power to move people. We never lose sight of that mission."

THE PYRAMID PERSONIFIED. THE SECRET LIFE OF A LAWNBOY PISTON. DALLAS NEON AT NIGHT. API DOESN'T SIMPLY CAPTURE IMAGES, IT CREATES ART.

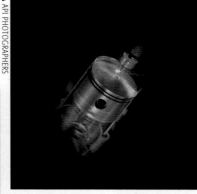

ost Memphians think of Belz Enterprises in connection with its ownership and redevelopment of the Peabody Hotel, a place that has become as much of a Mid-South institution as Beale Street or even the Mississippi River. But the Peabody is just one of many unique, first-class Belz Enterprises developments located around the country. ▲ As Memphis' foremost developer, Belz has built a portfolio that consists of major

warehouse/distribution centers, industrial parks, offices, hotels, shopping centers, and residential developments ranging from apartments to planned residential communities.

Unlocking Regional Potential

In 1946, company founder Philip Belz understood the vast untapped potential in the Memphis area. Belz and his son, Jack, turned their vision into warehouses, shopping centers, and neighborhoods to meet the needs of a growing city.

In the early 1950s, the industrial core of north Memphis was booming. Industry demanded infrastructure and large-scale warehousing, and Belz built some of the first warehouses and industrial parks in Memphis. On the Mississippi River, Belz developed the 433-acre Rivergate Industrial Port, one

of the largest privately owned industrial ports in the country.

Since that time, Belz Enterprises has never lost sight of the importance of

distribution, and today offers more than 11 million square feet of warehouse, distribution, and industrial space. The company's efforts have played a big role in Memphis' emergence as North America's distribution center.

In 1979, Belz pioneered a new concept in shopping with the opening of the Belz Factory Outlet Mall in Lakeland, Tennessee. Belz's second mall, the Belz Factory Outlet World in Orlando, is today the second-busiest tourist destination in Orlando and one of the largest nonanchored factory outlet centers in the country. Belz has developed more than 3 million square feet of factory outlet malls, including locations in national tourist destinations such as Las Vegas; St. Augustine, Florida; and Pigeon Forge, Tennessee. Belz has even taken the concept offshore with the 2001 opening of a Belz Factory Outlet World in Canovanas, Puerto Rico.

Fueling the Downtown Renaissance

There are few places where the Belz commitment to Memphis is more evident than downtown. Belz's reopening of the Peabody Hotel and construction of the massive

JACK BELZ AND HIS WIFE, MARILYN, OPENED THE PEABODY PLACE MUSEUM TO SHARE THEIR COLLECTION OF CHINESE ART AND SCULPTURE WITH MEMPHIS (RIGHT).

BELZ'S REOPENING OF THE PEABODY HOTEL AND CONSTRUCTION OF THE MASSIVE PEABODY PLACE MIXED-USE COMPLEX HAVE BEEN PART OF MORE THAN $2 BILLION IN PUBLIC AND PRIVATE FUNDS PUT INTO THE DOWNTOWN AREA FOR DEVELOPMENT.

The most recent phase of the Peabody Place project was the opening of a vast, multifaceted entertainment complex in the heart of the city's tourist district. The Peabody Place Entertainment and Retail Center contains a 21-screen, state-of-the-art movieplex with a six-story-tall, large-screen-format theater for special viewing options. Jillian's, a multi-dimensional food and entertainment retailer on three levels, features a sports video café, more than 150 electronic simulation games, a bowling alley, a dance club, private party rooms, 11 tournament-quality billiard tables, and banquet facilities.

But perhaps no part of Peabody Place demonstrates the Belz commitment to the city of Memphis more than the Peabody Place Museum. Jack Belz and his wife, Marilyn, who wanted to share their collection of Chinese art and sculpture with the city and its visitors, founded the museum in 1998. The collection has grown and—in addition to including one of the largest assemblies of rare Chinese art in the country—now features Russian lacquer boxes, European contemporary glass, and selected Judaica.

It is difficult to imagine that Belz Enterprises could do any more to enhance the prosperity and quality of life for Memphis' residents and visitors. But rest assured, the company is at work on it already.

THE TOWER AT PEABODY PLACE, A 15-STORY, 185,000-SQUARE-FOOT, CLASS A OFFICE BUILDING, IS ONE OF BELZ'S SIGNATURE DOWNTOWN DEVELOPMENTS.

Peabody Place mixed-use complex have been part of more than $2 billion in public and private funds put into the downtown area for development.

The Peabody Hotel, one of Belz's most recognized developments, is considered to be the cornerstone of an unprecedented, 20-year period of growth in downtown Memphis. In 1981, Belz extensively renovated and reopened the Peabody, which was originally built in 1869. The hotel's lavish lobby, exquisite restaurants, and ceremonial daily duck march have become perennial tourist favorites. Listed on the National Register of Historic Places, the Peabody has been cited by the Department of the Interior as one of the country's most outstanding preservation case studies. The success of the Peabody Memphis led Belz to develop the Peabody Orlando, a 981-room, luxury convention/resort hotel located directly across from Orlando's 1.4 million-square-foot convention center.

Peabody Place, considered to be one of the largest mixed-use developments in the country, is anchored on the east by the Peabody Hotel and to the west by AutoZone's corporate headquarters of nearly 1,000 people. In between, Peabody Place is comprised of a variety of multifaceted properties that are bringing a new vitality to downtown. These include Pembroke Square and 50 Peabody Place—a pair of office buildings that are also home to an eclectic mix of retail shops, offices, and restaurants. Other key components include the Gayoso House, an apartment building/retail center built on the site where the historic Gayoso Hotel was located; and the Tower at Peabody Place, a 185,000-square-foot, 15-story, class A office building that is considered one the signature office addresses in Memphis.

THE PEABODY HOTEL, ONE OF BELZ'S MOST RECOGNIZED DEVELOPMENTS, IS CONSIDERED TO BE THE CORNERSTONE OF AN UNPRECEDENTED, 20-YEAR PERIOD OF GROWTH IN DOWNTOWN MEMPHIS.

*I*t's rare for a company to know for a fact that it changes lives every day. Wright Medical Group, Inc., however, is one such company. An Arlington, Tennessee-based orthopedic company with expertise in hip, knee, and small joint implants, as well as calcium-sulfate-based bone graft materials, Wright has earned an international reputation for focus and innovation. ▲ Wright's products command an impressive segment of the markets they

serve, and the company's lean, people-oriented operational philosophy has helped it launch a new era of success.

Half a Century of Changing Lives

Wright Medical, founded in 1950, can trace its heritage back to a Memphis company started on Jackson Avenue by Frank Wright. Then a sales representative for another local orthopedic company, Wright developed and secured the patent for an all-rubber walking heel for leg casts. Encouraged by the positive reception his invention received, Wright and his wife, Carolyn, launched Wright Manufacturing Company.

Following its success with the all-rubber walking heel, Wright Manufacturing Company went on to develop orthopedic implants for knee and hip joints, as well as such related accessories as bone plates, screws, and pins. In 1977, two years after Frank Wright's death, Dow Corning Corporation purchased the company. The company was renamed Dow Corning Wright and small joint implants were added to its line.

The company regained its independence in 1993 when an investor group purchased most of the assets of Dow Corning Wright and incorporated a new company, Wright Medical Technology, Inc. The new company set out to offer a broad line that included implants and instrumentation for spinal fixation, in addition to trauma, arthroscopy, and biotechnology products.

"In the mid- to late 1990s, the company's revenues and growth began to falter," says F. Barry Bays, president and CEO, who started out as a machinist in a local implant-manufacturing facility and is a longtime veteran of the orthopedics industry. "It became clear that the everything-to-everybody strategy wasn't going to pay off." Eager to regain its focus, Wright Medical Technology began seeking ways to recapitalize its business. In December 1999, the company successfully attracted the major global private investment firm E.M. Warburg Pincus Equity Partners, who

acquired Wright. Through the partnership, Warburg Pincus would fund the redirection of Wright Medical's strategy. The company changed its corporate name to Wright Medical Group, Inc. in early 2000.

Today, Wright is focused on designing and manufacturing innovative hip, knee, and small joint implants, as well as a line of unique calcium-sulfate-based bone graft alternatives. Wright Medical's headquarters—which includes manufacturing facilities, administrative offices, and a distribution center that ships orders worldwide—occupies four buildings in Arlington.

The present company's mission still reflects the intent of its parent company's early beginnings: to restore function to, and alleviate pain for, those suffering from musculoskeletal injuries and defects. "Our key objective is to always do the right thing for our customers, employees, and shareholders," Bays says.

Focus and Precision

The proof is in the marketplace. Wright's Swanson finger-joint implants, for example, are the leading small-joint implants in the world, and have garnered the company an impressive 80 percent of that

TODAY WRIGHT MEDICAL GROUP, INC. EMPLOYS 450 AT ITS ARLINGTON, TENNESSEE HEADQUARTERS, WHICH INCLUDES RESEARCH AND DEVELOPMENT FACILITIES, A MANUFACTURING SITE, ADMINISTRATIVE OFFICES, AND A DISTRIBUTION CENTER THAT SHIPS PRODUCTS WORLDWIDE.

THE WORLD LEADER IN SMALL-JOINT ORTHOPEDICS, PRODUCTS LIKE THE ORTHOSPHERE® IMPLANT ALLOW SURGEONS TO MEND HANDS CRIPPLED BY ARTHRITIS, RESTORING FUNCTION AND SIGNIFICANTLY REDUCING PAIN FOR PATIENTS.

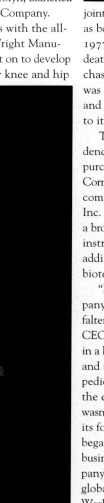

market. Hands disabled by arthritis gain a higher level of function with significant pain reduction with the implants, which are made from a medical grade of elastomer that is highly resistant to flexion fatigue.

Wright's PERFECTA® Hip System has also gained popularity among surgeons. Because the system is immensely versatile, surgeons can customize solutions based on the specific needs of each patient.

Wright's ADVANCE® Medial-Pivot Total Knee is also working wonders for patients and for the company. Remarkably successful at re-creating the natural movement of the knee, this product is one of the most innovative knee implants in the marketplace.

The company has also applied its research expertise and focus to pioneering in the area of biological skeletal repair with its OSTEOSET® line of bone graft materials. This calcium-sulfate-based product can be used in areas where trauma or disease has led to bone loss. As the body generates new bone, OSTEOSET pellets provide a framework for the new growth. The material is steadily resorbed by the body throughout the healing process, leaving nothing but healthy, new bone.

People Make It Happen

Our new era of success and innovation is being driven 100 percent by our people," Bays says. "We established the objectives, and then empowered our people to innovate, capitalize, and execute to serve customers and meet or exceed their expectations."

Wright Medical Group, Inc.'s philosophy recognizes that success and efficiency come from giving employees whatever they need to operate a smart and lean company. "Our company is accomplishing great things for customers and for shareholders, but the truly moving aspect of our newfound success is the remarkable, transforming impact we're able to have on more and more lives," says Bays.

Buying or selling a home can be very challenging. With prices to set, questions to ask, and terms to negotiate, a skilled, seasoned professional is essential to a successful transaction. "Getting the best price for your home has a lot to do with things you can't read in a book," says Fontaine Taylor, president of Coleman-Etter, Fontaine Realtors. "It takes a committed, experienced, full-time agent who knows the local market, and who's got the support necessary to do whatever it takes."

This is the philosophy that steers Coleman-Etter, Fontaine. From its emphasis on agent education to its investments in the latest technology, the company has built a reputation on service and expertise.

Founded on Personalized Service

Coleman-Etter, Fontaine was founded in Memphis in 1951 by Majorie Coleman and Frances Etter. It was the first real estate firm in the area to be founded by women. Taylor joined the company in 1983, became a partner in 1985, and bought out the remaining partners in 1987.

Today, according to Taylor, Coleman-Etter, Fontaine offers a number of advantages over other firms. "First—and really the most important—are our people," Taylor says. "We are extremely selective and hire only the best agents in the market."

On top of the rigorous selection process, Coleman-Etter, Fontaine ensures a high level of service by requiring all agents to be full-time agents. "Some other companies might have a lot of agents, but how many of them are part-time?" Taylor asks. "How

many homes do they actually sell? With full-time agents, buyers and sellers know that their agent is experienced, and they know that their agent is always available. From the very beginning, I wanted this company to be about exceptional service."

Education and Support

Because a large part of expertise is education, Coleman-Etter, Fontaine makes sure its agents have the most complete knowledge and skills possible. "I'm a huge believer in education," Taylor says. "It's crucial in this business."

Taylor herself is proof of this belief. Licensed in Tennessee, Mississippi, and Arkansas, she is a Certified Real Estate Specialist, a Certified Real Estate Broker, a graduate of the Realtors Institute of Tennessee, and a member of the Realtors Land Institute. Of the 34 agents who represent the company, all are licensed Realtors and nearly half are licensed brokers.

That same commitment to training extends to support staff and programs. "We constantly increase our level of service by adopting the latest technological advances," notes Taylor. Coleman-Etter, Fontaine was the first Memphis company to offer virtual tours

of homes on the Internet, and today, offers on-line tours of all its listed homes. The company has also developed an expertise in corporate relocation, and has become very successful at helping relocating employees find the right neighborhoods and the right homes for their lifestyles.

In addition, Taylor shares her expertise in a variety of other ways. She and her daughter, Fontaine Brown, have formed an in-demand sales team called The Fontaines, and Taylor continues to contribute to the industry. She has recently served as president of the Memphis and Tennessee chapters of the Certified Real Estate Brokerage Council; has served three times as chairman of the Memphis Area Association of Realtors Multiple Listing Service and Information Network; is a life member of the Multi Million Dollar Club; and is a past president of the Tennessee Real Estate Education Foundation. Taylor has been elected president of the Memphis Area Association of Realtors for 2001.

But nothing can distract Taylor from creating an environment where agents can provide an unmatched level of service. "Your agent is your adviser and your advocate," she says. "That's a role we will always take seriously."

WITH A HISTORY DATING BACK TO 1951, COLEMAN-ETTER, FONTAINE REALTORS IS TODAY ONE OF THE TOP REAL ESTATE FIRMS IN THE MID-SOUTH.

PRESIDENT FONTAINE TAYLOR AND HER DAUGHTER FONTAINE BROWN HAVE FORMED AN IN-DEMAND SALES TEAM CALLED THE FONTAINES.

ince 1952, Allen & O'Hara, Inc. has been in the business of developing, financing, building, renovating, maintaining, and operating successful commercial properties, with emphasis on college and university student housing, residence halls with food service, and hotels nationwide. Privately owned, this Memphis-based firm was founded by Harwell Allen Jr., a contemporary of Holiday Inn founder and fellow Memphian Kemmons Wilson.

The company built many of the early Holiday Inns and many other chain hotels and motels that followed.

"What Mr. Allen quickly noticed was that many of these hotel franchises were owned by doctors, dentists, lawyers, and other professionals," explains Paul O. Bower, Allen & O'Hara president. "The need for professional, on-site management became obvious pretty quickly, so we developed the expertise to provide turnkey development, as well as full-service hospitality management services."

Today, fully accredited by the Institute of Real Estate Management, Allen & O'Hara is engaged in the development, ownership, and management of hotels, student residences, apartments, and commercial properties throughout the United States.

Innovation on Campus

Riding the crest of the baby boom shift in demographics, Allen & O'Hara branched out from hotels into apartment development and management, and then turned its attention to the growing market for student housing on college campuses. In 1964, as the first national company to own, build, and operate student residence halls, Allen & O'Hara introduced the concept of privately operated student housing. "We more or less invented the privately owned student housing business," says Bower. Allen & O'Hara went on to develop and/or manage 57 student housing properties totaling some 31,000 beds at 42 university campuses across America.

Today, largely because of its experience in college student housing, Allen & O'Hara is on the leading edge of the privatization of student housing at the nation's colleges and universities. In addition to an aging inventory of dormitory rooms and increasing college enrollment nationwide, university administrators are faced with students who want more privacy than the standard dormitory allows.

"About 80 percent of college students now come from homes where they had their own bedrooms," explains Bower. "Colleges that want to be competitive are meeting this demand with innovative, private-bedroom, apartment-style housing offerings." Allen & O'Hara provides college administrators with an experienced partner to create affordable, contemporary housing for their campuses using off-balance-sheet, tax-exempt bond financing.

The company's expertise in so-called privatized college student housing has earned Allen & O'Hara developments at the University of North Carolina, North Carolina State University, Ohio State University, University of Louisville, and others. "Much like the hotel business, student housing is a complicated and demanding field," notes Bower. "Clients call us because it has to be done right, and they know they can count on us."

ALLEN & O'HARA, INC. IS IN THE BUSINESS OF DEVELOPING, FINANCING, BUILDING, RENOVATING, MAINTAINING, AND OPERATING SUCCESSFUL COMMERCIAL PROPERTIES, SPECIALIZING IN COLLEGE AND UNIVERSITY STUDENT HOUSING. PICTURED (LEFT) IS THE UNIVERSITY PARK STREET APARTMENTS AT SALISBURY STATE UNIVERSITY IN SALISBURY, MARYLAND.

TODAY, LARGELY BECAUSE OF ITS EXPERIENCE IN COLLEGE STUDENT HOUSING, ALLEN & O'HARA IS ON THE LEADING EDGE OF THE PRIVATIZATION OF STUDENT HOUSING AT THE NATION'S COLLEGES AND UNIVERSITIES. PICTURED (LEFT) IS BETTIE JOHNSON HALL AT THE UNIVERSITY OF LOUISVILLE, LOUISVILLE, KENTUCKY.

B eginning as a small publisher of local newspapers in 1935, Towery Publishing, Inc. today has become a global publisher of a diverse range of community-based materials from San Diego to Sydney. Its products—such as the company's award-winning Urban Tapestry Series, business directories, magazines, and Internet sites—continue to build on Towery's distinguished heritage of excellence, making its name synonymous with service, utility, and quality.

Community Publishing at Its Best

Towery Publishing has long been the industry leader in community-based publications. In 1972, current President and CEO J. Robert Towery succeeded his parents in managing the printing and publishing business they had founded four decades earlier. "One of the more impressive traits of my family's publishing business was its dedication to presenting only the highest-quality products available—whatever our market might be," says Towery. "Since taking over the company, I've continued our fight for the high ground in maintaining this tradition."

During the 1970s and 1980s, Towery expanded the scope of the company's published materials to include *Memphis* magazine and other successful regional and national publications, such as *Memphis Shopper's Guide*, *Racquetball* magazine, *Huddle/FastBreak*, *Real Estate News*, and *Satellite Dish* magazine. In 1985, after selling its locally focused assets, the company began the trajectory on which it continues today, creating community-oriented materials that are often produced in conjunction with chambers of commerce and other business organizations.

All of Towery Publishing's efforts, represented on the Internet at www.towery.com, are marked by a careful, innovative design philosophy that has become a hallmark of the company's reputation for quality and service. Boasting a nationwide sales force, proven editorial depth, cutting-edge graphics capabilities, ample marketing resources, and extensive data management expertise, the company has assembled the intellectual and capital resources necessary to produce quality products and services.

Urban Tapestry Series

Towery Publishing launched its popular Urban Tapestry Series in 1990. Each of the nearly 100 oversized, hardbound photojournals details the people, history, culture, environment, and commerce of a featured metropolitan area. These colorful coffee-table books spotlight communities through an introductory essay authored by a noted local individual, an exquisite collection of photographs, and in-depth profiles of select companies and organizations that form each area's business core.

From New York to Vancouver to Los Angeles, national and international authors have graced the pages of the books' introductory essays. The celebrated list of contributors includes two former U.S. presidents—Gerald Ford (Grand Rapids) and Jimmy Carter (Atlanta); boxing great Muhammad Ali (Louisville); two network newscasters—CBS anchor Dan Rather (Austin) and ABC anchor Hugh Downs (Phoenix); NBC sportscaster Bob Costas (St. Louis); record-breaking quarterback Steve Young (San Francisco); best-selling mystery author Robert B. Parker (Boston); American Movie Classics host Nick Clooney (Cincinnati); former Texas first lady Nellie Connally (Houston); and former New York City Mayor Ed Koch (New York).

While the books have been enormously successful, the company continues to improve and redefine the role the series plays in the marketplace.

▼ STEVE DAVIS

TOWERY PUBLISHING, INC. PRESIDENT AND CEO J. ROBERT TOWERY (LEFT) TOOK THE REINS OF HIS FAMILY'S BUSINESS IN 1972, MAINTAINING THE COMPANY'S LONG-STANDING CORE COMMITMENT TO QUALITY.

"Currently, the Urban Tapestry Series works beautifully as a tool for enhancing the image of the communities it portrays," says Towery. "As the series continues to mature, we want it to become a reference source that businesses and executives turn to when evaluating the quality of life in cities where they may be considering moving or expanding."

Chambers of Commerce Turn to Towery

In addition to its Urban Tapestry Series, Towery Publishing has become the largest producer of published and Internet materials for North American chambers of commerce. From published membership directories and Internet listings that enhance business-to-business communication, to visitor and relocation guides tailored to reflect the unique qualities of the communities they cover, the company's chamber-oriented materials offer comprehensive information on dozens of topics, including housing, education, leisure activities, health care, and local government.

The company's primary Internet product consists of its introCity™ sites. Much like its published materials, Towery's introCity sites introduce newcomers, visitors, and longtime residents to every facet of a particular community, while simultaneously placing the local chamber of commerce at the forefront of the city's Internet activity. The sites provide newcomer information including calendars, photos, citywide business listings with everything from nightlife to shopping to family fun, and on-line maps pinpointing the exact location of businesses, schools, attractions, and much more.

Sustained Creativity

The driving forces behind Towery Publishing have always been the company's employees and its state-of-the-art industry technology. Many of its employees have worked with the Towery family of companies for more than 20 years. Today's staff of seasoned innovators totals around 100 at the Memphis headquarters, and more than 40 sales, marketing, and editorial staff traveling to and working in an ever growing list of cities.

Supporting the staff's endeavors is state-of-the-art prepress publishing software and equipment. Towery Publishing was the first production environment in the United States to combine desktop publishing with color separations and image scanning to produce finished film suitable for burning plates for four-color printing. Today, the company relies on its digital prepress services to produce more than 8,000 pages each year, containing more than 30,000 high-quality color images.

Through decades of business and technological change, one aspect of Towery Publishing has remained constant. "The creative energies of our staff drive us toward innovation and invention," Towery says. "Our people make the highest possible demands on themselves, so I know that our future is secure if the ingredients for success remain a focus on service and quality."

*F*inding a financial institution that really listens to an individual's needs and dreams is a rarity. Many Memphians, however, have found such a place at Memphis Area Teachers' Credit Union (MATCU). MATCU is one of Tennessee's largest and most progressive credit unions. Taking the philosophy of people helping people to heart, MATCU continues to focus on the people side of each transaction. ▲ MATCU was founded in the basement of Memphis'

East High School in 1957. Led by James Brewster, a group of teachers began the credit union, having been inspired by a credit union model that Brewster had seen in Portland, Oregon. The goal was to assist educators with financial success in an atmosphere of familiarity and trust. In its first office, the credit union stored its records in a piano bench.

The credit union's friendly service and trust caught on quickly in the Memphis area, and MATCU now offers an affordable, top-quality financial institution to more than 75,000 members, with 11 branch locations and approximately 200 employees. MATCU was originally created for employees of educational facilities and companies related to education in Tennessee; DeSoto and Marshall counties in Mississippi; and Crittenden County in Arkansas. Other groups have since been added to the field of eligibility, including employees of federal government agencies; residents of zip codes 38017, 38018, 38138, and 38139; and family members of MATCU members.

People Helping People

MATCU is different from other financial institutions because it is a not-for-profit organization and members are part owners. MATCU's board of directors is a group of highly qualified, committed members who write policy and monitor services. These individuals are volunteers who are not compensated for the countless hours they serve for the benefit of the organization and its members. This structure allows credit unions, in most cases, to offer higher dividends on savings and lower loan rates to members.

"Your initial deposit of $25 makes you a stockholder," says Ray P. Algee, president and CEO of MATCU. "Because of our not-for-profit status, we can offer free and reduced-fee amenities that are very member friendly. And through our subsidiary, Members' First Financial Services, Inc., we provide quality insurance and investment products."

Members' First and MATCU team up to provide a one-stop financial institution. MATCU provides traditional banking services, while Members' First Financial Services, Inc. provides investment options, personal and property insurance programs, and financial planning, so members can take care of many needs with a financial institution they know and trust. Members' First is continually evolving and examining new programs that bring value to credit union members.

MATCU is also making technological advances with enhanced computer programs that allow quicker and smoother transactions. CU@Home, MATCU's Internet banking service, provides 24-hour access to account information for members with an Internet connection.

MATCU invests in the community as well, offering scholarships to high school students who are pursuing a future in education. CU Around Town, the credit union's community involvement organization, reaches out in the area to provide support for many programs and charitable events.

"We strive to provide a quality, full-service financial institution," explains Algee. "We keep pace with the competition so our members have up-to-date products and services. What sets us apart is the personal, hometown atmosphere."

stablished in 1959, Mid-South Specialties, Inc. has, for decades, been using the most up-to-date methods for restoring concrete, masonry, and associated structures— from parking garages to multistory buildings. The company's reputation for attention to detail and expertise in difficult areas has led to its emergence as a regional leader. ▲ "When my father founded this business, he knew that word of mouth was the best form of

advertising there is," says Randy Marchbanks, president. Mid-South Specialties has lived up to that philosophy, and has turned a strong reputation into a thriving company that employs some 70 people and has operations in five states.

Regional Expertise

When Memphis developers were building the innovative Pyramid arena, there was only one real choice for specialty coatings and waterproofing— Mid-South Specialties. The company provided painting, waterproofing, caulking, and floor coatings for the massive facility.

Industrial painting projects are a prime focus for Mid-South Specialties as well. The company has completed projects in industrial plants, institutions, hospitals, steel structures, and multistory buildings—new and old. Caulking is an area of equally strong expertise for the company. Mid-South Specialties also provides tilt-up panel and masonry urethane joints, silicone curtain wall glazing, and major building expansion joints.

If a waterproofing job is completed poorly, the results can be very expensive. That's why developers depend on Mid-South Specialties for

tough waterproofing jobs that can range from below-grade sheets and liquid membranes to horizontal cold- and hot-applied high-build membranes.

In addition, the company has experience in epoxy overlays and other floor coatings, and has completed coating projects ranging from 1,000 square feet up to 800,000 square feet.

A Delicate Science

There is perhaps no greater testament to Mid-South Specialties' reputation than the fact that the company has been tapped to handle refurbishing projects in some of the city's most important and cherished structures.

Mid-South Specialties has completed concrete and masonry refurbishing and repair for the Memphis International Airport, the AutoZone downtown parking garage, and even the renovated Central Station. And the company has completed tuck-pointing projects—which involve old materials removal and replacement—for the Peabody Place development downtown, University of Tennessee Medical Center, and Shelby County Hospital.

And the list continues. Mid-South Specialties has installed cementitious coatings, elastomeric coatings, and floor overlays for renovation cus-

tomers that include the Mid-South Coliseum, FedEx, Baptist Hospital, University of Tennessee, Le Bonheur Children's Medical Center, Sharp Industries, the U.S. Coast Guard, Cargill, and many more.

"We really have become experts in restoration," Marchbanks says. "You can jeopardize the funding and timetable of a project if you don't know the strict rules set up by the historical commission and other organizations. We have decades of experience working within those strict guidelines."

That's just one of the many reasons for Mid-South Specialties' leadership in the industry. And as word of mouth continues to spread, the future should prove even more successful for the quality-driven company.

MID-SOUTH SPECIALTIES, INC. IS A SIGNIFICANT PART OF THE REVIVAL OF DOWNTOWN MEMPHIS.

1961

St. Jude Children's Research Hospital 1963

Putt-Putt Family Park 1963

Guardsmark, Inc. 1963

Saint Benedict at Auburndale 1966

Fred L. Davis Insurance Agency 1967

Patton & Taylor 1968

PricewaterhouseCoopers 1971

The Memphis Group, Inc. 1971

Drexel Chemical Company 1972

Jameson Gibson Construction Company, Inc. 1973

FedEx Corporation 1973

Shea-Hubbard ENT Clinic, PC 1974

St. Francis Hospital 1974

1975

W hen the entrepreneurial bug hit Memphis college student Aubrey Smith in 1963, he had no idea where it would take him. The 21-year-old took over the lease on an area Putt-Putt miniature golf course and, over the course of the next 30 years, turned it into a massive, family-oriented entertainment center. Today, Smith welcomes approximately 700,000 locals and tourists each year to what has become one of the largest Putt-Putt

franchises in the world. Its 40 acres offer an overwhelming assortment of activities for families, as well as a level of quality and professionalism that rivals any recreational park in the country.

Something for Everyone

"T he bigger the mix, the better," Smith says. "Families have different tastes, and we can satisfy most of them because we have evolved into what I call a recreation mall." Three different Putt-Putt golf courses offer 54 holes of varying levels of difficulty, featuring aesthetic fountains and life-size animals in a jungle theme. A 100-plus tee golf driving range (rated by *Golf Range Magazine* as one of the Top 100 ranges in America) is one of the largest in the Mid-South, and includes 17 covered and heated tees for driving year-round. There's a 1/3-mile, two-bridge, go-kart track that thrills children and adults alike with its exciting race cars. The park also features bumper boats, batting cages, and a fully stocked pro shop for golfers. Putt-Putt even offers golf instructions from PGA pros associated with the Golf Academy of Memphis.

Step inside the glass doors, and the Memphis Putt-Putt offers a whole new level of activities. A video arcade houses 75 games, large party rooms, a full-

service concession stand, and a 7,500-square-foot LaserTron laser tag arena.

The mix has another big advantage. It has made Putt-Putt one of the most popular destinations for the city's corporate and church outings and family reunions. The park can accommodate groups of up to 3,000 people in four private, covered picnic areas.

Exceptional Facilities and Extraordinary Service

"T here's another aspect of Putt-Putt Family Park that, according to Smith, plays a crucial role in its success: the people. "We've got an unbelievable team here that puts the customer above everything else," he says. "They are extremely helpful and attentive, and they keep

the facility in immaculate condition."

When David Rose, operations manager, came on board, for example, the next two seasons set park records. "David and his team of assistant managers have operations running so well that nothing falls through the cracks," Smith says. Luther Allen Stanley, the park's chief engineer, and his assistant, Jeff Moore, also play a critical role by keeping all equipment and facilities in perfect running order. Ed Arnold, electronics technician, keeps the game room fully operational, while Ken Pfister, golf-range manager, and his team give the same level of intense attention to the driving range and grounds. Bob Snyder and Reggie Winbush deliver the specialized care needed to maintain the miniature golf courses. Todd Posey and his marketing team make sure groups are given all the special accommodations they need to have an outstanding group outing. Jenny Reeves is the office manager and assists in all aspects of the park.

"A lot of parks have come and gone in this industry," Smith says. "Our people and their dedication are what have made this place what it is." With such a strong mix of activities and experts, there's no doubt that Putt-Putt Family Park will be a fixture on the Memphis entertainment scene for decades to come.

AUBREY AND BRENDA SMITH ARE THE PROUD OWNERS OF PUTT-PUTT FAMILY PARK, MEMPHIS' NUMBER ONE ATTENDED FAMILY ENTERTAINMENT CENTER.

THE SUPERTRAK IS THE LARGEST, LONGEST GO-KART TRACK IN THE MID-SOUTH.

OPERATIONS MANAGER DAVID ROSE WITH WIFE SUZANNE

I n 1966, Mary Alice Smith founded a little school called Auburndale with a unique mission. Her goal was to develop an academic environment where children with all levels of learning ability could be educated on the same campus. Smith knew that integrating these children would have a particular effect: the children would teach to and learn from each other. ▲ The model was so successful that the 22-acre school in Cordova was purchased in 1988

by the Catholic Diocese of Memphis to meet the increasing demand for strong and innovative Catholic education. Renamed Saint Benedict at Auburndale, the school opened its doors as a new diocesan school in the fall of 1988. With the motto Quality Education with a Catholic Heart, Saint Benedict retains its original vision of strong, personalized instruction.

The Strength to Succeed

T oday, Saint Benedict is a coeducational college preparatory school of the Catholic Diocese of Memphis. The school offers traditional and special-learning educational programs for students in junior kindergarten through 12th grade. While it integrates content and competencies across all grades, the school is organized into an elementary school and a high school. The division gives students at Saint Benedict at Auburndale environments that are developmentally appropriate for their given ages.

The most innovative educational approach at Saint Benedict is the school's PLUS program for students with different learning needs. The primary goal of the PLUS program is to prepare these students to graduate from high school and to pursue a college degree through a rigorous course of study and academic diligence.

The PLUS program follows Saint Benedict's philosophy of instilling confidence in students and building on their strengths. Students are educated at their own level, and gain the firm base of academic knowledge that is necessary for academic achievement throughout high school and college.

Founded on Faith

R eligious education at Saint Benedict is a vital part of the overall school experience. Students not only experience the highest levels of academic training, but they also experience meaningful spiritual guidance and are challenged to high levels of moral development.

Although founded in the rich heritage of the Catholic faith, Saint Benedict opens its doors to students of all faiths. The school is truly an educational environment for any student, regardless of denominational background.

The strength of a Saint Benedict at Auburndale education comes from the school's belief that there is much more to a sound education than can be found in textbooks, including individualized attention, parental involvement, and a strong ethical and faith-based foundation. This whole-student approach continues to prepare students for success in the world, long after they graduate.

SAINT BENEDICT AT AUBURNDALE ENRICHES ITS STUDENTS SPIRITUALLY, ACADEMICALLY, ATHLETICALLY, AND MORALLY, AS THEY PREPARE FOR REWARDING AND SUCCESSFUL LIVES IN COLLEGE AND BEYOND.

ounded by entertainer Danny Thomas, St. Jude Children's Research Hospital opened in 1962. The legend of the world-renowned hospital began during a dry spell in Thomas' early career as a radio actor. Down on his luck and with just $7 in his pockets, Thomas knelt in a Detroit church before a statue of St. Jude of Thaddeus, the patron saint of hopeless causes. "Show me my way in life," he prayed, "and I will build you a shrine." Thomas soon turned

a corner in his career, and went on to become the wildly successful star of the television show *Make Room for Daddy*.

To fulfill his pledge to St. Jude, Thomas pulled together a team and raised the funds to start the nation's first institution with the sole purpose of research and treatment of catastrophic childhood diseases.

Shining across the World

St. Jude Children's Research Hospital opens its doors to more than 4,000 children each year. The children come to Memphis from across the United States and from more than 60 countries.

"Our commitment at St. Jude is threefold," says Arthur Nienhuis, M.D., the director of the hospital and a physician and scientist whose research is focused on the development of gene therapy. "We want to give the very best care. We also provide social support to the patients and their families

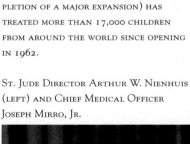

St. Jude Children's Research Hospital (as it will appear in 2005, upon completion of a major expansion) has treated more than 17,000 children from around the world since opening in 1962.

St. Jude Director Arthur W. Nienhuis (left) and Chief Medical Officer Joseph Mirro, Jr.

during this difficult time. And while the child receives treatment, we continue our research to find cures for the child's illness."

Children diagnosed with illnesses treatable under one of the hospital's treatment protocols are never turned away from St. Jude, regardless of whether the family can afford to pay the medical fees. All costs not paid by such third parties as insurance companies are absorbed by the hospital through its fund-raising arm, ALSAC, the acronym for American Lebanese Syrian Associated Charities. ALSAC, founded by Thomas, is the third-largest private health care fund-raising organization in the country. Its sole reason for being is to support St. Jude. The support of ALSAC and the community have meant that the hospital has been able to perform more miracles than anyone ever dreamed possible.

For example, 38 years ago, the cure rate for acute lymphoblastic leukemia—the most common pediatric cancer—was a mere 4 percent. By 2000, thanks to the advances made at St. Jude, the cure rate for this disease was 80 percent.

Research advances are commonplace at the facility, where world-class scientists complete research in all the

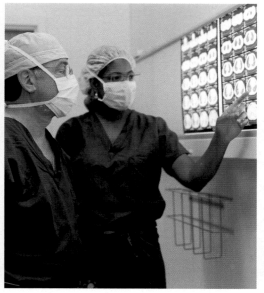
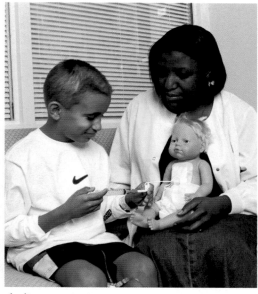

hospital's divisions. The staff includes Peter C. Doherty, Ph.D., chairman of St. Jude's immunology department, who won the 1996 Nobel Prize for Physiology or Medicine.

The hospital has treated more than 17,000 children from the United States and around the world. The findings at St. Jude are available at no cost to doctors and scientists all over the world, and the hospital's medical and scientific staff published more than 400 articles in academic journals in 2000 alone.

Reaching Ever Further

In May 1999, St. Jude celebrated a day that was second in importance only to its founding. On that day, the hospital and ALSAC announced the launch of a $1 billion expansion plan that will double its size and enhance its ability to find cures for catastrophic childhood diseases.

The expansion, already underway, is creating five new buildings, including a 500,000-square-foot patient care and research facility. The effort will also renovate and incorporate the 17-acre St. Joseph Hospital campus, which St. Jude acquired in 1997.

"The expansion will allow us not only to expand current research," Nienhuis says, "but also to move into additional areas of genetic and infectious disease research by creating a Children's Infection Defense Center (CIDC) and a Pediatric Genetic Diseases Center."

The CIDC will concentrate in the area of immunosuppression, AIDS, pneumonia, tuberculosis, and cholera, and will house a facility to develop vaccines and novel therapies for infectious diseases. The genetics center will continue the institution's focus on sickle-cell anemia and other diseases, as well as expanding into platelet disorders, hemophilia, and neurological diseases.

The hospital hopes to establish new programs in human immunology, chemical biology, and molecular biotechnology, and aims to close the gap between basic research findings and the clinical application of those findings. St. Jude is in a unique position to further the research and treatment of myriad rare pediatric disorders, many of which are overlooked by drug companies and other treatment facilities because there is little profit in developing drugs for these illnesses. In addition, insurance companies often decline to cover the costs of novel therapies.

"This expansion has taken the support of thousands of donors and volunteers throughout the country," says Richard Shadyac, ALSAC's national executive director.

On February 6, 1991, two days after celebrating the hospital's 29th anniversary, Danny Thomas died. However, his spirit remains as the force behind St. Jude. Thomas' creed was, "No child should die in the dawn of life." The miracle he built is helping to make that dream come true.

St. Jude researchers are searching for cures to catastrophic childhood diseases, including cancer, sickle cell disease, and AIDS (left and middle).

St. Jude nurses help educate their young patients about their illnesses and treatment (right).

The late entertainer Danny Thomas often spent time with the patients of the hospital he founded in 1962.

Guardsmark is one of the world's largest security services firms. The Memphis-based company is, by many accounts, the unmatched leader in the industry. TIME magazine has called Guardsmark the company that "many security experts consider the best national firm in the business." In the best-selling book LIBERATION MANAGEMENT, author Tom Peters describes Guardsmark as "the Tiffany's of the security business." ▲ In fact, Guardsmark has an

immaculate reputation as an unmatched leader in the private security industry, and its founder, Ira A. Lipman, is recognized as a global authority on both security and sophisticated business practices. *The New York Times*, *The Wall Street Journal*, *USA Today*, *The Washington Post*, *Reader's Digest*, *Business Week*, *People*, *U.S. News & World Report*, and news programs on NBC, ABC, CBS, and CNN have highlighted the company's role in redefining the security industry.

In 2001, the company has more than 16,000 employees who serve clients from more than 130 offices across the United States, Puerto Rico, and Canada. Guardsmark provides security for some of the most demanding clients in North America, including Fortune 1000 firms and the nation's largest banks, health care facilities, utilities, and transportation companies. Guardsmark security officers are entrusted with the protection of tens of thousands of people and billions of dollars in assets at banks, oil refineries, distribution centers, manufacturing plants, corporate offices, warehouses, public utilities, and hospitals.

There's no mistaking the source of this success: Guardsmark was founded on a commitment to exceptionally high standards and has never wavered from that ideal in almost 40 years of business.

Founded on a Vision of Excellence

Lipman, chairman and president of Guardsmark, was just 22 when he started the company. He was already a veteran in the business, having worked several years with his father, the late Mark Lipman, a well-known private investigator. During the course of thousands of sales calls on behalf of his father's business, Lipman recognized the growing need for quality uniformed security officers.

DEMANDING SELECTION REQUIREMENTS WITH AN EMPHASIS ON EDUCATION, PERSONAL INTEGRITY, AND CAREER PROFESSIONALISM MEAN THAT ONLY ONE IN 50 APPLICANTS IS SELECTED TO BECOME PART OF GUARDSMARK, INC.

IRA A. LIPMAN, CHAIRMAN AND PRESIDENT, PRESIDES OVER HIS SECURITY ORGANIZATION FROM THE NINTH-FLOOR CONFERENCE ROOM AT GUARDSMARK'S EXECUTIVE OFFICES IN MEMPHIS.

So in 1963—with just $1,000—he started a company whose focus would be providing the highest-quality security services.

Today, Guardsmark serves more than 400 cities across North America with a variety of services, including uniformed physical security, investigations, life and fire safety, and security consulting. The Mark Lipman Division comprises the investigative arm of the company, specializing in undercover investigations and preemployment background screening, while the Technical Services Division conducts sophisticated security surveys and offers consultation for contingency planning, executive protection, and sensitive white-collar crime investigations. Guardsmark's services also include a Worldwide Executive Protection Division to assist business leaders in the planning and implementation of overseas travel or high-profile events. The company's headquarters remains at the original home office in downtown Memphis—where Guardsmark now owns and occupies two buildings—but more than 96 percent of the company's business is conducted outside the Memphis area.

The industry has become crowded since Lipman started Guardsmark. In 1963, there were 3,000 firms in the security business; today, there are more than 13,000. But the growth of the industry has not necessarily led to a growth in industry-wide quality. In fact, the opposite has proved true. The demand for security services tempts many companies to relax their standards for screening officers. Not Guardsmark:

The company's continued dedication to employing the best has helped it become one of the largest security services companies in the world. With annual revenues of $400 million for the fiscal year ended June 30, 2001, Guardsmark's growth-without-acquisition strategy has averaged more than 12 percent growth, compounded annually, over the last 24 years.

Such impressive growth year after year results from Guardsmark's comprehensive focus on excellence in security service. The company protects not only a client's personnel and property, but also its bottom line. Guardsmark's high-quality security teams perform

increasingly sophisticated duties, including fire and life safety programs and more than 160 value-added services. By accepting these responsibilities, Guardsmark enables the client to focus on its core business. This innovative, proactive approach to security services provides Guardsmark customers with unmatched value.

And as further testament to the company's excellence, Guardsmark has achieved ISO 9001 registration at its headquarters and a growing number of branch offices. The highest level of compliance under the ISO 9000 International Quality Standard series, ISO 9001 registration means the

FEATURED ON EVERY SECURITY OFFICER'S UNIFORM, THE GUARDSMARK CREST PROMINENTLY DISPLAYS THE THREE QUALITIES THAT COMPRISE THE COMPANY'S PRINCIPLES OF BUSINESS: TRUTH, COURAGE, AND JUDGEMENT.

company has practices in place that reflect an internationally recognized level of quality management. Guardsmark is the only security services company to attain ISO 9001 registration at its U.S. headquarters and both U.S. and Canadian branch offices.

The firm's compliance-level process began in July 1999 when Guardsmark earned ISO 9002 certification. The initial registration was achieved in six months, an extraordinary accomplishment, and the upgrade to ISO 9001 came in another seven months. This rapid progression reflects the fact that quality systems were already firmly in place at Guardsmark. Attaining ISO 9001 registration reaffirms the company's compliance process, which has been in place since Guardsmark was founded.

THE LATE NBC ANCHOR JOHN CHANCELLOR SHARES A WORD WITH LIPMAN DURING A 1995 RECEPTION, AT WHICH LIPMAN ANNOUNCED THE ESTABLISHMENT OF THE JOHN CHANCELLOR AWARD FOR EXCELLENCE IN JOURNALISM®.

FOUNDED IN MEMPHIS, GUARDSMARK MAINTAINS MAJOR CENTERS IN CITIES SUCH AS NEW YORK (LEFT) AND LOS ANGELES, ALONG WITH MORE THAN 125 BRANCH OFFICES, TO MEET THE NEEDS OF CUSTOMERS FROM COAST TO COAST.

The Best of the Best

In security services, the product is only as good as the front line of security officers. Lipman knew that from the beginning and continues to put applicants through some of the most rigorous employment procedures in the industry.

Guardsmark's security officers must complete a 36-page employment application and are subject to one of the industry's most exhaustive screening and background checks. Of every 50 applicants, only one is accepted. Prior to employment, all employees are screened for drugs using a 10-panel drug test in an independent, federally approved laboratory. The program also includes testing for Ecstasy (3,4-methylenedioxymethamphetamine or MDMA). Guardsmark believes it is the only security firm or employer of size to test 100 percent of its employees using a 10-panel test. After joining the company, all employees—from the newest security officer to the CEO—are subject to ongoing random testing to ensure a 100 percent drug-free

workforce. Once employed, all personnel take the full Minnesota Multiphasic Personality Inventory-2™ test for career placement and development.

While some companies could never keep a full workforce with such stringent requirements, Guardsmark recruits and retains the "best of the best" with an unrivaled benefits package and commitment to employee development. As a result, the company's turnover is less than 25 percent of the industry average, as reported in independent estimates.

Full-time employees are eligible for annual wage increases, life and health insurance, tuition assistance, vacations, and the Guardsmark Wellness Team® program. Guardsmark is the only security services firm that offers free health coverage to 100 percent of its

full-time security officers, and the company offered the first 401(k) retirement savings plan in the industry, available to all full-time employees.

Employees come to Guardsmark with experience gained at the Federal Bureau of Investigation (FBI), the Secret Service, state and local police forces, and the military. Guardsmark is the largest employer of former FBI agents in the world, and its ranks include a deputy director and four assistant directors. Many employees graduated from Harvard University, the Wharton School of the University of Pennsylvania, Michigan State University, University of California-Los Angeles (UCLA), and other prestigious institutions of higher learning across the country. In fact, 95 percent of the company's management hold at least a four-year degree, and approximately 30 percent of the security officers have attended college, prompting a trade journal to name Guardsmark the employer with the best-educated workforce in the field. The company's tuition reimbursement program for all employees encourages continuing education.

Guardsmark employees' performance is further enhanced with an in-depth tracking and measurement program, and security officers receive ongoing learning and development through monthly publications and the use of Guardsmark's own interactive CD-ROMs. A special team of quality assurance professionals monitors the employees' performance.

Accepting only the highest-caliber employees fuels Guardsmark's reputation for excellence. The company's emphasis on career development can be seen in the personal and professional growth of its employees. Rewarding solely on the basis of performance, Guardsmark maintains a proud tradition of promotion from within. Many members of management, including vice presidents and regional managers, began their careers as security officers.

The company's employment policies have produced the highest-quality services, and the company continues to grow rapidly—proof positive that clients are willing to pay for quality and peace of mind. Guardsmark has an impressive client-retention rate of more than 92 percent year after year, which is believed to be the industry's best.

Changing an Industry

Guardsmark has led the security services field by example, and its standards have raised the bar in the industry. But Guardsmark does a lot more to make sure the entire security industry is serving the best interests of clients.

In the early 1970s, Lipman began the movement to disarm private security officers, an innovation that drew national attention, including editorial praise in *The New York Times* in 1982. From the outset, company management was convinced that the key to effective security was not guns, but painstakingly high recruiting standards, rigorous learning and development programs, and innovative services. At the time, this dramatic new policy cost Guardsmark a significant amount of business. In the long run, however, the practice to disarm officers paid off.

The company has also been a champion of strong, active organizational ethics codes. Guardsmark's corporate Code of Ethics was first adopted in 1980, before ethics statements were prevalent in American industry. The code is reviewed and renewed annually, when all employees are invited to give input. Each year, employees demonstrate their support by signing the new Code of Ethics. The code addresses relations between Guardsmark employees and all the people they interact with, including each other, clients, competitors, the government, and vendors.

Honor, honesty, and responsibility form the foundation of the code, along with support of employees by the company and support of the company by the employees. In addition, certain types of behavior are clearly denounced, including alcohol and drug abuse and

discrimination of any kind. Widely recognized as a leader in the corporate ethics movement, Guardsmark has been featured in many publications on business ethics. Lipman's leadership and the company's Code of Ethics have received praise in *Eighty Exemplary Ethics Statements* by Dr. Patrick Murphy at the University of Notre Dame and *Ethics Matters: How to Implement Values-Driven Management*, published by the Center for Business Ethics.

In 1996, Guardsmark was the private company recipient of the American Business Ethics Award. Sponsored by the American Society of Chartered Life Underwriters and Chartered Financial Consultants, the presenters lauded Guardsmark for its commitment to quality and safety, for its active pursuit of strong workplace ethics, and for taking the lead in calling for federal legislation to regulate the security industry.

A Recognized Authority

Lipman's transformation of the security services industry has led to numerous requests for advice and counsel, and he is widely regarded as an authority in a number of fields. Lipman's book, *How to Protect Yourself from Crime,* was first published in 1975 and was reprinted by the U.S. Department of Justice in 1981 as a government manual. Three more

editions have followed, the fourth published by Reader's Digest.

Lipman's articles have appeared in numerous national publications and on the editorial pages of major newspapers. He is also the editor of Guardsmark's highly regarded monthly security newsletter for management, *The Lipman Report®*. Focusing on topics from corporate espionage to white-collar crime, the report helps companies maintain an up-to-date perspective on security.

Lipman's achievements have been featured in 42 books. His biography is included in *Who's Who in America*, *Who's Who in World Jewry*, *Who's Who in the World*, and *Contemporary Authors*.

Changing the World

Passionate corporate citizenship is a big part of Guardsmark, and the company reaches beyond the security services industry to address the social and cultural needs of the nation as a whole.

The company was an equal opportunity employment pioneer and established a specific Equal Opportunity Policy in 1965, long before minority participation became a mandate. Today, almost 25 percent of management are minorities, and 21 percent are women.

Before joining Guardsmark, every employee signs the company's Diversity Policy and Statement, published as part of the employment application.

Widely disseminated throughout the company, this policy includes a sunset clause mandating its annual revision and renewal, similar to the Guardsmark Code of Ethics.

Lipman's personal passion for diversity and equality is well known outside the walls of Guardsmark. The story of Lipman's role in the desegregation of Little Rock Central High School—in which he helped NBC reporter John Chancellor share the truth with the American public—is retold in David Halberstam's book *The Fifties*.

Lipman has devoted considerable time and personal effort to United Way of America, where he has served in several capacities, including first chairman of the organization's Ethics Committee, chair of the steering committee of the United Way Leadership Conference 1996, and member of the board of governors.

Lipman—who has been honored by the Urban League; the National Conference of Christians and Jews, now the National Conference for Community and Justice (NCCJ); and the NAACP—is today a Trustee and a member of the Executive Committee of the Simon Wiesenthal Center, the international human rights organization.

Lipman is honorary chairman and past national chairman of the NCCJ, chairman emeritus of the National Council on Crime and Delinquency, and a member of the board of overseers of the University of Pennsylvania's Wharton School.

Lipman and Guardsmark are leading names in Memphis philanthropy. Affirming his belief in supporting the broad spectrum of causes that United Way reaches, Lipman served as general campaign chairman for United Way in Memphis in 1985-1986. That year, Memphis was recognized for the largest percentage increase in contributions among the 50 largest cities in the United States. Under Lipman's leadership, employees at Guardsmark's Memphis headquarters support United Way with impressive generosity, and, in 2000, contributed the highest amount per capita to United Way among all companies in the nation in the organization's corporate category. Lipman's philanthropic efforts also have helped organizations such as Junior Achievement of Greater Memphis, the Urban League, and the Memphis Shelby Crime Commission, which he helped found.

Guardsmark also preserves fine art for future generations. The Guardsmark Collection includes works by Henri Matisse, Pierre Bonnard, Helen Frankenthaler, Pablo Picasso, Edouard Vuillard, and others, but the works of Henri de Toulouse-Lautrec dominate—mostly drawn from the painter's observations of the French cabaret scene during the 1890s.

The Guardsmark Collection includes one of the finest and most complete collections of Toulouse-Lautrec's original posters, including important pieces recognizable around the world. The company has hosted groups from museums around the country. Lipman has generously loaned these works on several occasions to the Dixon Gallery and Gardens in Memphis, the Museum of Modern Art in New York City, and various other local and national galleries.

Few companies have changed their industries and communities like Guardsmark has. The company's longtime commitment to doing things right without exception has made it the choice for companies who put a high priority on security and will ensure continued growth and success for years to come.

LIPMAN ADDRESSES THE PRESS AFTER MEMPHIS CITY MAYOR W.W. HERENTON ANNOUNCED THE RESPONSE OF HIS ADMINISTRATION TO THE *Memphis and Shelby County Crime Report 1996*, SPONSORED BY GUARDSMARK. AS A RESULT OF THIS STUDY AND A FOLLOW-UP REPORT ISSUED IN 1997, LIPMAN HELPED FOUND THE MEMPHIS SHELBY CRIME COMMISSION, SERVING AS THE FIRST CHAIRMAN.

O n a wall in Fred Davis' office is a picture of Davis with Martin Luther King Jr.—taken while King was in Memphis in 1968, negotiating on behalf of striking city sanitation workers. At that time, Davis had just been elected to the city council—as one of only three African-American members—and he went on to play a key role in helping the city survive the crisis that followed King's assassination later that year. ▲ "I went on to fight a lot of

battles in my 12 years on the council, but building the insurance agency— that's been harder," Davis says. Fred L. Davis Insurance Agency was the first African-American-owned insurance agency in the region, and the company broke major ground in financial services for African-Americans in the South. "Before we opened in 1967, there wasn't a black person in six states who could write a standard policy for fire, auto—anything," says Davis.

But obstacles have never stopped Davis, and today, Fred L. Davis Insurance is one of the leading providers of comprehensive personal and commercial insurance products in the Mid-South. The agency's three licensed agents offer property, life, health, casualty, commercial, and investment insurance products. And, as one of only a few NASD-registered property and casualty agents in Tennessee, Davis

▼ ERNEST WITHERS

ONE OF THREE AFRICAN-AMERICAN MEMBERS OF THE CITY COUNCIL DURING THE 1968 SANITATION WORKERS' STRIKE, FRED L. DAVIS PLAYED A KEY ROLE IN HELPING MEMPHIS SURVIVE THE CRISIS FOLLOWING THE DEATH OF DR. MARTIN LUTHER KING, JR. HIS INSURANCE COMPANY, FRED L. DAVIS INSURANCE AGENCY, HAS BEEN SERVING ALL MEMPHIANS, BLACK AND WHITE, FOR MORE THAN 30 YEARS.

can help businesses and individuals by integrating investment vehicles, giving him further flexibility to offer strong pensions, IRAs, and other deferred-compensation packages.

Working for Clients, Serving the Community

D avis' client base includes some of Memphis' best-known entities, including Memphis Light, Gas & Water; Memphis International Airport; and Cook Convention Center. Davis also serves a long roster of small businesses and an even longer list of individuals.

"There's no real secret to our success," Davis says. "We've just built our reputation on personalized, high-quality service."

According to Davis, too many insurance companies focus on writing expensive policies, and fail to pay attention to clients' comprehensive needs. "There are some people who won't do anything unless there's money in it," Davis says. "That's not how I approach business. That's not how I approach life." Fred L. Davis Insurance Agency focuses on building relation-

ships with clients, and that approach has paid off.

While working for his customers, Davis has also continued in his role as community servant. He was a founding member of the Mid-South Minority Business Council, and he serves as a director on the board of the Assisi Foundation. Davis also serves on the boards of the foundations of the University of Memphis and Southwest Tennessee Community College; was one of a five-member commission that built Mud Island; and has twice served on the board of directors of the Memphis Area Chamber of Commerce. And although he went to jail during a 1960s protest to integrate the Fairgrounds, he ended up—decades later—as a member of the Memphis Park Commission, which has supervisory authority over that operation.

"You could say that my job has been opening doors," Davis says. "I hope my business has opened doors for my clients, and I hope my success has opened doors for other small-business-minded people. I've always tried to inspire people to be the best people they could. Hopefully, I've accomplished that."

O n April 17, 1973, Federal Express began operations from Memphis, providing overnight express delivery of just 186 packages, bound for 25 U.S. cities and carried on 14 small Falcon jets. That night, 389 FedEx employees made history—not just for Memphis, but for businesses around the world. ▲ Today, FedEx Corporation is a thriving global business—and household name—that includes six companies. On any given business day,

nearly 200,000 FedEx employees and contractors deliver more than 5 million packages to destinations in some 210 countries. Back in 1973, no one could have conceived of the technological changes that would occur over the next three decades, such as laser package scanning for real-time information, and shipping and tracking with desktop convenience on the FedEx Web site at www.fedex.com.

As FedEx has grown, so has the Memphis economy and the city's reputation as America's Distribution Center. "The FedEx impact on the local economy reaches far beyond the households of nearly 30,000 employees in this city," says Frederick W. Smith, chairman, president, and CEO. "A FedEx hub is also a magnet for other companies, and economic impact studies have shown that, either directly or indirectly, FedEx can be linked to one out of every 11 jobs in the Memphis area."

A Multifaceted Company

T oday, Memphis serves as worldwide headquarters for FedEx and four of its companies. FedEx Express provides time-definite express delivery to some 210 countries. With some 665 aircraft, FedEx Express is the world's largest all-cargo airline, and its largest hub operation makes Memphis International Airport the world's leading cargo airport.

FedEx Services consolidates sales, marketing, and technology support for the FedEx family of companies. The FedEx Services group also includes the subsidiary FedEx Supply Chain Services, based in Hudson, Ohio, which provides comprehensive logistics and transportation management.

FedEx Freight specializes in regional, less-than-truckload freight transportation. Established in March 2001, this new FedEx company oversees the operations of American Freightways, based in Harrison, Arkansas, and Viking Freight, based in San Jose.

FedEx Trade Networks, which facilitates global trade with its customs brokerage and freight forwarding services, includes subsidiaries Tower Group International of Buffalo, Worldtariff Ltd. of San Francisco, and Caribbean Transportation Services of Greensboro.

In addition, two other FedEx operating companies serve the Memphis

area. FedEx Ground, based in Pittsburgh, provides small-package ground delivery service, including FedEx Home Delivery. FedEx Custom Critical, based in Akron, offers exclusive-use, expedited, door-to-door delivery.

After some 30 years of service to the Memphis economy—and to the world—FedEx Corporation continues its commitment to growth and leadership. Supporting community events such as the FedEx St. Jude Classic golf tournament and numerous local charitable organizations, FedEx remains committed to being a good neighbor and a great place to work.

FEDEX CORPORATION IS TODAY COMPRISED OF SIX COMPANIES—FEDEX EXPRESS, FEDEX GROUND, FEDEX FREIGHT, FEDEX CUSTOM CRITICAL, FEDEX TRADE NETWORKS, AND FEDEX SERVICES.

Clyde Patton, Bruce Taylor, and Paul Ryan are known throughout Memphis for their hands-on approach to construction management and residential development. In a business where attention to detail can make or break a project, these men have a reputation for letting nothing fall through the cracks. It is a philosophy that has brought them much success. ▲ In fact, the three now lead a trio of successful companies that

are changing the face of Memphis. Patton & Taylor Construction Company; Patton, Taylor & Ryan Residential Developers; and Patton & Taylor Commercial Developers bring that eye for excellence to a variety of new construction, development, and renovation projects.

Patton and Taylor formed the construction company in 1968. Beginning with upper-scale, custom homes in the East Memphis area—including Germantown and Collierville—the company built more than 700 homes before 1982, when it transferred to the commercial arena. Since then, Patton & Taylor has been engaged in almost all phases of construction, from tilt-up warehouses to the renovation of loft warehouses and office towers. Other projects successfully undertaken include an armory, a fire station, retail centers, and a long list of apartment projects.

A sampling of Patton & Taylor projects includes the Grove Apartments, BPI Office and Distribution Center, Burch Porter & Johnson office

PAUL RYAN, BRUCE TAYLOR, AND CLYDE PATTON, STANDING IN FRONT OF ONE OF THEIR NEW RESIDENTIAL DEVELOPMENTS, ARE PRINCIPALS OF PATTON TAYLOR & RYAN.

THE LEASING BUILDING AT THE BAILEY CREEK APARTMENTS SETS THE TONE FOR THE 232-UNIT GARDEN APARTMENT COMMUNITY DEVELOPED BY PATTON & TAYLOR.

▼ DAVID SPARKMAN

STERLING SQUARE
AT SCHILLING FARMS

renovation, Calvary Street Ministry, Southaven Hampton Inn, Cotton Exchange Building renovation, Defense Depot Dining Facility, Homewood Suites Hotel, Paperworks Loft Apartments, Sleep-Out Louie's Restaurant, Wolf River Retail Center, Tennessee National Guard Armory, Yacht Club Condominiums, Saddlery Lofts

Apartments, and Registry at Wolf Chase Apartments.

Patton & Taylor Construction's experience enables the company to assist its customers in achieving cost-effective design, as well as in maintaining tight construction budgets for all types of residential and light commercial buildings. Experience means nothing to customers if they don't have access to the experts. That's why Patton & Taylor is proud of its reputation as a firm where clients work directly with the company's principals.

Patton, Taylor & Ryan

Memphis' growing reputation as a great home for corporate headquarters and service centers has led to a growing need for upper-scale communities to house these companies' executives. Patton & Taylor stepped in to meet this need with the addition of Paul Ryan to the company in 1985. The three formed an affiliate company, Patton, Taylor & Ryan in 1992.

Patton, Taylor & Ryan develops all types of single-family subdivisions, from zero-lot-line, in-fill developments to large estate lots. The company has

▼ DAVID SPARKMAN

developed a strong reputation for a sensitivity to the environment and the communities in which it builds. That is a growing concern, especially on in-fill projects, and Patton, Taylor & Ryan is proud of its reputation for respecting the history and the architectural and design patterns of a community.

Over the years, Patton, Taylor & Ryan has developed more than 3,000 lots in the Mid-South area, creating such prestigious communities as Richwood, Shelby Crossing, Cordova Woods, Quail Ridge, Fletcher Park, Wilsford, Kimbrough Grove, the Fairways, Sterling Square, Collierville Station, and Forest Shadows.

Patton & Taylor Developers

Building on their reputation and experience, Patton & Taylor launched a development arm called Patton & Taylor Developers. Developing retail centers and multi-family housing takes in-depth skill and keen management. Patton & Taylor Developers has leveraged its experience into some of the area's most successful strip commercial projects, including Saddle Creek North Shopping Center, Wolf River Retail Center, and Sycamore View Shopping Center.

Patton & Taylor Developers has also developed more than 3,000 garden apartment units with a long list of successful communities, including The Madison at Schilling Farms, Bailey Creek, and Dogwood Creek of Collierville, as well as Church Lake and the Civic Center Apartments in Southaven.

All three principals have earned honors for their skills and expertise. Patton was elected Builder of the Year in 1979, and is past president of the Memphis Area Home Builders' Association. He has served on the boards of the Home Owners Warranty Council of Memphis and the

Memphis Area Chamber of Commerce, and he currently serves as a board member for Regions Bank of Memphis and Nehemiah Community Development Corporation.

Taylor has served as chairman of the Multi-State Transportation System Advisory Board of the Memphis Area Chamber of Commerce, and has been a board member of the Memphis Area Homebuilders Association, the Hutchison School, VictoryBank & Trust Company, the Economics Club, and the Germantown Rotary Club. He also has been a board member of Opera Memphis, WKNO, and the vestry of Calvary Episcopal Church.

Both Patton and Taylor have experience in real estate sales, development, and financing, and are past directors of the Homebuilders Asso-

ciation of Memphis and past board members of Les Passees Children's Rehabilitation Center.

Ryan is a former chairman of the Bartlett Planning Commission. He is active in the Memphis Area Home Builders' Association, having served as chairman of the Vesta Home Show and the Developer's Council. In 1992, he was named Builder of the Year and served as president of the association in 1996.

But the most compelling proof of Patton & Taylor's expertise is standing all over Memphis. From downtown office renovations to all-new housing and shopping developments in the growing suburbs of East Memphis, the company is continuing to shape the city with successful project after successful project.

THE YACHT CLUB CONDOMINIUMS, CONSTRUCTED BY PATTON & TAYLOR CONSTRUCTION COMPANY, IS ONE OF THE LANDMARKS OF THE PRIZE-WINNING HARBOR TOWN COMMUNITY (LEFT).

SADDLE CREEK NORTH SHOPPING CENTER IN GERMANTOWN IS AN EXAMPLE OF A PRIME COMMERCIAL PROJECT DEVELOPED BY PATTON & TAYLOR (RIGHT).

THE MANAGEMENT TEAM OF PATTON & TAYLOR CONSTRUCTION COMPANY ASSEMBLED ON THE STEPS OF THE MADISON AT SCHILLING FARMS, A 324-UNIT MULTI-FAMILY COMMUNITY, DEVELOPED AND CONSTRUCTED BY PATTON & TAYLOR.

presence in the Memphis business community since 1971, PricewaterhouseCoopers has become an indispensable partner for many of the world's most respected companies. Reinvented in 1998 after the merger of two firms—Price Waterhouse and Coopers & Lybrand—PricewaterhouseCoopers has emerged from a role as a prestigious Big Six independent global accounting firm to become a trusted multifaceted business adviser.

One of 866 PricewaterhouseCoopers offices across the globe, the Memphis office was the nation's first fully integrated PricewaterhouseCoopers office, and continues its progressive leadership as the city's largest business services firm with some 115 employees. Today, the Memphis office provides clients with expertise in a long list of consulting areas, including audit, accounting, and tax advice; management, information technology, and human resource consulting; financial advisory services, including mergers and acquisitions, business recovery, project finance, and litigation support; business process outsourcing services; and legal advice through affiliated law firms.

"Businesses today look a lot different than they did even 10 years ago," says Vincent Robinson, managing partner for the PricewaterhouseCoopers office. "As they get bigger, more global, and more reliant on technology, we've maintained our commitment to keeping up with the services they need to operate smarter, faster, and stronger."

JAY ADKINS

A Partner in Business

With a heritage as one of the leading independent accounting firms in the world, PricewaterhouseCoopers has a reputation for delivering the information and advice that firms need to streamline and grow. As clients began to develop needs that fell outside of the traditional realm of CPAs, the company stepped up to serve them with consulting for a variety of aspects of their businesses. PricewaterhouseCoopers today handles not only complex audits and tax matters, but also consults and assists in such major business transactions as mergers, acquisitions, and corporate reorganizations. The firm provides valuable insight on business processes, and even counsels companies on e-commerce.

Using powerful technology and an expertise in business processes, the Memphis office is a clear example of the strength of this approach. In recent years, for example, the Memphis office of PricewaterhouseCoopers structured and proposed multistate tax plans designed to minimize a client's state tax liabilities. The office helped another client integrate its computer systems in a large-scale project that is changing the corporation's network from mainframe to a more agile client/server system.

WITH A HERITAGE AS ONE OF THE LEADING INDEPENDENT ACCOUNTING FIRMS IN THE WORLD, PRICEWATERHOUSECOOPERS HAS A REPUTATION FOR DELIVERING THE INFORMATION AND ADVICE THAT FIRMS NEED TO STREAMLINE AND GROW.

JAY ADKINS

Nationally, PricewaterhouseCoopers' technology leadership is clear across its whole family of services. And to see the firm's e-commerce expertise, one only has to look as far as Pricewaterhouse-Cooper's 550 "e.conomy" clients. These clients—including firms like Oprah Winfrey's Harpo Productions, Inc.—have access to the latest in new-economy services from Price-waterhouseCoopers and its affiliates.

But in spite of all its advances in technology, PricewaterhouseCoopers remains the preferred partner for leading companies in the world's most traditional market sectors in consumer and industrial products, energy and mining, financial services, entertainment, and the services industry. In the retailing and consumer products sector, for example, Pricewaterhouse works with 30 percent of that industry's major companies. The firm also provides services to 50 percent of the major corporations in the entertainment/communications industry.

Here in Tennessee, Pricewaterhouse-Coopers' expertise in both governmental and health care sectors landed it in a high-profile auditing job. The State of Tennessee hired the firm to complete a detailed analysis of the financial condition of the TennCare program and to help project future expenditures and funding needs.

Serving Clients and the Communities

In addition to expertise, Pricewater-houseCoopers puts a high value on service. In the arena of client service, few can match the firm's reputation. Independent polls by the Emerson Company, for example, have placed PricewaterhouseCoopers in the number one spot for overall client satisfaction among both banking and high-tech clients.

But service extends beyond clients at PricewaterhouseCoopers. The company is committed to the communities it serves, and plays a vital role in a variety of community programs. Nation-ally, the company is well known for its Minority Scholars Program. The program provides more than 40 grants per academic year to aid minority college students with their educational expenses. Students are selected each year on rigorous criteria that include a student's GPA, success in key courses, academic achievements, and a required interview with a member of the firm. In existence for more than 10 years, the Pricewater-houseCoopers Minority Scholars Program is one of the most substantial minority scholarship efforts in terms of award grants alone, and also one of the most enduring.

In Memphis, that tradition continues as PricewaterhouseCoopers supports a number of community organizations and serves as a visible member of the Volunteer Center of Memphis' Corporate Volunteer Council.

It's a formula that won't change any time soon. As technology and consolidation continue to transform the global marketplace, PricewaterhouseCoopers will continue its role as a leader in commerce, consulting, and communities.

TODAY HEADQUARTERED IN THE MORGAN KEEGAN BUILDING DOWNTOWN, PRICEWATERHOUSECOOPERS HAS BEEN A FIXTURE IN THE MEMPHIS BUSINESS COMMUNITY SINCE 1971.

THE MEMPHIS GROUP, INC.

hen traveling by air, many people simply board the plane, settle back, and wait to reach their destinations, never wondering what it takes to keep the plane flying safely. Very often it takes the products and services of The Memphis Group, Inc. (TMG). A leading supplier to the aviation industry, The Memphis Group conducts a thriving international business, serving thousands of travelers each day who enjoy the benefits of TMG's behind-the-scenes work.

The Memphis Group was founded in 1971 by John Williams, president, who was joined a year later by John Temple, executive vice president. Established under the name Memphis Avionics, the company sought to buy and sell surplus avionics equipment, specifically any equipment having to do with electronic communications or navigation in an airplane.

Finding New Markets

At first, TMG sold to a niche market, providing refurbished parts for personal and corporate private planes. Later, the company expanded and began selling new parts through Mid-America Avionics Distributors.

In 1979, the company created its own software and revolutionized the aviation products aftermarket. Called Inventory Locator Services (ILS), the program consisted of a database that provided one of the largest inventories of airplane parts in the world, giving TMG and other ILS clients access to a wealth of parts information.

JOHN WILLIAMS IS PRESIDENT (RIGHT) AND JOHN TEMPLE IS EXECUTIVE VICE PRESIDENT OF THE MEMPHIS GROUP, INC. (TMG).

In the early 1980s, the company consolidated its divisions, changing its name to The Memphis Group, Inc. Today, The Memphis Group companies include TMG Airepairs, formerly known as Aero Electronics, a majority owned subsidiary providing component maintenance services; and Memphis International, Inc. (MI), which is based in Atlanta and provides contract installation services worldwide.

TMG significantly expanded its activities at this time, adding engine and airframe components to its already diverse offering. The company built its own airport facility in Greenwood, Mississippi, to dismantle airplanes for the purpose of reselling the components. Aircraft dismantled by the firm include Boeing 727s, 737s, and 747s; Lockheed L1011s; Airbus A-300s; McDonnell Douglas DC-10s and DC-9s; and numerous commuter and corporate aircraft.

A Market Giant

Today, TMG's market has expanded to include the commercial airlines and air transportation companies, and the firm supplies nearly every part needed for airplane maintenance. With combined warehouse space totaling 400,000 square feet, TMG employs approximately 300 people, including agents in all major aviation hubs and employees in sales offices in the United Kingdom, China, Indonesia, France, and Ireland.

The company ranks among the top 10 buyers and sellers of surplus inventory

TMG'S ELECTRONIC DATA INTERCHANGE SERVICE PUTS BUYERS AND SELLERS IN TOUCH WITH INVENTORY AROUND THE GLOBE, ELIMINATING PAPERWORK AND OTHER COMMUNICATIONS NECESSARY TO OPERATE OTHER PRESENT SYSTEMS.

more of their management tasks and ultimately perform only passenger-related functions in-house.

Innovation at Its Best

TMG has a leading edge in the aviation supply business on several fronts. To adapt to the constant technological changes of today's society, the company created a new industry software package called BComm—an abbreviated form of International Business Communications, a division formed to market the product. This electronic data interchange service puts buyers and sellers in touch with inventory around the globe, eliminating paperwork and other communications necessary to operate other present systems. Additionally, TMG continues to offer such innovative services as leasing and pooling, which provide airlines with the possibilities of enormous savings in inventory cost and management.

The company's culture is geared toward customer support, with a straightforward approach to growth. TMG is proud of its reputation in the industry as an honorable company. One of its informal mottoes has been "We are the good group to know." Without satisfied customers, TMG doesn't have a business. With its policy of flexibility, the company is customer minded, always striving to accommodate the customer's requirements rather than TMG's systems.

The Memphis Group, Inc.'s mission is to be the aviation industry's recognized quality supplier of spare parts and support to identified markets—providing a stable, yet creative, work environment that promotes employee morale, growth, security, and loyalty.

in the world, with a customer list that includes most major airlines and maintenance facilities worldwide.

The combined capabilities of TMG and its related companies enable them to offer aftermarket services, including component overhaul, manufacture of avionics test equipment, avionics repair and maintenance, airframe structures repair, materials management, and professional consulting.

Williams' achievements in the management of the company earned him the *Memphis Business Journal*'s Executive of the Year award in 1991. He is now planning the company's next innovative moves, many of which will allow airlines to outsource more and

THE COMPANY BUILT ITS OWN AIRPORT FACILITY IN GREENWOOD, MISSISSIPPI, TO DISMANTLE AIRPLANES FOR THE PURPOSE OF RESELLING THE COMPONENTS (LEFT).

TMG'S MARKET HAS EXPANDED TO INCLUDE THE COMMERCIAL AIRLINES AND AIR TRANSPORTATION COMPANIES, AND THE FIRM SUPPLIES NEARLY EVERY PART NEEDED FOR AIRPLANE MAINTENANCE.

ince 1972, the Drexel Chemical Company has been an integral part of modern agriculture, both in the Mid-South and around the world. Founder Robert Drexel Shockey has catered to his customers since the company's birth, providing a wide variety of quality agricultural pesticides to control weeds and insects—always doing so at the best price possible. This approach, along with solid business practices and aggressive attention to

technology and marketing, has earned Shockey's company a sure place in an industry replete with huge, global entities.

"It still boils down to certain basics," Shockey says. "The bottom line is that the grower has to use chemicals to help produce a healthier, more bountiful crop. If we can supply him those products at a more economical price, then he stands a better chance of making a profit. Helping the grower to succeed is imperative to the long-term success of the entire agricultural industry."

Reaching across the Globe

After several years of experience in sales and management with other agricultural chemical companies, Shockey founded Drexel Chemical in Memphis in 1972 with a capital investment of $2,500. Initially, Drexel only distributed to suppliers and co-ops, but when demand increased, the company began manufacturing chemicals under its own label.

The company has been growing strong ever since. Since 1990, Drexel's management team has doubled sales, expanded warehousing, and watched the number of employees grow to more than 250 and the number of products to some 200. Today, the firm boasts annual sales in excess of $80 million. Drexel's products fall into four broad categories—growth regulators, herbicides, insecticides, and fungicides—used primarily on crops including corn, tobacco, and cotton.

Today, Drexel's reach spans the globe. The company serves a number of markets across the United States from a 215,000-square-foot facility on Presidents Island, which houses the company headquarters and its major distribution center. The strategic Memphis location—with major land, air, and water transportation facilities—plays a vital part in the quick and efficient distribution of Drexel products throughout the United States.

Drexel's exporting business has grown as well. While sporadic in the beginning, the export business has grown to a healthy balance of 10 to 12 percent of its annual sales. Drexel ships products to more than 30 countries, including Australia, Thailand, Zimbabwe, South Africa, and Chile.

Drexel serves all its markets from six facilities in four states. In addition to the Memphis facilities, the company operates a second production facility and another large warehouse in Cordele, Georgia. The company also has a third major plant in Tunica, Mississippi, and operates a third large warehouse in Mobile.

A Bright Future

Shockey attributes his company's success to several factors, including its broad product line and its efficiency. Also, the company responds quickly to customer needs, a quality that major multinational operations lack. Shockey believes that a willingness to put money back into

DREXEL CHEMICAL COMPANY FOUNDER BOB SHOCKEY HAS CATERED TO HIS CUSTOMERS SINCE THE COMPANY'S BIRTH, PROVIDING A WIDE VARIETY OF QUALITY AGRICULTURAL PESTICIDES TO CONTROL WEEDS AND INSECTS—ALWAYS DOING SO AT THE BEST PRICE POSSIBLE.

▲ SWEENEY SOUTH

HUD ANDREWS

THE MANAGEMENT OF DREXEL INCLUDES (FROM LEFT) BOB SHOCKEY, OWNER AND VICE PRESIDENT OF FINANCE; JAMES OLIVER, NATIONAL SALES MANAGER; LEIGH SHOCKEY, CEO AND CHAIRMAN; JIM PELT, VICE PRESIDENT OF MARKETING; AND BEN JOHNSON, PRESIDENT AND COO.

the operation has contributed to the health of the company and to its present fluid economic position.

Perhaps Drexel's most important asset is that the firm is well capitalized, making the company ready to respond at a moment's notice to large orders when customer needs dictate. It is not unusual for Drexel warehouses to hold merchandise worth $40 million.

Drexel is well prepared to face the challenges that the future holds. What will some of those challenges be? Shockey speculates that a big challenge will be additional federal regulations spawned by a public ignorant of the truth about agricultural chemicals. "Critics of pesticides treat them like people treated witchcraft 100 years ago," Shockey says. "They make a mistake calling pesticides a poison. They should call them a medicine. We treat for fungi and bacteria on plants. Sometimes molds and the like are more dangerous to humans than a small residue from pesticides."

Whatever the challenges, though, Shockey and his management team plan to keep the company strong by focusing on the agricultural end-users of Drexel Chemical Company's products. "We must all do whatever it

takes to provide an effective product the growers of any size can afford," Shockey says. "If we can help the

growers ensure a healthy, profitable crop, then that's good business for them, for us, and for the country."

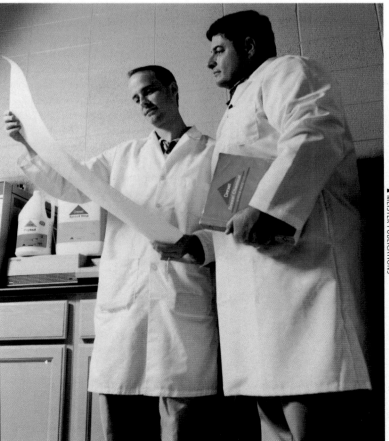

HUD ANDREWS

DREXEL'S PRODUCTS FALL INTO FOUR BROAD CATEGORIES—GROWTH REGULATORS, HERBICIDES, INSECTICIDES, AND FUNGICIDES—USED PRIMARILY ON CROPS INCLUDING CORN, TOBACCO, AND COTTON.

MEISTER PUBLICATIONS

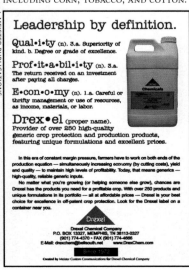

ameson Gibson Construction Company, Inc. is a Memphis business through and through. Born and raised in Memphis, the company's family owners and managers continue the tradition of shaping their community. ▲ Working in the family construction business, original partners E.P. "Gene" Gibson Jr. and David Jameson decided in 1972 that they would launch their own construction company. Some 30 years later, Jameson Gibson has

steadily grown to become one of the city's leading construction firms, with annual revenue in excess of $60 million. Although David Jameson remains as general superintendent, his son Chris Jameson now shares ownership with Gibson. Gibson oversees estimating and marketing while Jameson supervises project management, field operations, and accounting.

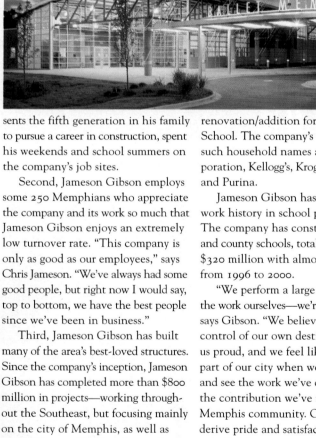

JAMESON GIBSON CONSTRUCTION COMPANY, INC. HAS LEFT ITS MARK ALL AROUND MEMPHIS WITH PROJECTS SUCH AS THE BALLET MEMPHIS DANCE STUDIO.

Community Success

Jameson Gibson won the *Memphis Business Journal's* 19th annual Small Business Award as the number one business in the 100-plus-employees category for several reasons. First, Gibson and the Jamesons are lifelong Memphians who grew up in the construction business. Collectively, they offer more than 116 years of construction experience. Gibson and David Jameson both began as apprentice carpenters and quickly advanced in skill and training. Chris Jameson, who repre-sents the fifth generation in his family to pursue a career in construction, spent his weekends and school summers on the company's job sites.

Second, Jameson Gibson employs some 250 Memphians who appreciate the company and its work so much that Jameson Gibson enjoys an extremely low turnover rate. "This company is only as good as our employees," says Chris Jameson. "We've always had some good people, but right now I would say, top to bottom, we have the best people since we've been in business."

Third, Jameson Gibson has built many of the area's best-loved structures. Since the company's inception, Jameson Gibson has completed more than $800 million in projects—working throughout the Southeast, but focusing mainly on the city of Memphis, as well as Shelby County. "We'll work out of town if we need to, but as long as we can make a living in Memphis, we'll stay right here at home," says Gibson.

Jameson Gibson's résumé is crowded with notable projects: the National Civil Rights Museum, the Lichterman Nature Center renovation, Chucalissa Archaeological Museum, St. Francis Hospital, Tim McCarver Baseball Stadium, the Mud Island parking structure, Memphis' Wonders Series' *Napoleon* and *Tombs of China*, and a renovation/addition for Carver High School. The company's clients include such household names as FedEx Corporation, Kellogg's, Kroger, Wal-Mart, and Purina.

Jameson Gibson has an impressive work history in school projects alone. The company has constructed 64 city and county schools, totaling more than $320 million with almost half built from 1996 to 2000.

"We perform a large percentage of the work ourselves—we're not brokers," says Gibson. "We believe in staying in control of our own destiny. It makes us proud, and we feel like an integral part of our city when we look around and see the work we've completed and the contribution we've made to the Memphis community. Our employees derive pride and satisfaction from it as well. They get a real kick out of it, almost as much as we do."

Versatility and Excellence

Jameson Gibson's experience in all types of construction is extensive. The firm's versatile approach, as evidenced by the wide variety of projects, has allowed it to become a major player in Mid-South construction. "We don't specialize in any one type of building," says Jameson. "We'll build just about anything, from heavy

ONE EXAMPLE OF THE FIRM'S VERSATILITY IS THE INTERIOR OF SACRED HEART SCHOOL'S CHAPEL.

JAMESON GIBSON CONSTRUCTION
COMPANY'S CLIENTS INCLUDE THE
TENNESSEE AIR NATIONAL GUARD (TOP
AND BOTTOM LEFT) AND THE NATIONAL
CIVIL RIGHTS MUSEUM.

concrete to the ornate detailing and gold leafing of a museum." Jameson Gibson has completed more than 50 million square feet in a wide range of building types, including offices, retail structures, entertainment venues, restaurants, hotels, casinos, hospitals, schools, jails, churches, community centers, industrial centers, manufacturing plants, warehouses, distribution areas, museums, and exhibitions. "If it has anything to do with buildings, we've done it," says Gibson.

Jameson Gibson also offers construction management and design/build services to its clients. "Working with clients to provide preconstruction services such as planning, designing, estimating, scheduling, and value

engineering can be the key to a successful project," says Jameson. Once a project is under construction, an experienced staff assures quality control, and data processing capabilities closely track and monitor costs.

The partners have also developed two other construction-related companies. Advance Manufacturing Company is a 36,000-square-foot, custom architectural millwork manufacturing facility. Standard Maintenance Company provides millwright and pipe-fitting services to industrial and manufacturing clients. "Having these resources to draw on can be an advantage for Jameson Gibson and its clients," says Gibson.

Through combining versatility with an attention to detail, expert

craftsmanship, and a blending of abilities and interests, Jameson Gibson provides its customers with a top-quality construction product.

A Memphis Legacy

Jameson Gibson has become one of the most successful and efficient construction companies in the Mid-South. The company has a strong reputation for successfully completing projects that are on time, to specifications, and within budget. "The proof is in the repeat business, which we get a lot of," says Gibson. "We build a quality project every time with no surprises. That way our customers ask us to come back and build their next project."

F or almost 40 years, Shea-Hubbard ENT Clinic, PC has been a leading medical group in Memphis, dedicated to quality care and to providing the community with excellent service. In 1962, after 10 years of active duty in the U.S. Navy Medical Corps, Dr. Martin Coyle Shea Jr. joined the Memphis Otologic Clinic. In 1967, Shea founded the Shea Otologic Group. As the practice grew over the years, it was renamed Shea, Hubbard and

Futrell Ear, Nose & Throat Group in 1985, introducing nose and throat care into the practice. Today, the clinic is called Shea-Hubbard ENT Clinic PC, and it specializes in otolaryngology and neurotology. These fields deal with the diseases, treatment, and surgery of the ear, nose, throat, and balance system.

A Wealth of Experience

P eople all over the nation have come to rely on the wealth of experience at Shea-Hubbard. The two principals, Shea and Dr. Ron E. Hubbard, have more than 80 years of combined otolaryngological experience. Both Shea and Hubbard are certified by the American Board of Otolaryngology, and both are fellows of the American College of Surgeons, members of the American Academy of Otolaryngology-Head and Neck Surgery, and associate clinical professors for the Department of Otolaryngology and Maxillofacial Surgery at the University of Tennessee Center for the Health Sciences.

Shea received a bachelor of science degree from the University of Tennessee-Knoxville, and then graduated from the University of Tennessee College of Medicine in Memphis. He completed his postgraduate studies at the U.S. Naval School of Aviation Medicine, where he was designated a naval flight surgeon. His residencies were in general surgery and otolaryngology at the U.S. Naval Hospital in Bethesda. He received his licensure in Tennessee in 1953 and his board certification in 1961 before founding the clinic.

The American Academy of Otolaryngology-Head and Neck Surgery honored Shea with the Distinguished Award for Humanitarian Efforts in 1992 for his many years of medical mission work in Peru. He is on the board of directors for the South America Mission, Inc., and is a participating surgeon in the Implantable Soundtec Direct Drive Hearing System Research Program. Shea is also a member of the American Laryngological, Rhinological, and Otological Society.

Hubbard joined the organization in 1974, when it was still Shea Otologic Group, and added his name to the masthead in 1985. Hubbard, who is from Little Rock, received a bachelor of science degree from Hendrix College in Conway before studying medicine at the University of Arkansas Medical School. He completed his residency in general surgery at the Veterans Administration Hospital in Memphis and his otolaryngology residency at the University of Tennessee, Memphis. Hubbard received his licensure in

PEOPLE ALL OVER THE WORLD HAVE COME TO RELY ON THE WEALTH OF EXPERIENCE AT SHEA-HUBBARD ENT CLINIC, PC. PICTURED (FROM LEFT) IS DR. RON E. HUBBARD, DR. MARK A. MILBURN, AND DR. MARTIN COYLE SHEA JR.

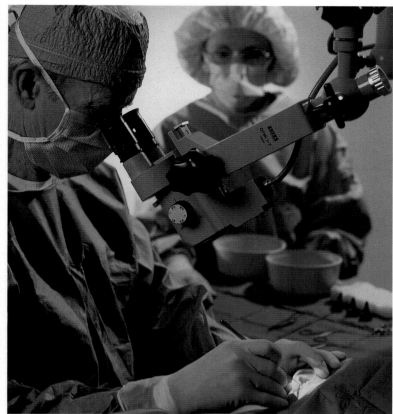

services," says Hubbard proudly. "This allows us to continue to grow while maintaining that standard."

Serving More and More Patients

This impressive array of experience has drawn more and more patients to Shea-Hubbard and has resulted in phenomenal growth. The company has grown to provide a whole spectrum of services related to the ear, nose, throat, and balance system.

"We do the complicated things that many ENTs just don't have the experience to do," says Shea. "For example, Hubbard is one of the most experienced doctors in the United States for pituitary tumors. Plus, we have the equipment and technology necessary to do everything. We get referrals from ENTs all over the country."

Patient problems run the gamut: hearing loss; ear infections; equilibrium disorders; infections and allergies of the nose and sinuses; infections of the mouth, throat, and larynx; breathing, swallowing, and voice disorders; and tumors of the ear, nose, throat, and neck. Additional services include allergy testing, hearing aids, custom-fitted earplugs, and surgery for the ear, head, and neck.

"We basically cover everything on the head and neck, except the eyes and the brain," says Hubbard, "and we are committed to offering the highest level of care available in the region. We will continue to pursue excellence in our work and in our service."

Tennessee in 1970 and his board certification in 1974.

In addition to the experienced principals, Shea-Hubbard employs highly skilled physicians and an excellent staff, many of whom have been with the organization for nearly 40 years. Shea-Hubbard's newest partners are Dr. Mark A. Milburn, who studied at the University of Tennessee College of Medicine, and Dr. John Touliatos. While at the University of Tennessee, Milburn completed his residencies in general surgical and otolaryngological, head, and neck surgery; the faculty voted him outstanding chief resident in 1998. Touliatos, a graduate of the University of Tennessee, Memphis, completed his residency in otolaryngology at Southern Illinois University in Springfield, Illinois.

"The longevity and vast expertise of our combined staff speaks to the quality and viability of our organization and its

FOR ALMOST 40 YEARS, SHEA-HUBBARD ENT CLINIC, PC HAS BEEN A LEADING MEDICAL GROUP IN MEMPHIS, DEDICATED TO QUALITY CARE AND TO PROVIDING THE COMMUNITY WITH EXCELLENT SERVICE.

THE CLINIC SPECIALIZES IN OTOLARYNGOLOGY AND NEUROTOLOGY—FIELDS DEALING WITH THE DISEASES, TREATMENT, AND SURGERY OF THE EAR, NOSE, THROAT, AND BALANCE SYSTEM.

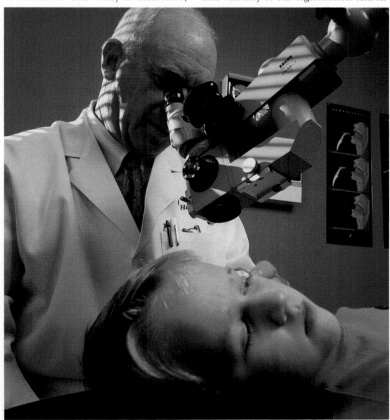

W hen Saint Francis Hospital opened its doors in 1974, it became the first full-service hospital in the fast-growing East Memphis area. In little more than a quarter century, Saint Francis has gone on to deliver a number of additional firsts to the Memphis medical community, including the city's first stroke emergency and chest pain emergency centers. ▲ While the technology and breadth of services offered by Saint Francis are truly remarkable,

the compassion and commitment of the hospital's doctors and nurses make it stand out. Since its founding, Saint Francis has remained focused on personalized and compassionate attention to the families it serves.

Services for a Long List of Needs

W hen patients inquire about the services offered at Saint Francis' 42-acre, East Memphis campus, they are reassured to discover that almost all of their health care needs can be addressed by the hospital.

Saint Francis' Chest Pain Emergency Center, the first in the city, provides emergency care for heart and heart-related problems. The hospital's new Cardiac Care Center features 32 of the Mid-South's top cardiologists, providing a full range of inpatient and outpatient care for the heart.

The Stroke Emergency Center delivers the same level of expertise in treating the symptoms of stroke and restoring function as quickly as possible. Other clinical and specialty areas at Saint Francis include Behavioral Health Services; a Diabetes Care

Center; a Cerebrovascular Center; Level II Trauma care; a Family Birthing Center with a pediatric intensive care unit; a new Heartburn Center; Home Health and Hospice; and a Senior Healthcare Center.

Department after department delivers exceptional care tailored to the individual needs of patients and their

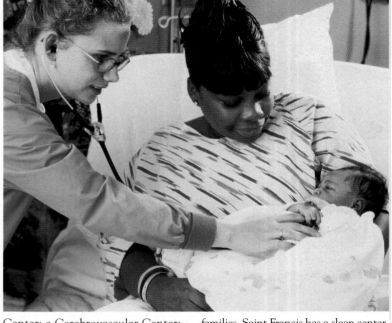

families. Saint Francis has a sleep center, since sleep disorders affect more than 18 million Americans; a women's center, providing individualized service and advice for women's needs; and an advanced wound healing center.

Saint Francis' expertise and resources make the system an invaluable community resource. Part of the Tenet

WHILE THE TECHNOLOGY AND BREADTH OF SERVICES OFFERED BY SAINT FRANCIS HOSPITAL ARE TRULY REMARKABLE, THE COMPASSION AND COMMITMENT OF THE HOSPITAL'S DOCTORS AND NURSES MAKE IT STAND OUT. SINCE ITS FOUNDING ALMOST 30 YEARS AGO, SAINT FRANCIS HAS REMAINED FOCUSED ON PERSONALIZED AND COMPASSIONATE ATTENTION TO THE FAMILIES IT SERVES.

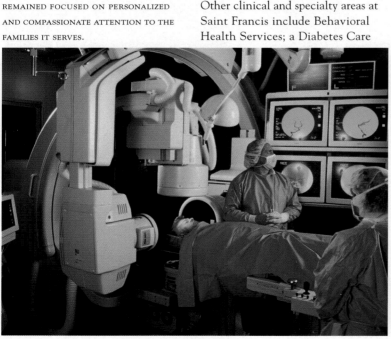

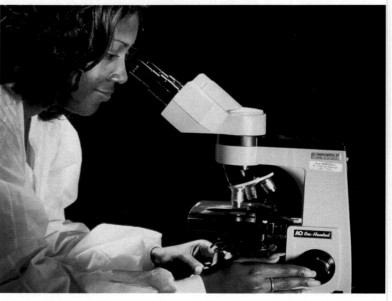

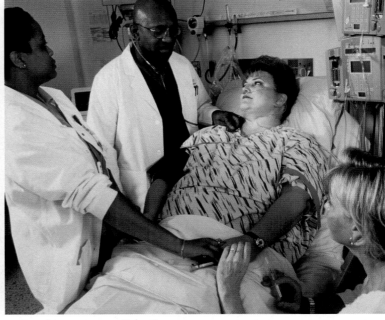

Healthcare System, Saint Francis is a member of the nation's second-largest family of hospitals and health care facilities. Many of Tenet's some 110 acute care hospitals have been nationally recognized as top-quality facilities for achievements in quality of care, efficiency of operations, and sustainability of overall performance. Saint Francis lives up to that tradition with a reputation for excellence and compassion.

But what continues to differentiate Saint Francis is the hospital's commitment to the treatment of the whole person. This commitment is evident in places like the Saint Francis Community Cancer Resource Center, where patients have access to a large collection of cancer-related literature and resources under one roof. The library staff provides direction and answers questions to help simplify a patient's search for information.

Today's active families can depend on additional programs, such as the Saint Francis Sports Medicine and Rehabilitation Centers. Operating in locations in East Memphis, Collierville, Millington, and Bartlett, the centers offer expertise and personalized treatment for a number of injuries. And many families also find great comfort in the compassionate services offered by the Saint Francis Nursing Home, where a skilled staff serves patients with around-the-clock attention and compassionate care.

A Strong and Compassionate Neighbor

There is no question that Saint Francis Hospital provides an invaluable service to the Memphis community. But the organization goes beyond just meeting the area's health care needs. Saint Francis is also extremely steadfast in community involvement.

The Memphis City Schools' Adopt-A-School program is an integral part of the community outreach efforts at Saint Francis. The hospital supports Kirby and Ridgeway high schools, is actively involved in Junior Achievement, and provides mentors for youth. Maintaining a strong outreach to the Latino community, Saint Francis prints brochures in Spanish, and holds Spanish classes for employees to help enhance their communication and customer service for Latino patients.

For almost 30 years, Saint Francis has been serving the Mid-South as a vitally important member of the community. From its exceptional facilities to the expertise of its staff to the long list of programs built to serve today's families, the hospital is truly a health care leader. But what makes Saint Francis unique is its personalized approach. Modeled on the life of compassionate service led by the saint for whom the hospital was named, Saint Francis Hospital is an incredible asset both to the thousands of families it serves and to the Greater Memphis community.

WHAT CONTINUES TO DIFFERENTIATE SAINT FRANCIS IS THE HOSPITAL'S COMMITMENT TO THE TREATMENT OF THE WHOLE PERSON.

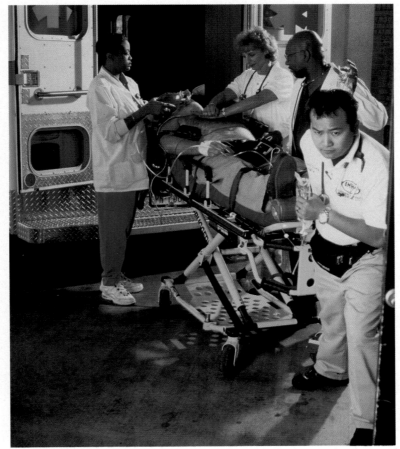

FROM ITS EXCEPTIONAL FACILITIES TO THE EXPERTISE OF ITS STAFF TO THE LONG LIST OF PROGRAMS BUILT TO SERVE TODAY'S FAMILIES, THE HOSPITAL IS TRULY A HEALTH CARE LEADER.

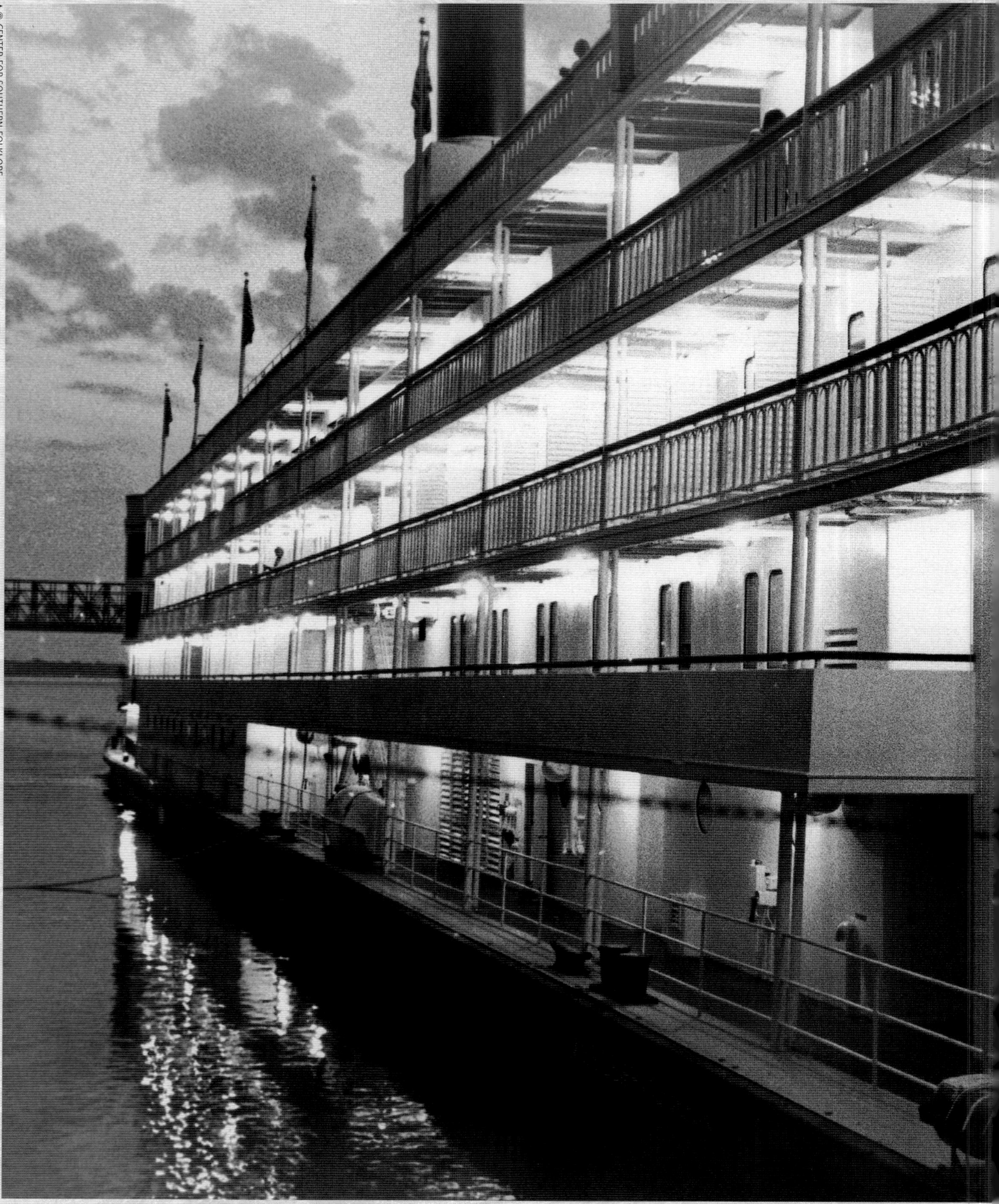

1976

1985

EDIC Management Group, Inc. is an investment real estate management firm that has specialized in multifamily properties for more than 20 years. As a large, multifamily property management firm, LEDIC faces pressures common to the property management industry, including the countless details that could mean big costs for the owner if they are missed or mismanaged. LEDIC's clients know the company's management team pays close attention to details.

Founded in 1977, LEDIC offers clients a variety of multifamily investment services, including general property management, acquisition analysis, market research, cash management, financial analysis, construction management, and property renovation. The company has an exceptional reputation and is considered a major participant in the national multifamily investment industry with clients across the country, including New York City, Charlotte, Atlanta, Santa Barbara, and Los Angeles. LEDIC was one of the top 30 largest managers of apartments in the United States in 2000.

LEDIC's managed properties range in size from 50 units to 800 units, with an average property size of about 250 units. The income- and rent-level spectrums are equally broad, ranging from exclusive residential communities to a portfolio of more than 20 affordable housing properties that LEDIC has renovated for Bank of America. Since 1990, LEDIC has supervised in excess of $200 million in construction, renovation, and repositioning of multifamily properties.

A Business Built on Relationships

Responsibility and trust are the foundations on which LEDIC has built its success, and the company's management roster offers a clue as to why many global investors trust the company.

David L. Shores, president and chief executive officer, is responsible for all aspects of the operation of the company. Shores has been heavily involved in client acquisition and due diligence efforts for many of LEDIC's institutional clients, and through his 15 years at LEDIC, the company has seen significant expansion and growth from a small, Memphis-based company to a large, regional firm. Shores' expertise is recognized by the National Multi-Family Housing Council and the National Housing Conference, both of which have named him to their board of directors. Shores' prior experience as a tax consultant in an international public accounting firm shaped the skills he uses today in his work with LEDIC's clients.

Davy Johnson Jr., LEDIC's executive vice president and chief administrative officer, is responsible for the day-to-day functions of LEDIC, including operations, insurance, legal, human resources, information technology, construction management, training, communications, marketing, and quality assurance. Johnson has more than 20 years of comprehensive property management experience, including tenure with a large, national management company as its manager over a large, regional portfolio of properties.

Jim Sellers, executive vice president and chief financial officer, is responsible for the financial management of the firm, as well as the timely, accurate generation of financial reports for distribution to the property owners. Sellers has 26 years of experience in the financial and operational theaters of growth-oriented companies. Public accounting experience with national and local accounting firms provided him with nine years of exposure to systems design, technology enhancements, compliance reporting, and multisite operations.

"This team delivers results for its clients," says Shores. "Brent Garrett, director of Client Services and senior vice president, is responsible for leading a team approach to all apartment management operations, and providing results and quality services for our clients. His role is key to the growth and success of our company, and satisfaction of our clients." Few owners think exactly alike, because all have different needs. Some want their properties managed for maximum cash flow, some for long-term appreciation, and some for highest near-term resale value.

LEDIC MANAGEMENT GROUP, INC. IS LED BY (FROM LEFT) CHIEF ADMINISTRATIVE OFFICER DAVY JOHNSON JR., CHIEF EXECUTIVE OFFICER DAVID L. SHORES, AND CHIEF FINANCIAL OFFICER JIM SELLERS.

Some owners have additional financial resources to use on the property, and some require that their properties stand on their own cash flow.

"In short, properties and their owners vary, so we have to be passionate about developing and executing a management program that is not only strong, but also customized," Shores says. "That means we must listen to our clients, understand their needs, and be astute enough to help formulate a plan to reach their goals."

Meticulous Research and Reporting

LEDIC is a recognized leader in the consistent study of apartment markets and operations. "We believe the greatest contribution we make to the value of a property is the level of intensive and sophisticated analysis that precedes any change," Sellers says.

An experienced real estate company staff researches details about the physical, marketing, and financial aspects of each new property assignment. Then, knowing what type of value enhancement the owner wants to accomplish, the firm can determine the best way to position or reposition the property to most efficiently meet this value objective.

With the growth in tax credit and bond financing for property acquisition, LEDIC has developed a reputation for its experience in managing the many complex regulatory issues facing these types of properties. Working directly with state agencies, LEDIC can provide the property owner with prepurchase compliance inspections, postpurchase training, certification, and audit assistance.

A Giant Family

LEDIC has grown steadily since its 1977 founding. Today, the company employs more than 800 people across the country. More than half work in the Memphis area, either in the headquarters operation or in Memphis communities.

"What's as impressive as our growth is our low employee turnover rate," Johnson says. "We have created a great atmosphere where people can develop their skills, enjoy their job, and grow in their careers."

To that end, the company has a number of innovative development programs, including LEDIC University. From instruction in high-quality property management practices to emerging leader workshops, LEDIC University helps employees offer exceptional service to clients while investing in their own careers.

LEDIC Management Group, Inc.'s committed approach to progressive property management strategy has meant more than 20 years of growth and success. It is that passion for excellence that has laid the foundation for the company's continued strength and growth in the years to come.

*M*emphis' emergence as a global distribution hub has led to the emergence of a long list of advanced support industries. The city is home to state-of-the art logistics and inventory companies, so it's no surprise that one of the nation's most progressive pallet companies is headquartered in Memphis as well. With 120 employees and four plants strategically located throughout the Mid-South, The Pallet Factory, Inc. is a full-service provider of pallet solutions.

Providing advanced manufacturing, recycling, design, and even outsourced pallet program management, The Pallet Factory is helping companies across the region store and move products more efficiently—and more profitably.

The Pallet Factory was founded in 1977 by Michael Doyle as an in-house pallet operation for his large juice-distribution franchiser. Doyle knew that embracing automated manufacturing and advanced design technology would save the company money in the long run, and his instinct proved true. In fact, he received such interest in the company's pallet operation that he sold his share of the juice business in 1982 to focus on The Pallet Factory.

Today, the company is an industry leader. It has been cited for its progressiveness by *Pallet Enterprise* and *Forest Products Equipment* magazines, and its expertise has led to a customer roster that includes some of the biggest names in distribution, including Kroger, Sara Lee Corporation, Amazon.com, Barnes & Noble.com, Thomas & Betts, Dollar General Stores, Fleming Foods, and Wal-Mart.

ON A WEEKLY BASIS, THE PALLET FACTORY, INC. SORTS, SEPARATES, AND REPAIRS APPROXIMATELY 100,000 PALLETS AND, AT THE SAME TIME, MANUFACTURES MORE THAN 10,000 NEW PALLETS (TOP).

LED BY CONTROLLER RANDY AVERESCH, VICE PRESIDENT JOSHUA DOYLE, AND PRESIDENT MICHAEL DOYLE, THE PALLET FACTORY IS A FULL-SERVICE PROVIDER OF PALLET SOLUTIONS (BOTTOM).

A Total Solution

On a weekly basis, The Pallet Factory sorts, separates, and repairs approximately 100,000 pallets and, at the same time, manufactures more than 10,000 new pallets.

Many of the pallets are for traditional distribution customers, but more and more of them are processed for customers who rely on The Pallet Factory's pallet management program. As part of the program, the Pallet Factory's fleet of tractors and more than 200 trailers provides pallet removal and delivery, and the company's advanced manufacturing center replaces worn and damaged pallets with recycled or new pallets.

Because The Pallet Factory can offer extremely efficient recycling and rebuilding, customers generally experience significant cost savings on disposal costs and new pallet purchases.

Unlike in the past, today's recycled pallets don't require a sacrifice in quality. Because of its commitment to technology in manufacturing, The Pallet Factory offers quality recycled pallets that provide the same function as new pallets, but cost less. The pallets are repaired to the National

Wooden Pallet and Container Association's repair standard using an advanced automated system.

The technology also makes it possible for The Pallet Factory to provide "combo" pallets that are built with a mixture of new and used components. Combo pallets can have new stringers and used deck boards or new deck boards and used stringers. These pallets are extremely popular with The Pallet Factory customers because of the savings they offer over new pallets.

In addition to recycling and manufacturing, The Pallet Factory often delivers additional, value-added services, such as pallet banking and on-site pallet sorting.

"Every company has different pallet needs," Doyle says. "At The Pallet Factory, we are experts when it comes to analyzing the needs of our customers and setting up programs tailored to those needs."

State-of-the-Art Service

When The Pallet Factory isn't working to deliver the best in pallet management solutions, the company can be found giving tours of its automated Memphis manufacturing and recycling center. "We've hosted customers, prospects, and even trade groups here," Doyle says. "No amount of describing can make up for the opportunity to see the automation in action."

More than 10,000 damaged and odd size pallets are disassembled every week with The Pallet Factory's automated Wood Recovery System (WRS). Components are processed and then sorted according to size and classification. They are then reused in the repair and manufacturing processes. Pallets are repaired using The Pallet Factory's Automated Sort & Repair System (ASR), which ensures total pallet quality throughout the repair process. "Customers can be certain that if a pallet passes inspection in our ASR system, it will go through their palletization system without a problem," Doyle says.

The Pallet Management program at The Pallet Factory allows customers to quantify the new level of efficiency they are experiencing. All pallet management customers receive computerized reports of pallet activity with detailed breakdowns and cost analysis. These itemized monthly reports include pallet bank balances, total pallets received, total pallets shipped at repair and regular prices, and precise cost per unit.

For even greater long-term operating savings, many pallet management customers turn to The Pallet Factory for computer-aided examination of the efficiency of their current pallet design, as well as the design of new pallets. The Pallet Factory staffs experienced users of the new Pallet Design System (PDS), the premier computer-aided design tool developed by Virginia Tech University and the Department of Wood Science and Forest Products. Whether customers charge The Pallet Factory with improving pallet safety, lowering costs, or forecasting next year's pallet costs, the company delivers.

PDS is especially useful in helping customers meet a specific level of performance, such as certain load-carrying capacity of the pallet based on the environment in which the pallet will be stored and handled by customers. PDS is an incredibly powerful and versatile tool that allows The Pallet Factory to customize pallet designs for specific handling challenges.

Founded on harnessing the power of technology for operational savings, The Pallet Factory has not only lived up to its mission; it is redefining an industry. And as more customers experience the impact of an advanced pallet management partner, the company is sure to continue its remarkable success.

edical technology and treatments seem to change every day. In spite of the advances, there's an aspect of cancer that is ongoing: the physical and emotional toll the disease takes on victims and their families. ▲ A special knowledge of the complexities of cancer treatment is the hallmark of Boston Baskin Cancer Group, the region's largest and most comprehensive cancer care centers. The group provides inpatient and outpatient oncology services, including

ancillary laboratory testing office-based chemotherapy administration, the latest clinical trials research program, and a bone marrow transplant program.

In addition to this leading spectrum of treatment technology and expertise, the clinic also emphasizes the power of social work services, psychological services, and pain management. "Our success today, I believe, is a direct result of our two-pronged approach to treatment," says Dr. Barry Boston. "We are dedicated to the latest in treatment techniques and also to helping our patients and their families cope with cancer diagnosis. The results are often miraculous."

Strength and Expertise

Dr. Barry Boston and Dr. Reed Baskin have strong and long-standing reputations in the oncology field, and are well known throughout the medical community.

Boston and Baskin, who began practicing in Memphis in 1976 and 1974, respectively, are leaders in their fields. Today, the practice's 11 doctors and a full-service staff of more than 100 make it one of the largest cancer treatment and blood disorder groups in the Mid-South.

Boston Baskin Cancer Group's resources are unmatched. The group, for example, provides exceptional gynecological oncology services in collaboration with the University of Tennessee (UT). Dr. Joseph Santoso, director of gynecological services at UT, joined the group in early 2001 and is the only provider of gynecological oncology in the Midtown area of Memphis.

And that's just the beginning of the clinic's unmatched expertise. The clinic offers the skills of eight additional oncology specialists.

In conjunction with the skills

these physicians have developed during advanced training, they have the expertise that comes from the involvement in ongoing research projects. The research program has been developed as a vital component in providing the best possible care for patients by offering a wide spectrum of oncology related clinical trials. Treatment options are available through clinical trials conducted in collaboration with academic institutions, private research organizations, and the pharmaceutical industry. That's a benefit for patients, many of whom enroll in these clinical trials when optimal treatment of their illness is uncertain or unavailable.

Boston Baskin physicians are also active in the advanced treatment regimen known as stem cell transplantation. This state of the art treatment is available in Memphis as the Blood & Marrow Transplant Center of the

DR. BARRY BOSTON (LEFT) AND DR. REED BASKIN, FOUNDERS OF BOSTON BASKIN CANCER GROUP, HAVE STRONG AND LONG-STANDING REPUTATIONS IN THE ONCOLOGY FIELD, AND ARE WELL KNOWN THROUGHOUT THE MEDICAL COMMUNITY.

The doctors of Boston Baskin Cancer Group's Methodist location include (from left) Dr. Sohail Minhas, Dr. Joseph Santoso, Dr. Jarvis Reed, Dr. Thomas Ratliff, and Dr. Ronald Lawson.

Mid-South. This unique outpatient center is a collaborative effort between Boston Baskin Cancer Group and Methodist Hospital.

Adding Quality to Life

The combined firm expects to see about 2,500 new patients each year, and serves patients within a 150-mile radius of Memphis. The group maintains two large offices in Memphis and a network of other offices throughout Memphis and the Mid-South with locations in West Memphis, Arkansas; Union City, Tennessee; and Southaven and Grenada, Mississippi. The primary office is located in Midtown Memphis in the heart of the Medical Center. Each patient benefits from the practice's unique attention to both body and spirit.

Boston, who was active in the early days of the hospice movement in the 1970s, was certified in the new field of palliative care in 1998, just one year after the Palliative Medicine certification became available. The somewhat holistic approach to treatment, combined with the more traditional techniques, creates a good mixture for the benefit of the patient. "Our focus is to mix high-tech and low-tech treatments into a big-picture treatment plan for the patient," Boston says.

Another part of that approach is the Families Adapting to Cancer through Education and Support (FACES) program. FACES is a support group for patients and their families. The group holds educational sessions on pain, eating, and technology advances, which are open to patients, caregivers, family members, and friends.

"Devastating diseases like cancer leave patients feeling helpless sometimes," Baskin says. "Education and empowerment can make a real difference when it comes to a patient's state of mind."

And that is the driving force behind Boston Baskin Cancer Group. Whatever it takes to treat patients and enhance their quality of life, that's what the group will do. As long as cancer continues to take tolls on families, the group will continue with their big-picture and big-hearted approach to cancer treatment.

The doctors of Boston Baskin Cancer Group's St. Francis location include (from left) Dr. Margaret Gore, Dr. Kathleen Spiers, Dr. Drew White, and Dr. Furhan Yunus.

t Flinn Broadcasting Company, innovation is just what the doctor ordered. More than a mere slogan, this statement is a key factor in the growth of this bold, innovative Memphis company. Since 1978, at one time or another, the firm's founder and owner, Dr. George Flinn, has brought more new broadcast formats to the city than any other person in Memphis. Flinn Broadcasting's radio and television formats are legendary,

and each of them was a new idea when Flinn brought them to Memphis: all children's, all sports, heavy metal, modern rock, alternative rock, hot talk, adult alternative, relationship talk, all blues, hip-hop, Top 40, all '80s, home shopping, all oldies, and all Christmas.

Success Built on Research

Over the years, Flinn's diverse selection of programming has been vital to the company's success. Flinn Broadcasting has always been willing to experiment, adjust, redefine, and evolve. And this willingness to change has fueled Flinn's growth—from its beginning, as a tiny AM radio station on the outskirts of Memphis, to an influential group of AM, FM, and television stations. The company's success results from extensive experimentation and research.

In a relatively short time period, Flinn's agile, continuous format adjustments have helped the company become a major player in the regional radio market. Today, Flinn Broadcasting's listenership figures are impressive, and its share of local broadcast advertising dollars is significant.

Given Flinn's tremendous enthusiasm for the business, his willingness to try new things, and his determination to succeed, it was really only a matter of time before Flinn Broadcasting became an important part of the Memphis area's broadcast industry. Flinn simply needed to discover the right formula.

"I like to stay on the cutting edge, and I've paid a price for that," says Flinn. "I've had to go through a lot of trial and error to find things that work."

Not only does Flinn now know what works, but he also finds that

other Memphis stations have begun to imitate things that Flinn Broadcasting does. When some of the company's formats—such as alternative rock or all-blues—have proved highly successful, other stations have altered their formats to match Flinn's.

A Passion for Innovation

While radio has always been a passion of Flinn's, he did not enter the profession until 1978, when he created his first station, WGSF-AM in Arlington, Tennessee. The station was the first in the Memphis area to air an oldies format. Flinn launched the station 10 years after he graduated from the University of Tennessee Medical School, interned at Barnes Hospital, was a radiology resident at Methodist Hospital, and was on the staff at the National Institutes of Health in Bethesda.

▼ T. GURLEY

WHEN WHBQ—THE FIRST RADIO STATION EVER TO AIR AN ELVIS PRESLEY RECORD— WENT UP FOR SALE IN 1988, GEORGE FLINN GRABBED IT. TODAY, AS PART OF FLINN BROADCASTING COMPANY, THE STATION IS THE CITY'S ONLY ALL-SPORTS STATION, FEATURING LOCAL AND NATIONAL CALL-IN SHOWS, AS WELL AS LIVE, PLAY-BY-PLAY BROADCASTS.

Flinn, a lifelong Memphian who owns five successful radiology clinics and helped develop a component of the ultrasound diagnostic technology, always wanted to be in radio, but he did not always have the necessary financing.

"At first, my mission was to save AM radio," says Flinn, who has an appreciation for and an understanding of the history of radio in his hometown.

When WHBQ—the first radio station ever to air an Elvis Presley record—went up for sale in 1988, Flinn grabbed it. Today, the station is the city's only all-sports station, featuring local and national call-in shows, as well as live, play-by-play broadcasts.

Although Flinn enjoys hands-on management and being involved in the selection of formats, he has had to distance himself from the process.

"I loved being in the middle of everything, and it was very difficult for me turn the job over to others," Flinn says. "But I have learned over the years that I am not a radio programmer. My goal is to have successful radio stations, so I have gotten some of the best people in the country to accomplish that. The second step is to let them do their jobs without interfering."

One very important step in that direction was the hiring of Steve Smith and Jeny Clifton, New York and California consultants, respectively, to produce the hip-hop format of Hot 107.1, which has become one of the

most popular stations in Memphis' highly competitive FM market. Chris Taylor helped launch 107.5 KISS FM, and it has become a major local and national force in Top 40 radio.

Flinn Broadcasting first became involved in television in the early 1980s, when Flinn and Holiday Inn founder Kemmons Wilson established WLMT-Channel 30. Since then, the company has created a home shopping channel, a Christian music video station, and a channel that offers programming for the disabled.

Along the way, Flinn Broadcasting has developed broadcast stations in other cities including Little Rock; Chicago; Denver; Jackson, Mississippi; Reno; and Alexandria, Louisiana. But Memphis is definitely where the company's heart and soul lie. Music has been an integral part of the River City for more than a century. That legacy is safe with Flinn Broadcasting and George Flinn, who will continue to be a positive musical influence and an industry innovator in Memphis in the years to come.

107.1 (TOP) HAS BECOME ONE OF THE MOST POPULAR STATIONS IN MEMPHIS' HIGHLY COMPETITIVE FM MARKET. THE SAME HOLDS TRUE FOR 107.5, TODAY A MAJOR FORCE IN TOP 40 RADIO.

During the past few decades, technology has radically changed the printing business. Digital printing, file exchange over the Internet, and high-power design software have transformed many printers into companies that look very different from the way they did 25 years ago. Unfortunately, though, many of these companies have changed their technology without reassessing the way they approach the printing business in the new economy.

Graphic Systems, Inc. has not fallen into that trap.

"Today, printers have an amazing opportunity to be real business partners with their customers," says Dennis Kopcial, founder of Graphic Systems, Inc. "Because we've combined a variety of technologies into a total integrated package, we can sit down with customers and devise innovative and efficient solutions for any kind of business communication project. At Graphic Systems, we think of ourselves as the solution looking for a challenge."

A One-Source Solution

Graphic Systems is a one-source solution for quality print-related products and services; document distribution and fulfillment; and premium Internet

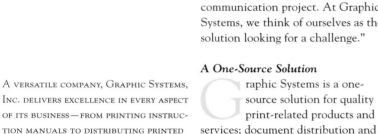

A VERSATILE COMPANY, GRAPHIC SYSTEMS, INC. DELIVERS EXCELLENCE IN EVERY ASPECT OF ITS BUSINESS—FROM PRINTING INSTRUCTION MANUALS TO DISTRIBUTING PRINTED MATERIALS WORLDWIDE.

services. The company's print-related products and services run the gamut from simple letterheads to custom promotional items. From logos to brochures to national ads, Graphic Systems can deliver virtually any corporate printed material.

The company also combines its printing skills with logistics expertise to form strong document fulfillment solutions. The company can house documents and promotional materials, shipping them on an as-needed basis. Graphic Systems can even add the Internet to the package, giving customers an Internet ordering system for literature that allows end users to request documents on their own.

Because of its expertise and focus, Graphic Systems has become one of the largest independent graphic communications management companies in the country, with offices in Memphis and Jackson, Tennessee. The combined power of several business units operating as one seamless system of services enables the company to manage the creation, production, and distribution of business communications products from beginning to end.

Quality, Innovative Service

In November 1978, Graphic Systems began business in the back room of a Memphis warehouse. The company started out as a traditional business forms distributor, but with a twist. Kopcial knew that customer service was a priority in the industry, and developed a better way to process business forms orders. The new system sped up production and gave customers more control over the process.

This innovation was the key to the company's early success, and the management has not lost sight of that early lesson: Improving services improves sales.

In 1998, the company celebrated its 20th year in business with revenues of $20 million and a team of some 70 experts. While the company's numbers have changed, its philosophy has not. Graphic Systems experts work with clients to help them design and implement solutions to their business communication challenges.

Versatile Solutions

A printing company at heart, Graphic Systems delivers excellence in the printing of commercial communication materials such as stationery, custom envelopes, presentation folders, brochures, catalogs, and direct mail projects.

The company also specializes in binders and index tabs. Businesses unaware of all the possibilities often spend too much time and money on binder production. Graphic Systems can assist customers in choosing the

right size, binder material, metal specifications, decoration process, options, and accessories.

Graphic Systems continues to build on its expertise in pressure-sensitive labels. Using high-tech materials and adhesive systems, the company creates labels for even the most demanding applications, such as product labels, bar code labels, continuous rolls, laser sheets, and multi-ply coupons. Graphic Systems often acts as a service bureau for overprinting of blank label stock, and even oversees label application, if necessary.

The company also continues to leverage its early leadership in business forms, and assists clients not only with the printing of forms, but also with their design. "Companies don't realize that poorly designed, confusing forms can cost them big in lost time and dissatisfied customers," Kopcial says. "We pride ourselves on helping customers develop smart forms."

Graphic Systems also offers high-speed digital printing, which makes it possible to print four-color documents in small quantities with an efficient budget. This capability also makes it possible to print variable data, resulting in customized versions of the same job. The company prints small runs of brochures, newsletters, transparencies, labels, manuals, and more, with the same cost efficiency as large-press projects.

But the real power of a partnership with Graphic Systems comes when the company combines available services into a total graphic communications management solution. With its network of experts and technology, the company can offer a powerful turnkey approach to the communications process—from concept through fulfillment and distribution to Internet applications.

"I think our success and growth come from our fundamental belief that customers need a partner who can eliminate headaches and provide them the freedom to focus on their businesses," Kopcial says. That focus on the customer will serve Graphic Systems, Inc. well for years to come.

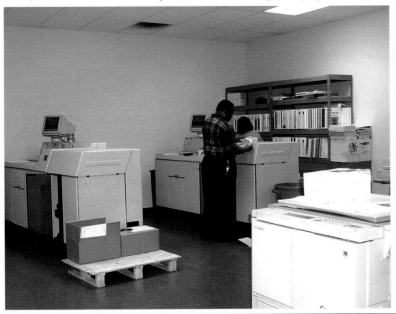

emphis knows Sharp Manufacturing Company of America. Not only is Sharp known by consumers across the city for its advanced consumer electronics, but the company also enjoys a reputation as one of the city's most progressive employers. Since 1978, the multinational manufacturer has produced—on a 107-acre property in southeast Memphis—some of the world's most advanced consumer electronics products. At Sharp's 700,000-square-foot

Memphis facility, its employees assemble the company's market-leading carousel microwave ovens, toner and developer for Sharp copiers, and high-definition television (HDTV)- and digital television (DTV)-compatible projection TVs for the U.S. market.

Sharp's Memphis operation is part of Japan-based Sharp Corporation, a consumer electronics giant that continues to be known for high quality and technological innovation. Sharp's complete product line includes more than 700 items, the majority of which are manufactured in 35 countries outside of Japan for distribution worldwide. The company's annual sales total is more than $14 billion, of which Memphis contributes some $293 million.

Sharp's Memphis facility, for example, produces more than 1.4 million microwave ovens each year, and plays a big role in Sharp's leadership in that market. Sharp has innovated a number of the features that have led to the ongoing popularity of microwave ovens, and the company today has approximately a 25 percent share of the microwave oven market in the United States. For the copier market, Sharp assembles approximately 400 tons of toner cartridges every year.

SHARP MANUFACTURING COMPANY OF AMERICA'S MEMPHIS FACILITY HOUSES THE COMPANY'S ADMINISTRATION BUILDING AND MICROWAVE OVEN PRODUCTION PLANT, WHICH IS ONE OF ITS FOUR MANUFACTURING FACILITIES LOCATED ON 107 ACRES AT THE CORNER OF RAINES AND MENDENHALL.

SHARP'S CONTINUING SUCCESS AND EXPERTISE LED THE COMPANY TO TAP THE MEMPHIS FACILITY TO START AN IMPORTANT PROJECT—THE PRODUCTION OF HDTV- AND DTV-COMPATIBLE PROJECTION TVS. AND IN JULY 2001, SHARP BEGAN COPIER PRODUCTION IN ITS MEMPHIS FACILITY.

In July 2001, Sharp began copier production in its Memphis facility. The digital copiers and fully configured, multifunction units include printing, copying, scanning, E-mail, and faxing capabilities for complete office automation.

A High-Definition Future

Sharp's continuing success and expertise led the company to tap the Memphis facility to start an important project—the production of HDTV- and DTV-compatible projection TVs. The Memphis facility unveiled two widescreen, rear-projection TVs in early 2001. Each unit shipped and sold is being built by the Memphis team.

Both HDTV- and DTV-compatible projection TVs offer Sharp's latest technology in picture quality, as well as a variety of video inputs that provide customers with crystal-clear digital images from a set that is designed as the centerpiece of rear-projection television (RPTV) home-theater systems. While there is some reluctance among many manufacturers to invest in expensive digital technology, Sharp recognizes customer demand for the latest DTV and HDTV picture quality. The company has been a longtime supporter of digital television, and is pushing forward with the state-of-the-art model introduction.

Displaying all DTV and HDTV signals in full high-definition (1080i) resolution, these models utilize the new Sharp digital and HD Color Purity Processor and digital and HD Contrast Enhancer to optimize the picture quality of all digital sources. In addition, these systems feature Sharp's proprietary, second-generation Digital

Double Format Converter (DDFC) that "upconverts" analog signals to enhance their appearance on the high-resolution screen. The new models also come fully equipped with composite inputs to accommodate signals from a variety of sources, including DTV and HDTV decoder boxes and digital video disc (DVD) players. By incorporating a next-generation, 10-bit, 3D-Y/C comb filter, these sets are able to enhance picture detail by filtering out artifacts inherent in broadcast signals at a rate four times better than conventional filters.

In addition, these Sharp models offer a twin picture that employs two National Television Standards Committee (NTSC) tuners. The dual tuners allow viewers to watch two programs side by side on the rectangular screen, and also drive a conventional picture-in-picture feature. A four-way speaker system with 24 watts total audio output further enhances the home-theater appeal.

These next-generation televisions are made exclusively in Memphis. And to keep up with the demand, local employees now turn out more than 100 sets daily. The introduction of the 3-CRT rear-projection TV occurs as the TV market in the U.S. changes to digital broadcasting for video viewing. Future plans are also in place to develop and produce the liquid-crystal display (LCD) rear-projection TV, utilizing the leading-edge LCD technology that was developed by Sharp.

Delivering More than Technology

In addition to a steady supply of high-tech jobs, Sharp contributes a variety of resources to its home community. Sharp management in Memphis spends many hours in board meetings for educational, cultural, and philanthropic purposes. Employees also invest time and effort into such projects as the March of Dimes Walkathon.

Corporate support goes to numerous deserving organizations, such as the Metropolitan Inter-Faith Association (MIFA), Goodwill Industries, and American Cancer Society. Other sponsorships include such functions as the Memphis in May Sunset Symphony and Junior Achievement bowling teams.

It's clear that Sharp and Memphis make a strong match. The city's workforce helps Sharp bring its world-famous technology to life, and the company shows its corporate citizenship with high-tech jobs and community support. The combination has produced exceptional results over the years, and is sure to continue delivering success for many more years to come.

CLOCKWISE FROM TOP LEFT:
PICTURED ARE MEMBERS OF THE ENGINEERING PROJECT TEAM FOR SHARP'S HDTV AND DTV COMPATIBLE PROJECTION TVS.

SHARP'S TOP MANAGEMENT IS VERY COMMITTED TO SAVING THE ENVIRONMENT BY PARTICIPATING IN THE COMPANY'S ANNUAL TREE PLANTING CEREMONY IN RECOGNITION OF EARTH DAY.

SHARP HAS BEEN AN ADOPT A SCHOOL SPONSOR OF SHARPE ELEMENTARY FOR THE PAST 20 YEARS. PICTURED ARE THE SCHOOL'S PRINCIPAL, ARNETTA WILSON, AND SHARP'S VICE PRESIDENT OF HUMAN RESOURCES, T. C. JONES, JR. WILSON AND JONES RECOGNIZED SHAQUILLE FULLER, ONE OF THE SCHOOL'S FIFTH GRADERS, FOR HIS DRAWING THAT DEPICTS THE "PARTNERSHIP" RELATIONSHIP BETWEEN THE SCHOOL AND SHARP.

PROUDLY "MADE IN THE USA," SHARP'S MICROWAVES OWN ABOUT 25 PERCENT OF THE U.S. MARKET.

he rapid advancements in voice and data networking since 1990 have enabled businesses of all sizes to connect and communicate with their customers and partners faster and more efficiently, while also giving them access to technologies that drastically improve their business operations. ▲ *However, progress has come so quickly that many businesses, especially small and midsize companies, have struggled to keep up with the new demands of*

the marketplace. They face many challenges that didn't exist before the communications revolution: setting up high-speed network connections for remote offices and telecommuting employees, answering E-mail and Web inquiries from customers, and developing Web pages that can serve customers worldwide, 24 hours a day, seven days a week. To compound the situation, businesses are faced with a dizzying array of choices for networking products and services.

For businesses like these, a company with a size and scope unmatched in the industry, Expanets, has come to the rescue. Expanets—whose name is derived from the descriptor

Experienced at Networked Solutions—helps lift the burden from small and midsize businesses by applying its experience, expertise, and a wealth of industry-leading products and services to solve its clients' most pressing technology issues.

A National Resource for Growing Companies

ost businesses with fewer than 500 employees don't have the in-house information technology expertise that's needed for the management of today's networks," says Keith Dyer, vice president and general manager of Expanets. "They look to us to help manage their

current systems and develop solutions with new technologies so they can concentrate on the business at hand."

Expanets has some 200 offices nationwide, with a regional office in Memphis overseeing operations in Tennessee, Alabama, Kentucky, Louisiana, and Mississippi. The company is one of the nation's largest providers of networked communication services to businesses with 20 to 500 employees, and is uniquely capable of serving small and large businesses as well.

While national in scope, Expanets provides service through its some 200 local offices and its some 4,300 team members, who are experienced in

EXPANETS—WHOSE NAME IS DERIVED FROM THE DESCRIPTOR EXPERIENCED AT NETWORKED SOLUTIONS—HELPS LIFT THE BURDEN FROM SMALL AND MIDSIZE BUSINESSES BY APPLYING ITS EXPERIENCE, EXPERTISE, AND A WEALTH OF INDUSTRY-LEADING PRODUCTS AND SERVICES TO SOLVE ITS CLIENTS' MOST PRESSING TECHNOLOGY ISSUES.

working with clients in a wide range of industries, including finance, manufacturing, health care, hospitality, transportation, real estate, and professional services, such as legal, engineering, and commercial printing services.

Expanets was built through the acquisition of 26 leading local networking companies, including ATS Telephone and Data in Memphis, and the Growing and Emerging Markets division of Lucent Technologies. The company is a partner entity of NorthWestern Corp., a Fortune 500 energy and communications company.

Custom Solutions

According to Dyer, what makes Expanets different is the company's focus on how entire small and medium-sized businesses operate. The firm views its role as much more than just a technology vendor, and helps clients take a big-picture view of their internal processes—showing them where they can increase efficiency and often drive unnecessary costs out of the business.

"Our first step in working with clients is to take a hard look at their business processes, which can include how they handle incoming voice calls or E-mails from customers, or how their back-office accounting processes flow," Dyer explains. "Once we identify a problem area, we develop technology-based solutions to make that particular process run more efficiently."

That approach means that customers get a refreshing, unbiased partner. "We don't just show up to sell a new PBX system or a new router because that's what we happen to have on the shelf," Dyer says. Because Expanets is not tied to one particular vendor or service provider, the company can specify the exact system and components that are a match for each client. The company has relationships with

more than 140 industry-leading manufacturers and service providers, enabling the firm to create the right mix of products and services to fit the unique needs of its clients.

Whether a client is in need of local voice service, data transport, infrastructure hardware, Web hosting, or just phone sets, Expanets can draw on names like Avaya, NEC, Siemens, Cisco, BellSouth, and Lightyear to structure the best possible solution.

Expanets' nationwide capabilities and strategic partner relationships give it far more access to new technologies, research and development, and network carrier services—such as local and long-distance voice and Internet access—than other solutions providers. And because of the company's in-depth knowledge about medium-sized businesses, Expanets can work directly with manufacturers in the development of products that meet the unique needs of this market.

"Because we have alliances with so many providers, we also add convenience to our mix of services," says Dyer. "Our clients can do it all with one call, which frees up a lot of their valuable time."

emphis-based AutoZone has been a success in every sense of the word. The aftermarket auto parts retailer has charted phenomenal growth, and its brand name has become synonymous with quality parts and exceptional service. ▲ But ask any Memphian about the impact of AutoZone, and you're not as likely to hear about the company's remarkable performance in the marketplace. To Memphians, AutoZone is known for its hometown

performance. The company's unprecedented commitment to the City of Memphis and its citizens has made it a true hometown favorite.

A True Memphis Company

AutoZone's commitment to the city began back in 1979, when its first stores opened in Memphis. Twenty-one years later, the company cemented that commitment by being the lead sponsor of the gleaming AutoZone Park, a gem of a baseball stadium that immediately won the hearts of Memphians and garnered national acclaim.

Between the opening of that first store and the opening of the baseball park it helped finance, AutoZone's community involvement has been unparalleled by just about any corporation of its size in the nation. AutoZone has had a hand in everything from

the establishment of the National Civil Rights Museum in Memphis to college scholarship programs, the Memphis Food Bank, Partners in Education, and the Salvation Army's Angel Tree program.

AutoZone made an unprecedented commitment to Memphis in 1995, when it built its new corporate headquarters downtown at a time when many companies were following a trend to move to the outskirts of the city. Today, AutoZone's corporate headquarters stands on the banks of the Mississippi River, adding to the beauty of the Memphis skyline. Additionally, the company contributed the valuable property it left in East Memphis to the city's library system. That property is now home to the city's new Main Library.

However, considering all of AutoZone's contributions to the

community through the years, perhaps none has meant as much to the community as AutoZone Park, the $72 million, 15,200-seat masterpiece that sits only about six blocks from the company's corporate headquarters. The new home for the city's Class AAA baseball franchise was the key piece in a $2.3 billion downtown development effort that is revitalizing the entire Mid-South.

In its first season, the Memphis Redbirds broke every attendance record in the city's professional baseball history, which spans more than 100 years. In fact, the Redbirds came within only a few thousand fans of leading all of the minor leagues in attendance for the 2000 season.

For AutoZone, the company's success and Memphis' success are intertwined. "Our customer service, our quality parts, and our innovative

MEMPHIS-BASED AUTOZONE HAS BEEN A SUCCESS IN EVERY SENSE OF THE WORD. THE AFTERMARKET AUTO PARTS RETAILER HAS CHARTED PHENOMENAL GROWTH, AND ITS BRAND NAME HAS BECOME SYNONYMOUS WITH QUALITY PARTS AND EXCEPTIONAL SERVICE.

stores have taken us to the top of the automotive parts business," says John Adams, recently retired chairman and CEO. "But I always tell people we've had a silent partner and a secret weapon: Memphis.

"Memphis is the distribution capital of the free world, and that has played a role in our success," Adams says. "But AutoZone draws its strength from Memphis' people and its culture. Treating our customers like friends came naturally for us when we opened our first store, and 20 years later it's still the right thing to do."

Doing the Job Right, Nationwide

Indeed, service is the cornerstone of AutoZone's corporate culture. The letters WITTDTJR carry a special significance at the company.

They represent an AutoZone creed: What It Takes To Do The Job Right.

What AutoZone does, better than anyone else, is sell auto parts, accessories, chemicals, and motor oil to do-it-yourselfers and professional technicians through some 3,000 stores in 42 states and 16 *tiendas* in Mexico. The company also sells heavy-duty truck parts through 49 TruckPro stores in 15 states. AutoZone provides electronic diagnostic and repair information as well.

From its three stores in 1979, the company grew to 396 stores in 15 states by 1987, when it changed its name from Auto Shack to AutoZone. In 1991, with 598 stores in 20 states, it left its parent company, Malone & Hyde, and became its own publicly held firm. Only seven years later, AutoZone acquired Auto Palace with 112 stores and Chief

Auto Parts with 560 stores, including 400 in California. These acquisitions increased AutoZone's totals to 2,657 stores in 38 states. In 1999, it acquired 100 Express locations from Pep Boys and opened its first international stores in Mexico. That year marked another banner accomplishment for AutoZone: It was the year the company entered the Fortune 500.

"When you look back on this company's relatively short history, it's phenomenal to see that AutoZone really invented an industry," Adams says. "We transformed the aftermarket auto parts business into a service- and quality-driven retail phenomenon.

"Memphis made that possible," Adams insists. "And Memphis plays a big role in our continued leadership of this industry."

*E*nSafe Inc. made its name in the environmental consulting industry by bringing together a talented staff, and leveraging their knowledge and creativity toward solving clients' hazardous waste and safety issues. Now, EnSafe is further leveraging the capabilities of its multidisciplinary personnel and expanding into new business areas as the environmental industry matures. ▲ Since 1997, EnSafe has broadened its consulting horizons beyond its traditional

environmental and health and safety services to information technology, remediation contracting, and safety engineering and ergonomics. The company also has expanded its geographic horizons in that same time frame by adding offices in Tennessee, Ohio, Michigan, and the Slovak Republic.

These expansions of service areas and geographic coverage are the consequence of EnSafe's entrepreneurial spirit, as well as its ability to identify clients' needs and to provide innovative solutions to meet them. The company's principles are based on a foundation where nothing less than excellence is acceptable in serving clients' needs.

A Benchmark of Excellence

Excellence was the goal of EnSafe's founders when the company started with three employees in 1980, according to Phillip G. Coop, Certified Hazardous Materials Manager (CHMM), president. In some 20 years' time, consistently providing

that level of service has helped EnSafe grow to hundreds of technical and support professionals in numerous offices in the United States and overseas. In EnSafe's multidisciplinary atmosphere, a geologist in one office may be drawing up well-boring logs, while the computer application development specialist next door is devising Web-based database applications. Down the hall, an occupational safety specialist may be putting together a hazardous materials training course curriculum, while the remediation construction manager across from him is negotiating disposal costs for contaminated soil.

Communication and collaboration between professionals are critical to EnSafe's success. EnSafe encourages these professionals to cross their traditional boundaries, giving clients' solutions a broader perspective.

"We hire people with expertise and talent, and then do whatever is necessary to keep their skills sharp and their horizons broad," Coop says.

The Proof is in the Product

EnSafe's expertise and collaborative vision result in innovative and powerful solutions for its clients. One recent achievement was the company's unprecedented success in remediating a contaminant that was thought to be untreatable. Perchlorate, an energetics booster used in solid rocket fuel, was migrating from a weapons facility and threatening public drinking water supplies in central Texas. EnSafe not only developed a low-cost, fixed-bed biological treatment system, but also is now implementing the first-ever in-place remediation system for this recalcitrant contaminant.

EnSafe's achievement earned the Grand Award in the Consulting Engineers of Tennessee's 2000 Engineering Excellence Awards competition. The company was also a finalist in the American Consulting Engineers Council's 2000 national competition.

In addition to environmental awards, EnSafe also was recognized

THE PRINCIPLES LEADING ENSAFE INC.'S GROWTH AND DIVERSITY EFFORTS ARE (SEATED, LEFT TO RIGHT), PHILLIP G. COOP, CHMM, AND JAMES N. SPEAKMAN, PE, PH.D., AND (STANDING, LEFT TO RIGHT) MICHAEL A. WOOD, CPA; CRAIG A. WISE, PE; PAUL V. STODDARD, PG; AND GINNY GRAY DAVIS, PG.

▼ ALEX GINSBURG

on the information technology front as a winner in the Innovators in the Internal Revolution category of the 2000 Inc./Cisco Growing with Technology Awards.

EnSafe has aggressively integrated technology in all aspects of its internal business operations and consulting services. The company's state-the-art wide area network has established a virtual corporate office that has no geographical boundaries. EnSafe is using the World Wide Web, a corporate intranet, and client extranet Web sites as primary communication and collaboration resources.

Harnessing the Power of New Technology

By combining the expertise of its geographic information systems (GIS) staff and its information technology (IT) division, EnSafe is leveraging the capabilities it developed through traditional environmental work into new applications. Using advanced mapping capabilities in combination with database applications, EnSafe is helping urban police departments monitor crime not only by location, but also by time of day and a host of other variables. This project will give police departments a more accurate picture of the problems facing their communities so they can allocate resources more effectively.

Another application of EnSafe's IT expertise is the production and facility information tracking (ProFIT) system the company developed for a major food manufacturer. In the midst of a project designed to simplify the manufacturer's compliance reporting process, EnSafe saw opportunities to expand the capabilities of environmental engineer-

ing database applications to capture the types of information vital to decision support of a far more encompassing nature. EnSafe developed a way to pull production and facility data from the plant's information system into a database to automatically create needed reports. The results are placed on the client's intranet site, where they are accessible plantwide.

The plant maintenance manager, for example, is now able to pinpoint the top 10 sources of lost production to determine where best to focus preventive maintenance efforts. EnSafe's ProFIT system reduced the time it takes the manufacturer to generate daily production reports from three to four hours to a mere five minutes. In addition, EnSafe expanded the plant's intranet capabilities through the development of

an elaborate, yet user-friendly, intranet application, including upgrading the facility's intranet infrastructure.

"The IT division is a natural extension of our philosophy that when it comes to other environmental and advanced monitoring problems, there are no cookie-cutter solutions," Coop says.

Another natural extension of the company's solutions philosophy is EnSafe's remediation construction arm, EnSafe Ops, LLC. Ops gives EnSafe the ability to manage its customers' environmental liabilities on a turnkey basis, leveraging the company's extensive experience in environmental remediation projects with the expertise of its professional staff in compliance, engineering, hydrogeology, community relations, data management and visualization, and risk assessment. Through the addition of Ops to its stable of services, EnSafe can take a site from initial investigation to construction and operations and maintenance of remedial systems.

EnSafe's newest endeavor is its Safety Engineering and Ergonomics practice, which also takes a unique approach to business. "The ergonomics practice will focus on client solutions driven by productivity, not compliance," Coop says. "I like to call our solutions 'brainpower by the hour.' Clients with complex needs can call on EnSafe and count on us to put our seasoned, passionate professionals to work. We don't force their need to fit in a single, off-the-shelf program. We've built a reputation for delivering powerful and effective solutions, no matter what the challenge may be."

OCCUPATIONAL SAFETY SPECIALISTS USE A VARIETY OF INSTRUMENTATION IN PERFORMING INDOOR AIR QUALITY AND EXPOSURE MONITORING ASSESSMENTS.

AN ENSAFE GEOPHYSICIST USES A VARIETY OF NONINTRUSIVE TECHNOLOGY TO MAP CONTAMINATION UNDERGROUND (LEFT).

ENSAFE SCIENTISTS FROM DIVERSE DISCIPLINES, SUCH AS GEOLOGY, ENGINEERING, AND BIOLOGY, WORK IN TEAMS TO DEVELOP COST-EFFECTIVE SOLUTIONS FOR CLIENTS (RIGHT).

I*n the latter half of the 20th century, Memphis has emerged as a vital North American hub for the location of distribution centers for many Fortune 500 companies. A multitude of raw materials, goods, and products are shipped from this area to destinations all over the world. Since 1981, Mid-South Marking Systems, by offering bar coding expertise and superior service, has helped these companies ship and receive these products in an efficient and reliable manner.*

"Many of these companies have located distribution centers in Memphis to take advantage of the services of FedEx," says Rick Summers, owner of Mid-South Marking Systems. "These companies are committed to warehousing and shipping products quickly and efficiently, and more and more of them are realizing that, to accomplish these goals, bar code technology has to be used extensively through the receiving, inventory, and shipping processes."

And that's the specialty of Summers' company: It is a provider of integrated bar coding systems that help companies of all sizes label and track inventory with precision and efficiency.

Mid-South Marking Systems has been built on helping customers increase productivity. "We're not here to sell customers a product off the shelf and then vanish," Summers says. "Our strategy has always been to send a specialist in and to help the company select the most compatible, high-performance system for their business."

Mid-South Marking Systems then provides all the support the client needs to bring the system on-line, from installation expertise to on-site operator training. "As these businesses face increasing pressure generated by the new economy's speed, they don't have the time or the patience to deal with prob-

lems with the inventory labeling systems," Summers says. "They seem to value the one-stop aspect of our service. For installation, support, and supplies, they call us. It's an amazingly convenient way for them to do business."

And it's not just convenience that Mid-South Marking Systems brings to the table. The company is an authorized reseller for some of the most advanced labeling systems available. For example, the firm can offer products from Zebra Technologies, one of the world's leading manufacturers of bar code label printing systems. Zebra printers and software function in operations of all sizes worldwide. In fact, more than 60 percent of the Fortune 500 companies in some 80 countries use Zebra technology. Mid-South Marking Systems' product line includes Zebra direct thermal and thermal transfer printers, in fixed and portable models. These durable printers

produce high-quality bar codes and text on pressure-sensitive labels and tags in a wide variety of materials and sizes.

The company also offers various forms of data collection, including batch and radio frequency technology. From portable, handheld units to fixed terminals and a variety of handheld laser scanner devices, Mid-South Marking Systems helps customers assess their needs and select the appropriate solution. Mid-South Marking Systems also sells software for inventory control, asset tracking, and document tracking, as well as a variety of pressure-sensitive labels, tags, and ribbons in assorted materials and sizes. The company even offers expertise in highly specialized areas such as industrial, health care, and horticultural applications.

"And true to our customer-tailored philosophy, everything we do is backed by a customer support program that includes service and repair on all our products," Summers says. "In many situations, we go into companies and train their employees to operate and service the equipment."

The team at Mid-South Marking Systems loves to see new operations relocate to Memphis, which not only brings new business potential, but also a new level of health and vitality into the city. "People outside of the industry don't realize that more and more major companies are moving sophisticated operations here," Summers says. "And that benefits the whole community."

SINCE 1981, MID-SOUTH MARKING SYSTEMS, LED BY OWNER RICK SUMMERS (RIGHT), HAS BEEN OFFERING BAR CODING EXPERTISE AND SUPERIOR SERVICE TO MAJOR COMPANIES THROUGHOUT NORTH AMERICA.

he nation's most successful senior executives have a lot in common. They share an instinct for success in their industry. They share a tireless passion for their jobs. Ask Legacy Wealth Management President John Ueleke, and he'll add another trait shared by many successful senior executives. ▲ "Many of these successful people donate all their brainpower and energy to their companies," Ueleke says. "It leaves their

▲ SAJ CRONE

personal finances on the back burner, and can lead to a situation in which their personal affairs are dangerously out of control."

Ueleke should know. He is one of the nation's most respected financial advisors, and his counsel is sought by investors all over the country. In 1996, *Barron's* magazine named him one of the nation's 15 most powerful financial planners. He's a regular on the *Worth* magazine list of top financial planners and was named by *Medical Economics* magazine as one of the best advisors for medical professionals.

Financial Advisors and Personal Portfolio Builders

Ueleke founded Legacy Wealth Management in 1982 to serve a specific need he saw in the financial services industry. "Who wants to manage your money?" he asks. "Everybody. But who really wants to help you through the tough stuff? Difficult financial transitions are a part of life. The crowd thins when it's time to roll up your shirt sleeves and make the hard choices."

He founded the company as a fee-only, needs-driven personal finance practice. Where banks, investment houses, and insurance companies tend to focus on a portion of a client's financial picture, the professionals at Legacy Wealth Management consider themselves to be holistic wealth managers or, as Ueleke is fond of saying, "personal portfolio builders".

"Most folks are too busy to do the necessary research on the best available investment opportunities. We simplify things and streamline the process. We are not selling products, so our counsel is unbiased and objective. That's really important to our investment-minded clients," Ueleke says. "Other clients have different needs, including tax, estate, and retirement planning. Some

have large positions in employer stock options and need advice on the best way to exercise them. Ours is not a sales-driven approach. It's a needs-driven approach," he emphasizes.

The company's approach is immensely popular. Whether it's funding the future education for a new grandchild or retirement cash-flow planning, Legacy Wealth Management strives to meet the needs of each client and works to alleviate the headache and

worry associated with a wide variety of personal financial decisions. This frees clients to run the rest of their lives. Legacy Wealth Management's growth and exceptionally high client retention rate are evidence that the company is doing something right. Many of its clients would agree the company is a breath of fresh air in the financial planning world.

"This is a people business," concludes Ueleke, "We never forget that."

THE PROFESSIONALS AT LEGACY WEALTH MANAGEMENT WORK TO ENHANCE THE LIVES OF CLIENTS AND THEIR HEIRS BY ASSISTING CLIENTS IN PLANNING FOR THE FUTURE, HELPING THEM NAVIGATE THROUGH DIFFICULT FINANCIAL SITUATIONS, AND KEEPING THEM FOCUSED ON LIVING THEIR DREAMS.

▲ SAJ CRONE

▲ JAY ADKINS

sk people what they know about Memphis, Tennessee, and you're likely to notice a pattern. Across the nation and around the world, music fans of all ages know Memphis as the home of Elvis Presley. More than 650,000 visitors pass through Graceland's gates every year, generating an annual economic impact of more than $150 million for the city. Today, Elvis Presley's Graceland is one of the five most-toured homes in the United States—

and the most famous home in the country, after the White House. It is a phenomenon that is a testament to the captivating talent and life of one of the world's most recognized entertainers.

A Rising Star

On January 8, 1935, Elvis Aaron Presley was born to Vernon and Gladys Presley in a two-room house in Tupelo. He and his parents moved to Memphis in 1948, and Elvis graduated from Humes High School in 1953. In 1954, he began his musical career with the legendary Sun Records label in Memphis.

In late 1955, Elvis' recording contract was sold to RCA Victor. By 1956, he was an international sensation. Elvis' musical influences were the pop and country music of the time, the country gospel music he heard in church and at the all-night gospel sings he frequently attended, and the rhythm and blues he absorbed on Beale Street as a Memphis teenager. With a sound and style that uniquely combined his diverse musical influences and blurred and challenged the

ELVIS PRESLEY'S GRACELAND IS ONE OF THE FIVE MOST-TOURED HOMES IN THE UNITED STATES—AND THE MOST FAMOUS HOME IN THE COUNTRY, AFTER THE WHITE HOUSE.

social and racial barriers of the time, Elvis ushered in a new era of American music and popular culture.

Elvis went on to star in 33 films, make history with his television appearances, and break records with live concert performances on tour and in Las Vegas. Globally, more than 1 billion of his records have been sold, more than any other recording artist. Elvis is widely regarded as one of the most important figures of 20th-century popular culture. He died at his beloved Memphis home, Graceland, on August 16, 1977.

A Special Place

When Elvis purchased Graceland in 1957, it was the fulfillment of a child's promise to his parents that, one day, he would know success, bring an end to his parents' financial struggles, and

set them up in the finest house in town. Graceland was a tangible, permanent symbol of how much Elvis had overcome—and a monument to his achievement of the American dream. But, more than anything, Graceland was Elvis' home.

When Elvis died, his will named his father, Vernon Presley, as executor and trustee of his estate, including Graceland. The beneficiaries were Elvis' grandmother, Minnie Mae Presley; his father, Vernon Presley; and his only child, Lisa Marie Presley.

Vernon Presley died in 1979 and Minnie Mae Presley died in 1980, leaving Lisa Marie as the estate's sole heiress. Elvis' will stated that her inheritance was to be held in trust for her until her 25th birthday, February 1, 1993. Vernon Presley's will brought about the appointment of three coexecutors/ cotrustees to succeed him. They were

the National Bank of Commerce in Memphis; the Presleys' accountant for a number of years; and Lisa Marie's mother, Priscilla Beaulieu Presley, whose 1967 marriage to Elvis had ended in a 1973 divorce.

To preserve the home and ensure that it would always be there for Elvis' fans, Priscilla Presley and the executors elected to open Graceland to the public. In late 1981, they hired Jack Soden, an investment counselor from Kansas City, Missouri, to help plan and execute Graceland's public opening and to oversee the total operation. Graceland opened for tours on June 7, 1982. Today, Lisa Marie Presley, owner and chairman of the board, continues to play an active role with both Soden and the rest of the management team.

A New Generation

More than 20 years after his death, Elvis still captivates and moves fans around the world. A new generation of fans has fueled continued record sales, and the grounds of Graceland on any given day are swarming with young Americans, Asians, and Europeans, and many more who have traveled to Memphis to get a little closer to the myth of Elvis.

From the beginning, visitors could tour several main rooms in the mansion, plus Elvis' trophy building and racquetball building. With Elvis' ever growing popularity and the success of Graceland, new attractions and developments have come through the years. In 1984, Elvis' two jet aircraft—*Lisa Marie* and *Hound Dog II*—were added as tour attractions in the Graceland visitor center. In 1989 came the opening of Vernon Presley's office behind the mansion, as well as the opening of the newly constructed Elvis Presley Automobile Museum across the street. Within the main house, the kitchen and Elvis' parents' bedroom were added to the mansion tour in 1995 and 1998, respectively.

In 1999, the company introduced Elvis Presley's Heartbreak Hotel, a redesign of a former Wilson World hotel acquired on a nearby property. In early 2001, Graceland announced a new digital audio tour presentation, along with new and significantly expanded exhibits for the mansion tour. The company also became a high-profile player on historic Beale Street in downtown Memphis with the 1997 opening of its chic restaurant/entertainment venue, Elvis Presley's Memphis.

But, perhaps most appealing to the new generation of fans, is Elvis' official home on the Web, www.elvis.com. With news and information about Elvis and about Graceland's attractions and amenities, the site is also home to popular contests and other dynamic events. On August 26, 2000, the site broadcast live video of the candlelight vigil, the annual tribute to Elvis by his fans, who come from around the world to commemorate the anniversary of his death.

Today, Elvis Presley, his music, and his home are having an impact on fans who were born well after his death. There's no greater proof of his enduring talent.

TWO OF THE MORE MEMORABLE ROOMS HIGHLIGHTED ON THE GRACELAND TOUR ARE THE JUNGLE ROOM, COMPLETE WITH A WATERFALL CASCADING DOWN A BRICK FACADE; AND A CONVERTED RACQUETBALL COURT THAT DISPLAYS STAGE COSTUMES AND GOLD AND PLATINUM RECORD AWARDS.

VISITORS TO GRACELAND CAN STAY AT ELVIS PRESLEY'S HEARTBREAK HOTEL (LEFT).

THE MEDITATION GARDEN IS NOT JUST THE RESTING PLACE OF ELVIS AND MEMBERS OF HIS FAMILY—IT'S A PLACE FOR FANS TO REFLECT AND PAY THEIR RESPECTS TO THE KING OF ROCK-N-ROLL (RIGHT).

*W*hen patients have a condition that calls for a specialist, their first concern is usually the physician's knowledge and experience—Is the doctor aware of the latest procedures and medications? Does the doctor have access to other specialists for collaboration? Is the doctor recognized as an expert in the field? ▲ These concerns often bring patients to UT Medical Group, Inc. the group practice of the physicians who also teach at the University of Tennessee

College of Medicine. Comprised of almost 450 doctors in almost every field imaginable, UT Medical Group is where patients go for an advanced level of care and expertise.

"Helping patients is our number one concern, and we are exceptionally equipped to deliver a wide range of care," says Dr. Jeffrey Woodside, chief medical officer of UT Medical Group. "Our physicians are passionate leaders in their fields, and we can put into practice what's taught and discovered at the university."

On the Leading Edge

Thanks to those ties to the university, UT Medical Group has board-certified physicians in most medical fields. Many are recognized as leading authorities not only in the region, but also across the country. They are involved in many of the most advanced procedures that take place in the city. UT Medical Group physicians, for example, perform most organ transplants in the Mid-South. UT physicians also staff one of the most recognized burn, neo-

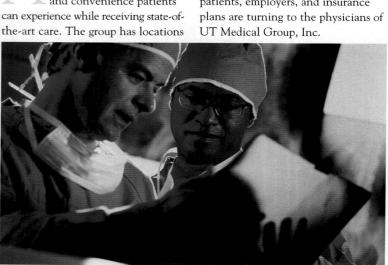

natal and high-risk obstretic, and pediatric medical centers in the south.

Many of the region's toughest cases are referred to UT Medical Group physicians for their expertise and—in the most challenging cases—access to leading-edge treatments.

Another benefit to the broad expertise of UT Medical Group is the frequent collaboration among physicians. Because advanced specialized treatments can impact other aspects of a patient's health, it is vital that a physician have access to other specialists who can assist in difficult treatments and diagnoses.

Convenient Care

Another rare aspect of UT Medical Group is the comfort and convenience patients can experience while receiving state-of-the-art care. The group has locations throughout Shelby County, including Midtown, East Memphis, Germantown, and Cordova. And the new, massive UT Medical Group specialty center in Germantown offers the first true multispecialty center outside of the medical center. It contains treatment and testing for cardiology, internal medicine, general surgery, psychiatry, ophthalmology, otolaryngology, urology, OB/GYN, cancer genetics, and more. There is also an on-site pharmacy, lab, radiology suite, conference center, and a preventive medicine center.

Patients rarely want to take chances with their health. And when a situation calls for a specialist, the concerns become even more serious. For expertise and compassion, more and more patients, employers, and insurance plans are turning to the physicians of UT Medical Group, Inc.

COMPRISED OF ALMOST 450 DOCTORS IN ALMOST EVERY FIELD IMAGINABLE, UT MEDICAL GROUP, INC. IS WHERE PATIENTS GO FOR AN ADVANCED LEVEL OF CARE AND EXPERTISE.

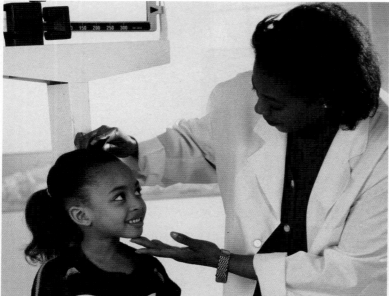

Today, tens of thousands of yearly trade shows give manufacturers valuable face-to-face time with prospects, and have helped make the trade show and exhibition industry one of the largest industries in the world. Right in the middle of that success is Arlington-based Exhibit-A, Inc. Founded in 1985 and today operating out of offices in Arlington, Orlando, and Eastern Europe, the company designs and manufactures trade show exhibits for major clients worldwide.

Exhibit-A offers a full line of portable exhibits and manufactures custom exhibits as well. The company offers a broad spectrum of displays, and has helped numerous clients with large-scale exhibits, portable exhibits, museum displays, interactive kiosks, and point-of-purchase displays.

Unparalleled Flexibility

What makes Exhibit-A different, though, is its flexibility and its impressive custom-exhibit capabilities. "Every client has a different need," says Don Furr Jr., president. "From budgets to customer demographics to show-space specifications, they have a long list of challenges to face. So, we don't think they should be forced into an off-the-shelf solution."

In addition to the top offerings in premanufactured exhibit lines, Exhibit-A serves customers with skilled designers and craftspeople who build custom exhibits in the company's 55,000-square-foot, Memphis-area manufacturing facility. The plant has a wide array of construction capabilities, as well as equipment for graphics production, cold process and thermal lamination, mounting, and large-format digital group-ware output. It's a powerful combination that yields impressive results.

The company, for example, built a massive, 20-by-40-foot, two-tiered, wood-paneled display for Thompson's Company, makers of retail and commercial wood treatment products. Exhibit-A also built an exhibit for National Football League Properties' presence at the National Sporting Goods Association show in Chicago. Exhibit-A has constructed specialty displays for a long list of clients, including SunCom, Toyota, and the U.S. Navy.

Service to the Extreme

Our capabilities give us the edge in production of displays, but also allow us to offer a rare level of service," Furr adds. If an unforeseen need arises at the last minute, for example, Exhibit-A can design and build a solution and then ship it out—all in a matter of hours, if necessary. This is an extremely valuable service for companies who have had displays damaged during the course of a show.

Exhibit-A has taken its high-service approach to the extreme by offering extensive installation and dismantling services to all of its clients. "For companies who want to completely outsource the headaches of exhibiting, we ship the display components to the venue in our own trucks, set up before the show, dismantle them after the show, and ship them to storage," Furr explains. "We're a turn-key service."

As trade shows continue as an indispensable component of national marketing programs, Exhibit-A, Inc. is sure to continue growing. "We feel extremely blessed that so many people have trusted us with such a vital part of their businesses," Furr says. "We look forward to continuing to serve them, whatever their needs may be."

EXHIBIT-A, INC., FOUNDED IN 1985 BY DON FURR JR. AND TODAY OPERATING OUT OF OFFICES IN ARLINGTON, ORLANDO, AND EASTERN EUROPE, DESIGNS AND MANUFACTURES TRADE SHOW EXHIBITS FOR MAJOR CLIENTS WORLDWIDE, INCLUDING THE TOYOTA CENTER AT AUTOZONE PARK; AZO, INC.; AND THE MEMPHIS BROOKS MUSEUM OF ART.

1986

1993

here are few pillars of Memphis' corporate community whose impact on the city compares to the role played by International Paper (IP). One of the largest forest products companies in the world, IP houses its operational headquarters in Memphis, which means some 3,100 jobs for the city's residents. ▲ But IP's relationship with the city is more than simply an employer-and-employee one. Since the company opened its doors in the

Bluff City in 1987 with only about 250 Memphis employees, IP has grown and prospered with multibillion-dollar acquisitions, massive revenue growth, and international market expansion.

Memphis has played such a vital role in this success that IP announced in 2001 that it planned to invest $66 million in its Memphis operation and lay the groundwork for an even stronger presence. From that point, the possibilities are endless.

The Path to Global Leadership

Incorporated in Albany, New York, on January 31, 1898, IP was a merger comprised of 17 pulp and paper mills. Holdings also included 1.7 million acres of timberland in the northeastern states and Canada. During its early years, IP was one of the nation's largest producers of newsprint, supplying 60 percent of all newsprint sold in the United States and exporting to Argentina, England, and Australia.

The company grew and, by the late 1920s, was constructing some of the world's largest newsprint mills. The company diversified into other product lines, adding kraft paper production mills in Louisiana and Mississippi, and corrugated container plants in Catania;

Bilbao; Arles; and Mortagne, France. These facilities improved IP's presence in the European market. The company also built new corrugated container plants in Pomezia, Italy; Guadeloupe; and Las Palmas, Grand Canary Islands.

By the late 1970s, IP had reorganized into functional business units: white papers, consumer packaging, industrial packaging, wood products, and specialty packaging. Today, IP ranks among the world's largest producers of high-quality printing and writing papers, serving growing markets for business, printing, and fine papers, including many grades of

recycled paper. The company's best-known brands include HammerMill, Springhill, Great White, Strathmore, Legacy, and Beckett, among others. IP's coated papers are used in magazines and catalogs, and the firm manufactures heavyweight papers used for folders, tags, and tickets.

IP also makes papers for office and consumer use under the brand names HammerMill, Legacy, Brite-Hue, Jet Print Photo, Invent It!, and Great White. The company's commercial papers include Accolade, Liberty 2000, and other brand names of coated papers for catalog, direct mail, book,

INTERNATIONAL PAPER'S INTERNATIONAL PLACE, LOCATED ON POPLAR AVENUE AND MASSEY, CURRENTLY HAS TWO EXISTING TOWERS. CONSTRUCTION FOR TOWER NUMBER THREE, STARTED JANUARY OF 2001, IS TO BE COMPLETED APRIL 2002.

FROM ITS SUCCESS AS ONE OF THE LARGEST FOREST PRODUCTS COMPANIES IN THE WORLD, TO ITS DEDICATION TO BEING AN ACTIVE MEMBER OF THE COMMUNITY, INTERNATIONAL PAPER IS ONE OF THE CORNERSTONES OF MODERN MEMPHIS.

magazine, publishing, and other print advertising end uses.

In addition, IP is one of the world's largest manufacturers of consumer and industrial packaging. The company's consumer packaging operation produces bleached board, which IP and its customers convert into a broad spectrum of packaging products. The firm produces food-service products such as cups, lids, plates, cartons, and containers for fast-food and other restaurants. In addition, the company manufactures

beverage packaging for dairy, juice, and specialty liquid products.

IP's industrial packaging includes containerboard, corrugated paperboard, and various kraft materials that are made into boxes, point-of-purchase displays, pallets, and dunnage bags. IP's kraft packaging also supplies paper bags, carryout bags, refuse bags, polyethylene refuse liners, and other products.

IP's product roster goes on and on, including pulp and a long list of

forest products that cater to families and industry all over the world.

IP is also the largest private forest landowner in the United States and manages 12 million acres of land under the principles of the Sustainable Forestry Initiative, a strategy that ensures the perpetual growing and harvesting of trees while protecting wildlife, plants, soil, and air and water quality.

Today, IP has operations in nearly 50 countries, employs some 113,000 people worldwide, and exports its products to more that 130 nations.

Growing with Memphis

In 1987, IP–headquartered in Purchase, New York–made the decision to move its operational headquarters to Memphis. The city was emerging as a global distribution center, and extensive research proved that the Memphis area would provide a hospitable and profitable base for the company's global customer service and support operations. Memphis was also attractive because of its well-connected airport, existing fiber-optic network, and affordable cost of living.

At the time, IP was a $6 billion company. About 250 employees moved to Memphis from New York, and went to work with some 200 new Memphis employees in a new office tower at International Place.

In 1989, IP consolidated its Alabama- and New Jersey-based Information Systems operations into a new Memphis facility. In 1990, the company opened a third facility–a Customer Commitment Center. In 1991, IP opened a fourth location and passed the 1,000 mark for number of Memphians employed. Soon, the company moved into a second tower at International Place and began to add new facilities all across the city.

By 2000, IP was almost a $30 billion company with some 3,400 Memphis employees at 14 facilities. The company pumps more than $226 million into the Memphis economy in local payroll and taxes, and spends approximately $10 million each year with Memphis-area minority vendors.

In the Memphis Community, International Paper supports many minority development programs such as Minority Market Place, which allows businesses to showcase their services (left).

Organizations such as Church Health Center, Inc., a non-profit health care clinic for people who are working but can't afford health care insurance, rely on International Paper volunteers like Hank Burterlson and Jerry Bower to make sure enough sample medications are available for patients who visit the clinic (left).

Mandy Young is an IT employee at the Business Process Technology Center who concentrates on the company's SAP project for accounting and finance processing (right).

INTERNATIONAL PAPER GAVE THE NATIONAL CIVIL RIGHTS MUSEUM A $1 MILLION COMMITMENT SUPPORTING PROGRAMS THAT HELP TEACH CIVIL AND HUMAN RIGHTS. THE 2000 FREEDOM AWARD WAS PRESENTED TO NELSON MANDELA FOR HIS COMMITMENT TO HELP PEOPLE WHO STRUGGLE FOR FREEDOM AND HUMAN RIGHTS (LEFT).

LARRY SIMMONS, GROUP LEADER, PURCHASING INITIATIVE AND DEVELOPMENT, ADDRESSES THE COMPANY'S SUPPORT TO HELP MINORITY VENDORS MAKE AN ECONOMIC IMPACT ON THE MEMPHIS COMMUNITY (RIGHT).

More Than an Employer

More than an employer, IP is a strong advocate for issues that improve the quality of life in Memphis, and ensure the community's long-term success and prosperity. For IP, that means focusing on two issues that the company sees as critical in the development of the city: education and diversity. In 2000, IP donated more than $1.6 million to support these issues.

The list of educational causes supported by IP includes active participation in the Memphis City Schools Adopt-a-School Program. After just a year in Memphis, IP adopted Coleman Elementary School. Today, some 40 employees serve as volunteer tutors and the company makes numerous financial contributions to the school. In further support of the Memphis City Schools, the IP Company Foundation has contributed $75,000 to support EDCORE grants for teachers in the classroom.

IP made a donation of $25,000 to aid in the construction of Memphis' new, state-of-the-art main library, and the company—in 1999 alone—

donated more than $45,000 to area colleges. IP funds arts programs in the local schools, and is a supporter of the city's WONDERS cultural exhibition program.

To support the enhanced acceptance and appreciation of diversity in the Memphis area, IP has provided employee volunteers and made donations to support diversity issues. Memphis is the home of the National Civil Rights Museum, and IP has been one of the museum's strongest supporters. Between 1997 and 2000, the company contributed $660,000 to the museum. In 2000, IP committed $1 million to support the museum's Freedom Awards program through 2004.

Each year, IP hosts the Minority Business Development Conference, and serves as the major sponsor of the Minority Business Development Marketplace. In 1999, the company donated $20,000 to the Memphis Urban League, and continues to provide funding to support diversity in the arts.

IP's unprecedented commitment to the community was recognized almost immediately after the company opened

Memphis operations. In 1990, IP was named Corporate Neighbor of the Year by the Volunteer Center of Memphis. In 1998, the company won the award a second time.

Shared Plans for a Bright Future

As impressive as IP's first decade in Memphis has been, IP recently assured the city that it was only the beginning. In early 2001, IP unveiled its $66 million plan to build a third tower at International Place and expand into two additional buildings at Willow Lake Business Park, as well as the desire to add some 950 jobs by 2003.

Memphis' critical role in the company's recent success has led to the development of a strategic plan that calls for significant investment in the company's Memphis infrastructure. The new mission for the Memphis operational headquarters is threefold.

The first goal is to become an even more effective provider of customer support services for the corporation. That means staff additions, enhanced

A FRESH COAT OF PAINT, PROVIDED BY INTERNATIONAL PAPER EMPLOYEES SUCH AS CAROLYN DAUGHERTY, HELPS NON-PROFIT AGENCIES IN MEMPHIS PROVIDE SERVICES TO PEOPLE IN THE COMMUNITY (LEFT).

INTERNATIONAL PAPER PLANTS MILLIONS OF TREES EACH YEAR TO CONSERVE FOREST LANDS. STUDENTS AT COLEMAN ELEMENTARY GATHER AROUND TO PLANT A SEEDLING DONATED BY THE COMPANY.

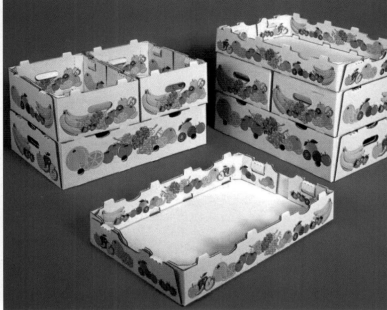

commitments to training and education, and innovative partnerships with the city and educators to ensure that the labor pool in Memphis is second to none.

The second goal for the Memphis operation is to consolidate the multiple facilities into three large campuses. The three towers at International Place will house consolidated global business management; five buildings at Willow Lakes will house global customer and employee support services; and the Southwind complex will serve as the home for consolidated global information technology services. The goal for consolidation is to enhance efficiency and build on the sense of employee community.

The third Memphis goal for IP is to step up its already impressive commitment to philanthropy. Already, half of the company's Memphis employees participate in the Volunteers of

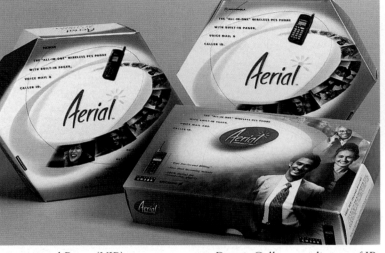

International Paper (VIP) program. Together, they donate more than 20,000 hours each year.

It's an ambitious program, but one that International Paper is extremely proud to be undertaking. "Memphis has been a big part of our success,"

says Dennis Colley, coordinator of IP operations in Memphis. "The city has been enormously receptive and our employee base here is exceptionally strong. We're looking forward to a long–and continually expanding–relationship with the city of Memphis."

INTERNATIONAL PAPER PRODUCES A VARIETY OF PAPER PRODUCTS SUCH AS PACKAGING FOR AERIAL PHONES, NEW ENGLAND APPLES, ETC.

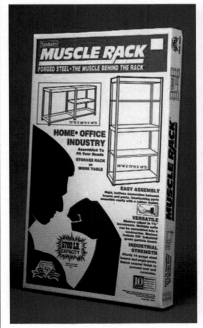

UNITED WAY OF MEMPHIS IS SUPPORTED BY MORE THAN NINETY-FIVE PERCENT OF INTERNATIONAL PAPER EMPLOYEES. CHRISTINE HEALY READS DURING HER VISIT AT THE SALVATION ARMY, A NON-PROFIT AGENCY TO SUPPORT NEEDY INDIVIDUALS AND FAMILIES.

I n the 1980s, the city of Memphis was looking for ways to capitalize on its cultural and tourism heritage to further enhance the education and quality of life in the region. Community leader Honey Scheidt encouraged then-Mayor Richard Hackett to investigate the impact a massive exhibit of Egyptian artifacts was having on a city in Canada. Hackett made the trip, and the rest is history. ▲ The mayor and private donors brought

Ramesses the Great to downtown Memphis in 1987. The exhibition, from the Egyptian Museum in Cairo, featured 74 Egyptian antiquities and a grand centerpiece—a colossal, 47-ton, 25-foot-tall statue of Ramesses the Great. Discovered at the site of ancient Memphis, the statue was restored in a joint project between the City of Memphis and the Egyptian Antiquities Organization funded by a grant from Coca-Cola, USA expressly for the exhibition.

A staggering total of some 675,000 visitors poured into the event. Building on this overwhelming success, city and community leaders developed WONDERS: The Memphis International Cultural Series. Designed to improve the quality of life in the city through education and revenue generation, the ongoing series of large-scale cultural exhibitions has become a fixture of the city's cultural, education, and tourism landscape.

A Glimpse into the Past

P resented in 40,000 square feet of galleries modeled after the architecture of the featured culture or historical era, WONDERS exhibitions offer a compelling and often overwhelming glimpse into the past.

The first official WONDERS exhibition in 1991 gave a powerful and personal look at Russia's Catherine the Great. Developed in conjunction with the Hermitage Museum in St. Petersburg, the exhibition featured 287 objects and the grand coronation carriage of Catherine the Great, restored especially for the Memphis showing. The exhibition attracted nearly 605,000 visitors from all 50 states and more than 65 foreign countries.

Then, in 1992, came *Splendors of the Ottoman Sultans*. Only twice in the history of Turkey had an exhibition of this magnitude been allowed to leave the country. Imperial caftans, weapons, and Iznik and Chinese pottery were among the 275 treasures that reflected the Ottoman sultan as statesman, military leader, and patron of the arts. The exhibition's grand centerpiece was the famous Topkapi Dagger, which was shown for the first time in the Western Hemisphere.

The Etruscans, composed of artifacts from the Vatican's Gregorian Etruscan Museum, followed shortly thereafter. The exhibition, which pieced together the mystery of the now vanished Etruscan civilization, was presented in association with the Memphis Pink Palace Museum.

WONDERS hit a giant home run in the summer of 1993 with *Napoléon*, a massive collection of 175 objects on loan from nearly 50 museums and private collections from France, the Vatican, Switzerland, England, and the United States. It was the largest exhibition ever presented in North America on Napoléon Bonaparte.

THE CULTURAL SERIES KNOWN AS WONDERS HAS BEEN BRINGING HISTORY TO MEMPHIS FOR MORE THAN A DECADE. INCLUDED IN THE SERIES WAS THE 1993 EXHIBIT *Napoléon*, WHICH SHOWCASED THE LIFE AND TIMES OF FRANCE'S MOST FAMOUS RULER.

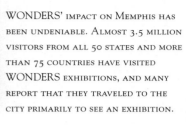

The centerpiece was a re-creation of the historic Council Chamber of the Château de Malmaison, with original furnishings restored especially for the exhibition.

In 1995, *The Imperial Tombs of China* showcased more than 250 objects from seven periods of Chinese history. The largest and most significant collection of tomb treasures ever to travel outside of China, the exhibition featured four life-size terra cotta warriors from the tomb of the first Chinese emperor, a jade burial suit sewn with gold thread, and the famous Dragon and Phoenix Empress Crown from the Ming dynasty.

In spite of the long series of successful exhibitions, no one was prepared for the impact of *TITANIC: The Exhibition* in 1997. From April 3 to September 30, a total of 634,935 people visited the Pyramid to see items collected from the ship's wreckage on the bottom of the Atlantic. Pieces were presented with a poignant narrative that gave a look into the lives lost during the tragedy. The largest single collection of *Titanic* artifacts anywhere, the Memphis exhibition went on to travel the country.

In 1998, *Ancestors of the Incas: The Lost Civilizations of Peru* offered an in-depth look at the mysteriously advanced ancient Incas. More than 300 objects—including three mummies—drew some 153,000 visitors.

In 1999, *World War II Through Russian Eyes* showcased never-before-shown memorabilia from the Central Armed Forces Museum in Moscow, including personal belongings of Hitler and Stalin.

In 2001, WONDERS debuted *Eternal Egypt: Masterworks of Ancient Art from The British Museum*. Approximately 150 artifacts—many of which had never been shown in the United States—were arranged chronologically to reveal the development of Egyptian art over 35 centuries, spanning the full range of pharaonic history from 3100 B.C. to the Roman occupation of the fourth century A.D.

Changing the Community

WONDERS' impact on Memphis has been undeniable. Almost 3.5 million visitors from all 50 states and more than 75 countries have visited WONDERS exhibitions, and many report that they traveled to the city primarily to see an exhibition.

The educational impact has also been immense, and tens of thousands of schoolchildren from across the region have received a once-in-a-lifetime look at history. The WONDERS format is especially useful for educators—the bigger and more interactive displays paint a picture that few museums and no classrooms could deliver.

The benefit has been so strong that community leaders began working in the late 1990s to take the series off the city's rolls and make it self-sufficient. With a grant from the Plough Foundation in 2000, WONDERS became an independent, not-for-profit organization. That same year, Hackett, one of WONDERS' original advocates, was named its first president and CEO.

"WONDERS has become an important piece of the fabric of this community," Hackett says. "I'm looking forward to continuing its powerful impact on Memphis."

A s the city of Memphis has emerged as North America's distribution center, area companies with an expertise in moving products efficiently have flourished. Pyramid Logistics Group is one such industry success story. Founded by Major Smith and Jeff O'Connor as a local provider of same-day courier service, the company has built a name for itself with its agility and acumen in an ever-changing marketplace. ▲ Pyramid Logistics Group

operates within two separate divisions. The first, Pyramid Couriers, handles on-demand, same–day delivery service, both in the Mid-South and throughout the continental United States. The second division, Pyramid Distribution and Warehousing, is a full-service logistics provider.

"Almost immediately, our customers began to ask for a broader range of delivery, warehousing, distribution and outsourcing services," says O'Connor. "And that's what we are focused on delivering today."

Service on Demand

The courier side of the business was built on a firm commitment to help customers achieve the impossible. "People use couriers because time and care are critical," Smith says. "So we developed a long list of services that takes this to the extreme."

Pyramid Logistics Group provides a 24-hour, seven-day-a-week service. It is equipped with up-to-the-minute Global Positioning Satellite (GPS) tracking technology that monitors a customer's package—from pick up to delivery.

The company offers real-time fax, providing proof of delivery upon receipt. Its services include one- and two-hour deliveries, daily route services, and next flight out air services. The company also specializes in same day, over-the-road

drive-outs anywhere in the continental United States.

"We have a fleet of more than 40 vehicles, ranging from cars to tractor-trailers. We have the capabilities of transporting 1 lb. to 40,000 lbs. Pyramid has also helped customers with international, same-day deliveries. The market moves at a blinding pace today, and we do whatever it takes to help our customers keep up," Smith says.

Logistical Solutions

Pyramid Logistics Group is the newest third-party logistics company for the e-commerce crowd. Its services are unique to each client's requirements, goals, and standards. The company creates logistical solutions designed to fit within its customer's operating parameters. "Distribution has become particularly complex, so we've stepped up with sophisticated and advanced solutions for our customers," O'Connor says.

Pyramid Logistics Group understands the importance for warehousing options—offering both short- and long-term storage. Its warehouse space is built to suit customers' needs, and the facility is protected with an alarm system and surveillance cameras. The company also offers designated areas separated by caged fencing. Pyramid Logistics Group can even provide a client company 24-hour access to its facility.

Pyramid Logistics Group specializes in managing its customers' inventory, offering the ability and technology to interface with customers' computer systems to transmit reports electronically. This service is popular with companies who want to maintain a centralized and accessible parts operation.

Pyramid Logistics Group is also a transportation management company, providing a one-stop solution for all transportation needs. Its services consist of shipment consolidation including zone pool distribution, line haul distribution, and intermodal services. Shipment consolidation is a cost-effective means of transportation. The benefits include reduced freight costs, secure shipments, decreased claims, and reduction in cycle times. The company is also fully insured and bonded.

"This company looks a lot different than it did eight years ago," Smith says. "And it will probably look a lot more different in another eight years. But what won't ever change is our commitment to doing whatever it takes to help our customers solve their distribution challenges."

Pyramid Logistics Group has created its own formula for success with a firm commitment to service and the flexibility to adapt to the changes in the market, There is no doubt the company will continue down the road towards even greater success in the years to come.

PYRAMID LOGISTICS GROUP PROVIDES AN END-TO-END LOGISTICAL SOLUTION FOR MANUFACTURERS AND RETAILERS NATIONWIDE.

sk Tom Hathaway about the success of Memphis-based *The Buyer's Agent,* and the modest entrepreneur will insist that he was simply the first to fill a growing need that was developing in the residential real-estate market. As the Missouri Real Estate Commission's Chief of Enforcement in charge of investigations and audits, he followed up on an endless list of consumer complaints made to the commission. "Time and time again," he says, "I saw

home buyers who were not satisfied with the outcome of their transactions." Some were confused by the process, he recalls, and many felt they had been misled outright.

"The root of the problem was clear," he says. "Real estate agents are obliged by law to represent the best interest of the seller, and no one is obliged to represent the best interest of the buyer. Once I realized that, the solution was really pretty obvious." He founded The Buyer's Agent in 1988, and today the company serves homebuyers through a network of 400 agents working from 60 offices worldwide.

Opening the Door for a Buyer's Advocate

As contracts have become more complicated over the years, homebuyers have found themselves increasingly confused about the process. Hathaway had seen it in his experience with the Missouri Real Estate Commission, and the Federal

Trade Commission (FTC) had begun to monitor the situation, as well. In 1983, the FTC completed a study showing that 72 percent of all homebuyers mistakenly thought that the agent who helped them buy their home was their agent and served their best interests. The same study

revealed that 74 percent of sellers mistakenly thought the agent who brought the buyer to the transaction was representing the buyer. "Not so," says Hathaway.

In the following five years, most state governments passed "agency disclosure" laws that that required the agents to inform buyers that they represented the sellers' interests. "But most of the laws were poorly crafted," Hathaway says, "and few were actually enforced."

And there was the opportunity. If someone stepped up with a new kind of real estate firm that represented buyers exclusively, customers would have the option of choosing a real-estate expert who was on their side. In 1988, Hathaway formed that new kind of company.

An Increasingly Popular Franchise

Today, Memphis-based The Buyer's Agent is a national franchisor of successful real-estate offices that serve buyers only. The company opened its first real-estate office in Memphis, and soon after added offices in Nashville, Tennessee; Jackson, Mississippi; and Little Rock,

TODAY, MEMPHIS-BASED THE BUYER'S AGENT IS A NATIONAL FRANCHISOR OF SUCCESSFUL REAL-ESTATE OFFICES THAT SERVE BUYERS ONLY.

Arkansas. Within two years, it had added offices in Orlando, Florida; St. Louis, Missouri; Minneapolis, Minnesota; Ann Arbor, Michigan; and Mobile, Alabama. The company has been featured in a long list of magazines, including *Business Week*, *Success*, *Smart Money*, *Kiplingers*, *Newsweek*, *Woman's Day*, and *Money*.

When asked about the phenomenal success of the operation, Hathaway again insists that the principle is not very complicated. "You don't have to mislead people to make money," he says. "Our customers love us, and they tell their friends."

Just ask Jon Boyd. Boyd purchased a The Buyers Agent franchise in 1992, and operates an eight-agent office in Ann Arbor. The opportunity to offer customers money savings and peace of mind is an irresistible package, he says. "In addition to the nearly $3 million that my office has been able to save home buyers over the years, I'm just as proud of the very high level of service we have been able to provide."

Big Savings for Customers

The franchise is able to save money for its customers in several key areas. First, a buyer's agent is required by law to negotiate the best price possible for the buyer. This obligation leads to lower prices.

Second, The Buyers Agent operates its own non-profit mortgage lender, Southmor Mortgage Corporation. Owned by the franchisees and licensed to lend in 42 states, the company saves customers thousands of dollars in fees that typically accompany a conventional mortgage. Another major area of savings is the repair and improvement requirements buyer's agents are often able to negotiate. As a representative solely for the buyer, the expert agent aggressively pursues an agreement that has more accommodations and fewer hidden surprises.

"We can literally save a buyer thousands of dollars," Hathaway says. "We have documented more than $90 million in consumer savings since the company closed its first transaction in 1988."

Hathaway knows he's making a difference, because he regularly sees The Buyers Agent criticized and attacked by the traditional real estate industry. Furthermore, he says the industry is working state-by-state to repeal disclosure laws. "If they can avoid committing to agency representation of the buyer or the seller," Hathaway says, "they can begin to operate like car dealerships and represent no one's interest but their own."

Even if all states eventually relieve real estate agents of their duty to represent one party in a transaction, Hathaway knows his franchisees have too much momentum to be stopped, or even slowed. "What the real estate industry has been incredibly slow to understand," he says, "is that customers in general hate the level of service they receive from traditional agents and typically feel that they pay too much. When they work with The Buyer's Agent, the opposite is usually true."

"As they continue to sing our praises and tell their friends," he adds, "I can't imagine anything but increased success for The Buyer's Agent, our franchisees, and our clients."

WHEN ASKED ABOUT THE PHENOMENAL SUCCESS OF THE OPERATION, OWNER TOM HATHAWAY INSISTS THAT THE PRINCIPLE IS NOT VERY COMPLICATED. "YOU DON'T HAVE TO MISLEAD PEOPLE TO MAKE MONEY," HE SAYS. "OUR CUSTOMERS LOVE US, AND THEY TELL THEIR FRIENDS."

THE COMPANY WORKS DILIGENTLY TO SAVE ITS CUSTOMERS MONEY AND MAKE THE OVERALL PROCESS OF PURCHASING A HOME A PLEASANT, STRAIGHTFORWARD ONE.

rother International Corporation, which has had a manufacturing and distribution presence in Memphis since the
late-1980s, has become a highly successful international
company by following a simple formula: combine innovation and quality to ensure that
customers are satisfied. But while the formula is simple, achieving the results can be
challenging. Brother has been successfully meeting that challenge for almost a century.

The company began manufacturing sewing machines in Japan in 1908, and by executing its formula of creating innovative, exceptional products while consistently exceeding customers' expectations, Brother now has 13 manufacturing bases and 33 marketing facilities located in 30 countries.

Today, Brother practices its innovation and commitment to quality in three core businesses: information, fashion, and communications. The list of products manufactured by Brother has grown steadily, and includes knitting machines, electronic typewriters, word processors, high-speed printers, facsimile machines, and electronic labeling systems. These products are well known throughout the world and are distributed in more than 100 countries.

Tapping the Region's Strength

Brother International Corporation was established in Memphis in 1989. Powered by its exceptional can-do attitude, the Memphis operation not only has grown dramatically, now employing several hundred people, but also has enhanced the city's reputation as America's Distribution

Center. Using its geographic location to full advantage, Brother's Memphis location has become the distribution center for North and South America, shipping some 250 products, as well as spare parts for all Brother goods.

Memphis offers direct connections with just about every possible form of transportation—air, water, ground, and rail—and Brother utilizes them all. The company's shipping capabilities range from overnight delivery services to

trucks that, in just two days, can reach 45 states, as well as major industrial sites in Canada and Mexico.

Manufacturing Excellence

Brother Industries, USA, Inc., a fully owned subsidiary of Brother International Corporation also taps Memphis' manufacturing expertise. Now employing some 500 people in its 225,000-square-foot manufacturing facility, the company provides every step of product development, from concept to distribution. Using state-of-the-art equipment and technology, the plant produces all the typewriters and word processors for the company's North and South American markets. In February 2000, the Bartlett facility produced its 10 millionth typewriter.

The Brother group also includes a research and development organization staffed by more than 50 engineers and support personnel who are available to confer with customers at any stage of development. This talented group is composed of electrical, mechanical, software, and manufacturing engineers with years of in-depth experience. Additionally, the team can draw on

BROTHER INTERNATIONAL CORPORATION
DISTRIBUTION CENTER (TOP)

CUSTOMERS CAN REST ASSURED THAT
THEIR ORDERS WILL BE QUICKLY AND
ACCURATELY FILLED WITH THE USE OF
BROTHER'S SOPHISTICATED, COMPUTERIZED,
MATERIAL HANDLING SYSTEMS (LEFT).

BROTHER'S STATE OF THE ART SYSTEMS ARE
EQUALLY CAPABLE OF HANDLING ORDERS
OF LARGE AND SMALL MACHINES OR PARTS
(RIGHT).

the experience of some 600 engineers employed by Brother in other parts of the world.

In 1996, Brother entered into a partnership with Pitney Bowes, manufacturing postage meters jointly designed by the two firms. The relationship has flourished, and in 1997 and 1998, Pitney Bowes recognized Brother as one of its Alliance Champions.

Brother also provides its customers with what it calls "100 percent visibility of their project." The company places personal computers with the appropriate software in clients' offices, enabling them to access their projects to see how many models are in production, to see how many are stored in the warehouse, and even to place orders.

Brother by no means considers its mission accomplished once a product has reached its destination. The effort to exceed customers' expectations can also be found in the areas of returns and refurbishment. The capable Brother team has set up a system to accept product returns and repairs. When a product is returned, a special technical team at Brother will inspect the model, make the proper repairs, place the product in new packaging, and return it to the customer.

Growing with Bartlett

To meet increasing customer demand, Brother International Corporation embarked on a major expansion of its warehousing operations in 1998. A state of the art, automated distribution facility and national call center was constructed on 102 acres in Bartlett's industrial park. This facility includes more than 1 million square feet of warehouse and office space that is fully air-conditioned and heated.

Brother Industries, USA, Inc., which has achieved ISO 9002 certification and is a winner of the Tennessee Quality Award, is also an involved member of the Bartlett community. The company is the single biggest contributor to the Bartlett Performing Arts Center, and it has donated the Japanese gardens at Bartlett City Hall. In 1996, the firm was named the Bartlett Corporate Citizen of the Year. In 2000, Brother was also the winner of the City of Bartlett Lawn Beautiful Award.

Obviously, Brother's philosophy, "Together, there is no limit to what we can achieve," applies not only to its attitude in business, but to the community as well—a fact the company continues to demonstrate.

BROTHER'S PRINTED CIRCUIT BOARD ASSEMBLY LINE UTILIZES STATE-OF-THE-ART SURFACE MOUNT TECHNOLOGY AS WELL AS THE MANUAL INSERTION OF ELECTRONIC COMPONENTS (LEFT).

A TYPICAL FINAL ASSEMBLY LINE FOR TYPEWRITERS (RIGHT)

BROTHER INDUSTRIES, USA, INC. MANUFACTURING FACILITY

ince the early 1990s, Memphis has experienced an economic boom, and at the heart of that growth and productivity lies Memphis' airport. In addition to its well-known cargo leadership, Memphis International Airport is also an international center for passenger traffic. Thanks to Northwest Airlines' Memphis hub, the city enjoys more nonstop services per capita than any other city in the United States. ▲ *And the Northwest partnership with*

Memphis is just beginning. With tens of millions of additional dollars committed to Memphis' infrastructure and service, Northwest Airlines has cemented its role as one of the brightest lights on the city's economic landscape.

An Airline Built on Innovation

Northwest Airlines first took off on October 1, 1926, flying mail between Minneapolis/St. Paul and Chicago. In 1927, Northwest took on its first passengers, and in 1947, the airline pioneered the great circle route to Asia. The airline's strong Asian presence and commitment to excellence led to continued growth, and in 1986, Northwest made a major commitment to domestic service when it acquired Republic Airlines. As a result of this acquisition, Northwest took over Republic's hubs in Detroit and Memphis.

In 1993, Northwest took another step that would change Memphis' transportation market forever—the airline partnered with KLM Royal Dutch Airlines to offer convenient and seamless service between the United States and cities around the world. The partnership led to Memphis' first nonstop international passenger flight: Memphis to Amsterdam.

In 1996, Northwest announced another alliance, this time with Continental Airlines. This alliance improved consumer travel options, and delivered an even wider range of benefits to millions of air travelers in the Americas, Asia, and Europe. Northwest also has marketing affiliations with several regional airlines; operating as Northwest Airlink, the airline offers dozens of connecting flights daily.

Today, Northwest Airlines is the world's fourth-largest airline, and, together with its global travel partners, serves more than 785 destinations in 120 countries on six continents. The airline's U.S. system spans 49 states and the District of Columbia. With frequent service to Tokyo, Seoul, Shanghai, and Manila, Northwest also remains an industry leader in service to Asia, operating more than 200 nonstop flights between the United States and Asia each week. The airline has more than 53,000 employees worldwide.

A Partnership with Memphis

The story in Memphis is equally impressive. When Northwest acquired Republic's hub in 1986, financial viability and service were suffering. In 1990, Northwest faced a crucial decision: close the hub or reengineer it to Northwest's high standards for service and community leadership. The airline decided to stay in the city, and set up an all-new flight pattern that focused on adding more options for connecting passengers and Memphis customers as well. The new schedule was a hit and traffic increased almost immediately. The Amsterdam connection in 1995 further boosted traffic.

In 1999, Northwest entered into an agreement with the Memphis-Shelby County Airport Authority to complete a $400 million renovation and

TODAY, NORTHWEST AIRLINES IS THE WORLD'S FOURTH-LARGEST AIRLINE, AND, TOGETHER WITH ITS GLOBAL TRAVEL PARTNERS, SERVES MORE THAN 785 DESTINATIONS IN 120 COUNTRIES ON SIX CONTINENTS.

expansion plan for Memphis International Airport. When the renovation is complete, the airport will have a new, regional jet facility on Concourse A, which will create 15 new gates and jet bridges. In addition, Concourse C is being redeveloped to accommodate the new Avro RJ 85 aircraft. By the end of the project, Northwest Airlines will have spent approximately $51.5 million on facility expansions and renovations, and an additional $152 million on airfield improvements.

Northwest recently completed a new, state-of-the-art WorldClub lounge at Memphis International Airport, and also helped fund a Concourse B and C passenger connector, which will help to decrease the time it takes for passengers to go from one concourse to the other.

Thanks to Northwest, Memphis was the first airport in the United States to receive video monitors at gate check-in positions. Other facility improvements include new ticket counters, new gate podiums, new carpets, expansion of the unaccompanied minor room, and a new baggage carousel. Northwest also announced in 2000 the addition of 48 new flights, the largest service expansion in Northwest history.

"The people of Memphis have made Northwest their preferred airline, and we are grateful to the community for its strong support and its appreciation for the power of this partnership," says Tim Griffin, executive vice president for marketing and distribution. "We believe that these new flights will create even greater value for our customers in terms of convenience and schedule flexibility."

Griffin insists that community support for Northwest's service has enabled the airline to grow significantly—from fewer than 140 daily departures in 1994 to more than 290. "We can't begin to say how grateful we are to have been embraced as Memphis' hometown airline," Griffin says. Today, some 2,800 Memphis employees and 1,500 Northwest Airlink employees help the airline continue that commitment to the city.

A Better Place to Live

Northwest's investment in Memphis goes well beyond flight service and employment. In addition to the hundreds of millions of dollars the airline pours into the community through regular operation, the company has contributed millions more to the many non-profit causes that make the city special. As an example, Northwest has funded projects at Le Bonheur Children's Hospital, St. Jude Children's Research Hospital, LeMoyne-Owen College, National Civil Rights Museum, Memphis Arts Council, Orpheum Theater, Memphis Museum System, Memphis Symphony, Brooks Museum, Memphis Zoo, Memphis Redbirds, and Memphis Cancer Foundation.

And there's more on the horizon. With Northwest Airlines actively planning the addition of new domestic and international flights, there is little doubt of one fact: those flights will continue to deliver prosperity and an enhanced quality of life to the city of Memphis.

IN ADDITION TO ITS WELL-KNOWN CARGO LEADERSHIP, MEMPHIS INTERNATIONAL AIRPORT IS ALSO AN INTERNATIONAL CENTER FOR PASSENGER TRAFFIC. THANKS TO NORTHWEST AIRLINES' MEMPHIS HUB, THE CITY ENJOYS MORE NONSTOP SERVICES PER CAPITA THAN ANY OTHER CITY IN THE UNITED STATES.

WITH FREQUENT SERVICE TO TOKYO, SEOUL, SHANGHAI, AND MANILA, NORTHWEST ALSO REMAINS AN INDUSTRY LEADER IN SERVICE TO ASIA, OPERATING MORE THAN 200 NONSTOP FLIGHTS BETWEEN THE UNITED STATES AND ASIA EACH WEEK.

*I*n a crowded convention hall at the 1999 annual meeting of the National Association of Personnel Services (NAPS), Dotty Summerfield was sitting next to Emmy-award-winning broadcaster and convention keynote speaker Deborah Norville when the president of NAPS called Summerfield's name from the stage. Though she had been active in planning the conference, Summerfield had no idea what was next on the agenda: she was to be presented

with one of the association's highest honors—the prestigious NAPS Norbert I.B. Fried Ethics Award.

"I was honored and surprised—and I still am," Summerfield says. "The most complimentary thing anyone could say about me, my company, or the people who work with me is that we do our business in an ethical manner. The award means more to me than I could ever put into words."

The Value of Integrity

Summerfield's company— Summerfield Associates, Inc.— is a Memphis-based recruiting, consulting, and staffing company. The company's staff specializes in national recruiting for information technology, human resources, finance and accounting, distribution and logistics, telecommunications, and corporate legal positions. Founded by Summerfield in 1989, the company serves a long list of local, regional, and national clients of varying sizes. With more than 60 years of combined experience in the recruitment of permanent, contract, and contract-for-hire personnel, Summerfield Associates has become a priceless partner for companies who are committed to doing whatever it takes to find the right people.

SUMMERFIELD ASSOCIATES, INC. OFFERS EXPERTISE IN HIRING TALENTED PEOPLE— A FACT THAT IS EVIDENT IN ITS OWN HIGHLY SKILLED TEAM. EMPLOYEES INCLUDE (FROM LEFT) LORRAINE STEINBERG, DOTTY SUMMERFIELD, PATRICIA NUSS, AND JANICE "CHICI" LEE.

Usually, hiring Summerfield's company is all it takes. "Many of our clients use us on an exclusive basis," she says. "I think that's because they have seen our commitment to integrity firsthand."

Recruiting has traditionally been a highly competitive industry, and it is becoming even more so. Because there are many needy clients out there, less-than-scrupulous firms often pop up to make a quick buck. Their clients learn tough lessons, though, when the same firms recruit already-placed employees a few months later to join other clients' firms. "We observe a strong code of ethics at Summerfield Associates," Summerfield says. "We will not recruit any candidate who has been placed by our firm, and we observe the highest level of confidentiality."

Summerfield's personal commitment to integrity goes back to her childhood.

"My father was a small-business owner, and he told me repeatedly about the value of honesty," she recalls. "'The only thing you've got is your name,' he used to say."

Summerfield's commitment has driven the way she runs her business, and it has also fueled her resolution to change the industry. She is a past president of the Memphis City Chapter of the Tennessee Association of Personnel Services, and she has served in a number of leadership roles in her profession. She joined the NAPS Board of Directors in 1993, and was elected to the organization's national executive board in 1997. That same year, Summerfield received the NAPS District Director of the Year Award.

But perhaps the most rewarding role for Summerfield was serving as the chair of the NAPS By-laws and Ethics

firm can meet client needs confidently and proactively. "We're doing things today that I would never have imagined 10 years ago," she says.

The firm, for example, has a strong Spousal Employment Assistance program, and even has developed a self-directed employment workshop that has been used by a Fortune 500 company. Summerfield Associates also offers Client-Identified Candidate screening services, where potential hires are screened before a company makes a final decision.

Summerfield Associates, Inc. is also doing some strategy consulting, in which the firm helps clients draft recruiting standards and tactics. "Many companies are being blindsided by sudden changes in their workforces and in the labor pool in general," Summerfield says. "We literally chart graduation rates, do projections for skills requirements, and do anything else that can help them prepare for future staffing needs."

And when you get to the bottom of it, Summerfield says, that's what the future of recruiting will look like. "While there will always be some commoditization in this industry, the truly successful firms will be the ones who make it their business to learn clients' operations—inside and out—and then do whatever it takes to help them staff for success," says Summerfield.

Committee for 1996-1997. "That year, we began a battle against 'temp-napping,' " she recalls. Temp-napping is a tactic practiced by some temporary placement firms; these companies secure contracts to handle all of their clients' temporary business, and then insist that the temps already on-site join the placement firms' rosters or risk losing their jobs. "There was some strong language in the policy and some strong resistance to it, but I was extremely proud when NAPS rolled it out in 1998," Summerfield adds.

It was this accomplishment, along with 20 years of commitment to promoting ethics in personnel services, that earned Summerfield the prestigious Fried award. "The award was a tremendous honor," she says. "But for me, the real honor comes from being recommended by a client to another client. Or having a major client decide to use us exclusively. Or having an employee say how refreshing and exciting it is to work here. These are the things that tell me we're doing things right."

New Services for a New Economy

Summerfield is passionate about her business. When she's not promoting the importance of integrity above all else, she'll tell you that the business world is changing. Personnel professionals who aren't committed to staying on top of the recent staffing strategies and developments, she says, are going to get left behind. "I'm a little nuts about training and education," Summerfield says, with

her characteristic smile. "Ask anyone here—they'll tell you."

Not a week goes by that the Summerfield staff doesn't do some kind of training or professional development; in addition, all eligible staff members sit for the test for the Certified Personnel Consultant (CPC) designation. It is important to stay abreast of industry trends, Summerfield insists, so that the

When young Adolph Coors came to the United States from Prussia in 1868, he had little idea that his name would become one of the most recognized in brewing. Using the rigorous brewing skills he had developed in his homeland, Coors opened the Golden Brewery in Golden, Colorado, in 1873. Today, the Coors Brewing Company, as it is now called, includes members of the third, fourth, and fifth generations of his family.

The company has also expanded across the country, and today calls Memphis one of its many homes. With more than 600 employees in the city and a need for Memphis' clear, pure, artesian water, Coors has developed strong ties to the city.

Meeting the Demand for Quality

The beer industry in America has undergone some major changes since 1873, especially in the last 50 years. By 1944, the industry had dwindled to only about 300 breweries, a number that decreased even more rapidly as the industry continued to consolidate.

Coors held its own in the diminishing arena, accommodating the rapid changes brought on by World War II. With the improvement of transportation and the advent of television advertising, brewers had to become more efficient producers. During this period, Coors pioneered two major innovations. In 1959, it was the first company to use aluminum cans. Shortly thereafter, Coors initiated the application of constant refrigeration, a variation of which is still unique to the company's high product quality.

Consolidations within the beer industry increased dramatically in the early 1970s. As competition escalated, the product lines began to expand. Light beer became extremely popular and, in 1978, Coors introduced Coors Light. Today, Coors Light is one of the top U.S. brands of light beer.

As demand for the company's products continued to surge, Coors added a packaging facility in Elkton, Virginia, in 1987, and another in Memphis in 1990. The expansion was a major undertaking for Coors, which up to that time was the world's largest single-site brewing and packaging company. As a result of the expansion, the company currently exports to more than 20 foreign countries, including

WITH MORE THAN 600 EMPLOYEES IN THE CITY AND A NEED FOR MEMPHIS' CLEAR, PURE, ARTESIAN WATER, COORS HAS DEVELOPED STRONG TIES TO THE CITY.

474

M E M P H I S

Puerto Rico, Greece, Guam, Japan, and the United Kingdom, plus U.S. military bases.

A Memphis Commitment That Runs Deep

Coors selected Memphis as the site of its packaging facility, and later a brewery, for three primary reasons. First, the city's central location, as well as its reputation as North America's Distribution Center, provides strong access to the brewery's international markets and its many regional niche markets. Thanks to these factors, Coors is able to respond to its customers with quick deliveries.

The second attribute that attracted Coors to Memphis was the operating brewery that already existed on Raines Road. And the third draw was the outstanding pure water supply for which Memphis and Coors are both famous. Coors has built its product reputation on quality, with an emphasis on fresh spring water—not an easy commodity to find in large quantities.

Coors continues to research and develop new products in order to add quality to its existing line of malt beverage products: Coors, Coors Light, George Killian's, Coors Extra Gold, Keystone brands, Coors NA (a non-alcoholic beverage), and Zima. Coors recently launched a new specialty beer, Blue Moon, which is brewed exclusively in Memphis.

But beer is not all Coors offers to the Memphis community. The Coors Belle, a banquet facility built right into the brewery, is a replica of a Mississippi River steamboat grand salon, and is available to the public for a nominal rental fee.

Since the complete renovation and subsequent start-up of the Memphis brewery in 1991, Coors has spent more than $107 million each year in the Memphis market in payroll-related expenses, taxes, money spent with Memphis vendors, and capital improvements. But Coors' ties to the community go well beyond the brewery's walls.

Memphis employees, retirees, families, and friends volunteer thousands of hours each year to projects ranging from conducting food drives for the Metropolitan Inter-Faith Association (MIFA) to visiting the children housed at Porter-Leath emergency shelter. Sharing Some Time Together—a group of Coors volunteers—raises more than $7,000 each year for holiday gifts for needy children, and a Coors group focused on veterans' needs visits the VA hospital at least once a month. The Memphis Coors volunteer program has received the Corporate Neighbor Award, and Coors Brewing Company is also a major donor to causes across the city. Coors has, for example, given more than $10 million to St. Jude Children's Research Hospital since 1994.

Recognized for both its strict brewing processes and its unwavering commitment to its home communities, Coors Brewing Company is sure to continue as a successful brewer and model corporate citizen for years to come.

*J*ust a little more than a decade ago, farmers in Tunica County, Mississippi, were attempting to scratch out a living by growing cotton, rice, or soybeans. In the 1980s, Tunica was one of the poorest counties in the United States, with unemployment at 26 percent. Things were so bad that, in 1985, television's 60 MINUTES devoted an entire segment to the area's depressed conditions. ▲ But that past is in stark contrast with the present, where

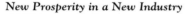

unemployment is now at less than 5 percent, and the county's per capita income is among the top 20 in Mississippi. The change has been stunning, and it is all thanks to tourism and entertainment—two things residents of the county could never have envisioned fewer than two decades ago.

Tunica County's economic reversal enabled Mississippi to become one of only three states to have reduced its number of welfare recipients in 1994. In the past decade, more than $3 billion has been invested in Tunica County.

"The turnaround has been nothing short of astonishing," says Webster Franklin, president of the Tunica Convention and Visitors Bureau. "If you weren't here to see what we call the Tunica Phenomenon, you wouldn't believe it."

New Prosperity in a New Industry

The county's remarkable transformation began in 1990, when Mississippi moved to permit casino gambling. The state's approach was to introduce regulations similar to those in effect in Las Vegas: 24-hour-a-day, nonstop action with no-limit wagering. Competition would determine the Mississippi casinos' suc-

cesses. By the beginning of 2000, there were 10 casinos in Tunica, each with luxurious hotel accommodations, totaling more than 6,000 rooms. Most of these hotels offer swimming pools, spas, fitness facilities, and entertainment venues that at one time or another have featured just about every big name or act in show business. The casinos feature more than 40 restaurants, many of which are open 24 hours a day, and which run the gamut from coffee shops and buffets to fine dining.

All of this growth has rocketed Tunica to its rank as the third-largest gaming resort destination in America.

In 1999, a Mississippi motor coach survey placed Tunica as the number one motor coach destination in the state, with 22,304 tours bringing 827,131 visitors to the area that same year. Tunica has also become a popular convention host. The area's 10 resort properties offer a total of some 120,000 square feet of flexible meeting space, with individual meeting facilities as large as 40,000 square feet.

Gaming revenues from Tunica casinos have provided funds to improve local community services, including streets and roads, the public school system, utilities, and fire protection.

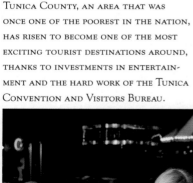

TUNICA COUNTY, AN AREA THAT WAS ONCE ONE OF THE POOREST IN THE NATION, HAS RISEN TO BECOME ONE OF THE MOST EXCITING TOURIST DESTINATIONS AROUND, THANKS TO INVESTMENTS IN ENTERTAINMENT AND THE HARD WORK OF THE TUNICA CONVENTION AND VISITORS BUREAU.

Total county revenues increased $48.6 million between 1992 and 1999, rising from $3.5 million to $52.1 million.

An expansion of the Casino Factory Shoppes and major renovations and expansions of the existing casinos and hotels was completed in 2000. The Paul Battle Jr. Arena and Exposition Center, named for a longtime resident of the area, and one of the largest arenas in the southeastern United States, also opened that same year.

"Our facilities offer a unique combination of amenities and services designed to accommodate anything from rodeos, horse shows, and concerts to banquets, sporting events, and trade shows," says A.C. Chapman, executive director of the facility. "Having this state-of-the-art, flexible arena will clearly enhance the rapidly growing casino resort destination in Tunica County."

With some 48,000 square feet of climate-controlled exhibit space on the main arena floor, seating for 6,000, and paved parking for 1,100 vehicles, the facility is the largest indoor arena in the state.

The expansion of the Casino Factory Shoppes will add 60,000 square feet to a facility that currently features more than 20 outlet stores. Upon completion of the project, the outlet center will span more than 200,000 square feet.

In addition, officials have approved construction of a Tunica County Airport that will include a 7,000-foot runway and support facilities. The economic impact of the airport, scheduled for completion in 2005, should be significant.

Tunica's rags-to-riches tale leaves no doubt as to why those who grew up in the area never tire of hearing the story of the Tunica Phenomenon. Any way you look at Tunica—past, present or future—it is an amazing story indeed.

THE MAJORITY OF CASINOS IN TUNICA
OFFER SWIMMING POOLS, SPAS, FITNESS
FACILITIES, AND ENTERTAINMENT VENUES
THAT AT ONE TIME OR ANOTHER HAVE
FEATURED JUST ABOUT EVERY BIG NAME
OR ACT IN SHOW BUSINESS.

*O*ne of the largest logistics outsourcing service providers in the Mid-South, Memphis-based Supreme Distribution Services, Inc. (SDS) serves approximately 50 major clients, employs some 100 full-time employees, and operates in several regions of the country. The company serves its customers from a cadre of some 3 million square feet of warehouse space nationwide, and its founder, Stephen M. Williams, was honored by the MEMPHIS BUSINESS JOURNAL as

the city's Small Business Executive of the Year in 1995, just three years after the company began operations.

In the face of this success, it's hard to imagine that Supreme Distribution Services was just a dream in 1992. Williams was employed as the director of distribution for a local warehousing firm, had just completed his college degree as a full-time business management student, and found himself spending a lot of time working to develop a plan to apply his degree, along with the experience he had gained, in a manner that would maximize future opportunities.

"That's when some intriguing things began to happen," Williams says. He was able to procure commitments from key industry associates, including his close friend, Keith Inman—current SDS vice president of operations—to join his newly formed entity. Timing couldn't have been better when a local business decision maker who attended church with Williams, Durell Hamilton, then of Continental

General Tire, Inc., said he would be willing to entrust his logistics needs to the care of Williams' embryonic organization, known as Supreme Distribution Services, Inc.

Another colleague, local commercial real estate professional Jerry Chandler, even loaned Williams $5,700, when financing for the new company's first lease agreement dissolved during some unanticipated developments in the 11th hour at the negotiating table at the offices of locally prominent Belz Enterprises.

Williams didn't take his blessings for granted. He proceeded to name the new company Supreme Distribution Services, Inc. as a continuing reminder of his eternal indebtedness to God. And Williams and his staff have never looked back.

Today, Supreme's logistics facilities handle dry and refrigerated products ranging from general commodities and hazardous materials to finished goods and raw materials. Goods are distributed by carton, container,

pallet, piece, and various other units of measure via all modes of modern transportation. In addition to its warehousing capabilities, Supreme's employees are trained in HazMat and a complete lift truck certification and safety program.

Flexibility Is the Key

Supreme operates under what Williams calls the Supreme Goal. That goal is to directly contribute to the ability of each customer to achieve a distinct competitive advantage in its respective industry as a result of a mutual business relationship with SDS.

The key to achieving that goal has been the ability to adapt. "Our main commodity is flexibility," Williams says. "The logistics outsourcing industry exists to a significant degree because manufacturers rarely produce the exact amount of product at the exact time it's needed. They rely on providers like SDS not only to store and distribute goods and products efficiently, but also to effectively disseminate pertinent supply chain information across distribution channels. That means we have to be prepared to accommodate wide variations in the amount of incoming inventory and the types of products we handle, as well as multiple distribution demands."

SDS' leadership also comes from a belief that customers need flexibility in payment and pricing structures. "We design cost structures specifically catering to the needs of each customer," Williams says. "Consequently, many customers find that higher levels of accountability and productivity can be achieved as a result of a logistics relationship with the Supreme Team."

More evidence of SDS' commitment to flexibility can be seen in its long list of value-added services.

SUPREME DISTRIBUTION SERVICES, INC. (SDS) SERVES APPROXIMATELY 50 MAJOR CLIENTS, EMPLOYS SOME 100 FULL-TIME EMPLOYEES, AND OPERATES IN SEVERAL REGIONS OF THE COUNTRY.

These include contract labor and supervision; cross-dock and trans-loading services; export shipping and documentation; container loading, blocking, and bracing; product consolidation and packaging; pick-and-pack order processing; rework and light assembly; reverse logistics; cycle audits; inventory monitoring; order tracking and verification; and retention-based employee training.

Growing with Memphis

Memphis is a big part of our success," Williams says. "It's no coincidence that more than 200 of the Fortune 500 companies have operations here." He cites Memphis' employee base, infrastructure, and location as foundations that have been instrumental in SDS' success.

Building on Memphis as a focal point, SDS has developed a chain of hub-city locations that connect the East and West coasts. Operations in southern California, South Carolina, and central Texas have helped to propel the company onto the national scene.

"Utilizing our strengths in information services while logically growing our cadre of physical space, we are capitalizing on the trends in the logistics industry," Williams says. "As more and more companies decide to outsource fulfillment, we are ready to deliver. As more and more manufacturers emerge technologically, we are ready to deliver. As time-sensitive food logistics requirements get more and more demanding, we are ready to deliver."

Where Word Is Bond

SDS' culture is built on a no-exceptions commitment to honesty and ethics, and the company's management is rooted in diversity appreciation and employee empowerment. At SDS, injecting a focus on character in the workplace not only benefits customers, but also makes the company a more satisfying place to work. "An often overlooked stress factor in the workplace is the presence of corrupting factors that influence employees' families, jobs, and reputations," Williams says.

SDS has been so successful in developing an ethics-based culture, the firm has launched a training division that helps other companies forge similar corporate environments. The Supreme Character Institute offers an employee-development program known as Character First®, which helps client companies improve work environments and cultivate achievement.

Supreme Distribution Services, Inc.'s employees and staff have worked diligently to develop and maintain their commitment to becoming a regional leader in third-party logistics outsourcing. Driven by a commitment to ethics, flexibility, and service, SDS will continue to be an industry leader for years to come.

TODAY, SUPREME'S LOGISTICS FACILITIES HANDLE DRY AND REFRIGERATED PRODUCTS RANGING FROM GENERAL COMMODITIES AND HAZARDOUS MATERIALS TO FINISHED GOODS AND RAW MATERIALS. GOODS ARE DISTRIBUTED BY CARTON, CONTAINER, PALLET, PIECE, AND VARIOUS OTHER UNITS OF MEASURE VIA ALL MODES OF MODERN TRANSPORTATION.

ocated just 15 minutes from downtown Memphis, Mid-South Community College (MSCC) is emerging as an integral player in the region's economic development. From basic literacy training for area residents to advanced skills development for the employees of large area companies, MSCC does whatever it takes to enrich the productivity and prosperity of eastern Arkansas, western Tennessee, and northern Mississippi. ▲ According to

Dr. Glen Fenter, president of the college, a two-pronged approach of helping people and helping industry is the key to the college's success. "To put it simply, we're based on the notion that education, economic development, and quality of life are all inextricably linked," Fenter says.

A History of Empowerment

MSCC is a two-year, public institution that has served Crittenden County, Arkansas, and surrounding counties since 1993. Although a young college, MSCC's founding marked the first local provision of higher education in a county that has been decades behind the more prosperous areas of the region in educational and economic development.

The college's pioneering spirit was immediately evident when MSCC began to set up alliances with both public schools and other institutions of higher education to increase college preparedness, as well as to provide local access to baccalaureate and graduate programs and professional training.

Today, the college offers five associate's degree programs, five one-year technical certificate programs, three certificate of proficiency programs, business and community education courses, developmental education, and adult education. Programs in business technology, information systems technology, general technology, child care, criminal justice, and practical nursing are available. The college employs some 30 full-time instructors and more than 70 full-time staff.

Credit enrollment has increased from approximately 100 students in the fall of 1993 to more than 1,200 in 2001. In addition, community and business education and adult education annually serve more than 2,000 students each.

And as needs grow, so does the college. MSCC has added many academic/technical programs in the past few years, including industrial technology, electricity/electronics, media broadcasting, A+ computer certification, Internet Webmaster certification, Cisco computer certification, and an associate's degree in nursing.

Further demonstrating its commitment to preparing tomorrow's workforce, MSCC supplements its diverse curriculum with an equally diverse approach to teaching. The college provides a variety of courses to county high schools during the school day, and delivers courses via the Internet and cable television to the students' homes.

Partnerships with four-year institutions include baccalaureate degrees in business, radiology, nursing, and education from Arkansas State University, and an on-line bachelor's degree in integrated studies from Emporia State University in Kansas. Graduate programs in education, business, nursing, and library science are available as well. The college's small classes average fewer than 20 students per class, and its flexible scheduling accommodates recent high school graduates through senior citizens.

Of further benefit to students is the recently completed, $12 million Donald W. Reynolds Center for Educational Excellence, which houses a library media center; a food service area; a bookstore; a state-of-the-art, multimedia conference room; and myriad other student support functions. The Reynolds center is also home to the innovative, high-tech Learning

MID-SOUTH COMMUNITY COLLEGE EMPLOYEES ENJOY WORKING WITH STUDENTS FROM THROUGHOUT THE MID-SOUTH. WHILE THE REGISTRATION PROCESS CAN SEEM COMPLICATED TO FIRST-TIMERS, IT GOES MORE SMOOTHLY THANKS TO WARM, FRIENDLY SMILES.

THE $12 MILLION DONALD W. REYNOLDS CENTER FOR EDUCATIONAL EXCELLENCE IS THE CENTERPIECE OF THE MSCC CAMPUS.

Success Center (LSC), which is designed to be the first-contact, one-stop center for providing information and assistance to MSCC students. The LSC includes such functions as student life facilities, one-on-one tutoring, advising, career counseling, study groups, and many more.

World-Class Transportation Training

The incredible diversity of opportunities for students at MSCC is impressive. But Fenter insists that the impact on students is just the beginning of the story. "We have an amazing opportunity in the Mid-South," he says. "We have the location, we have the transportation infrastructure, and we have the industry mix to emerge as one of the world's top distribution hubs. If we can offer an equally world-class workforce, there is no end to what we can accomplish."

To that end, MSCC opened a workforce development office to support an ongoing effort to train

current and potential employees for area businesses and industries. That same year, Richard Riley, U.S. Secretary of Education, acknowledged the progressive development programs at MSCC by holding a press conference on the college's campus.

In 1997, MSCC received $180,000 as part of a national grant from the U.S. Department of Education. Two years later, the college received more then $300,000 in Title III funds to boost student success and strengthen the educational and workforce resources of eastern Arkansas.

But the most notable of the college's workforce development initiatives has been its drive to establish the Transportation Technology Center at MSCC. A concept that would partner the college with area employers to offer state-of-the-art training for existing and prospective distribution and transportation employees, the center is already sparking intense interest.

At a Mississippi Delta Initiative conference in 1999, Fenter discussed

the idea of the Transportation Technology Center in a meeting with Rodney Slater, U.S. Secretary of Transportation. A month later, Fenter and two colleagues presented the plan to key administrative leaders at the White House. The final proposal was presented to national transportation officials at a December 1999 meeting at MSCC, with President Bill Clinton in attendance.

By April 2000, initial funding had begun to arrive in the form of a $500,000 grant from the State of Arkansas. Mid-South Community College educators are currently developing the curriculum in conjunction with leading national transportation companies with operations in the area, including FedEx and M.S. Carriers.

"There's no overestimating the power of education," Fenter says. "It can change a single person's outlook. It can change a family's future. It can supercharge a region's economy. Our mission is to help make these transformations possible."

A MSCC STUDENT TAKES A BREAK BETWEEN CLASSES TO USE ONE OF THE MANY RESOURCES AVAILABLE IN THE LIBRARY MEDIA CENTER (LEFT).

STUDENTS AT MSCC GATHER AROUND A MICROSCOPE TO COMPLETE AN ASSIGNMENT FOR A SCIENCE CLASS (RIGHT).

WHILE IMPRESSIVE DURING THE DAY, THE DONALD W. REYNOLDS CENTER FOR EDUCATIONAL EXCELLENCE IS EVEN MORE BREATHTAKING AT NIGHT.

1994

New Horizons Computer Learning Centers

Running Pony Productions

Baptist College of Health Sciences

Sam's Town Tunica

Compass Financial Advisors, LLC

Gold Strike Casino Resort

International Children's Heart Foundation

Borders Books

Bill Heard Chevrolet

Customized Staffing Services

Southwest Tennessee Community College

2001

One of the world's largest independent computer training companies has a strong presence right here in Memphis. Cited by FORTUNE *magazine as one of America's 100 fastest-growing companies, New Horizons Computer Learning Centers is a world leader in computer training. At 250 locations worldwide, the company offers training in software applications and technical certification to more than 2.4 million students each year. Its Memphis branch is*

CITED BY *Fortune* MAGAZINE AS ONE OF AMERICA'S 100 FASTEST-GROWING COMPANIES, NEW HORIZONS COMPUTER LEARNING CENTERS IS A WORLD LEADER IN COMPUTER TRAINING.

one of the biggest and most versatile in the region.

In 1994, David L. Weinstein, New Horizons president, started the Memphis operation with just four classrooms, as a franchise of the California-based venture. The location grew quickly, and in 1999, the parent company repurchased the Memphis franchise. Today, the Memphis operation is wholly owned by New Horizons. It has some 40 instructors, 23 classrooms, and four large conference rooms in the executive conference center on American Way, serving an average of 3,500 students monthly. It is one of the largest computer-training centers in the Mid-South, in terms of both space and students. And it is continually growing.

Phenomenal Growth, Phenomenal Service

One of the reasons behind this amazing growth is a strong focus on service. Most recently, New Horizons Computer Learning Centers named the Memphis operation the North American location of the year in medium markets (which includes those with fewer than 900,000 personal computers). The Memphis center also won a Novell Education 2000 performance award as the top Novell authorized education center (also in a medium market in North America), and Weinstein won the President's Cup award.

The dedication and diligence on the part of the course instructors is apparent. According to Weinstein, "They thrive on watching the lightbulb come on. They really care whether or not the students in their classes get it."

Shaping a New Workforce

With today's technology trends persistently emerging at breakneck speed, continuous training is a necessity. New Horizons attracts large volumes of business through its instructor-led courses, E-learning applications, customized course development, technical certification, and cutting-edge Internet training.

Many companies with a strong Memphis presence are recognizing the vast opportunities that open up when their employees are technologically savvy. Most students are sent to these training classes by their companies, since universities in general offer non-specific instruction, believing that different companies will train students in the specific technological practices of the industry.

For example, the Internet Professional program offers certifications in Internet commerce, enterprise development, server administration, and E-commerce, all of which provide the employee a more versatile, marketable set of skills. New Horizons is making an important contribution to the Memphis workforce—in fact, New Horizons services 75 percent of the Fortune 500 companies in the area. Such organizations include Federal Express, International Paper, and Marsh.

"Employers should invest in training—it really pays off," says Weinstein. "We serve a large and diverse audience—people changing careers, people who want to get promoted, people who need the training because the core aspects of their current jobs are changing. It's worth it to employers, because they get immediate results."

Something for Everyone

New Horizons prides itself on quality and convenience. High-demand job skills require the certification that New Horizons offers, and the trend in many large, successful companies is to outsource that training to experts like the ones at New Horizons.

STUDENTS GET TO CHOOSE FROM A VARIETY OF PACKAGES WITH FLEXIBLE TECHNICAL CLASSES, CLASSROOM TRAINING, WEB-BASED TRAINING, AND COMPUTER LAB OPTIONS THAT FIT THE SCHEDULE AND BUDGET— AND BEST MEET THE LEARNING NEEDS—OF EACH INDIVIDUAL STUDENT.

But, says Weinstein, New Horizons is more than just a training facility with seminars and classes. It's a technology center. Students get to choose from a variety of packages with flexible technical classes, classroom training, Web-based training, and computer lab options that fit the schedule and budget—and best meet the learning needs—of each individual student. There are qualified instructors, more courses throughout the day, and telephone assistance 24 hours a day, seven days a week. New Horizons also offers guaranteed results, allowing students to retake courses free of charge within six months. New Horizons Club Memberships enable companies and individuals to save money by offering packages that consist of a certain num-

ber of classes for a set fee. There's even an on-line exam preparation function that helps students practice for exams. Account executives help manage and guide each person's New Horizons experience in the most efficient way.

E-merging Trends

New Horizons is doing more Internet training than ever before. Of the some 3,500 students who train each month at the Memphis branch of New Horizons, 30 percent of them receive training in Internet skills.

The Internet program caters to three main groups of people: end users who need to use the Internet to research; Web creators and designers; and E-commerce and database professionals in

search of technical training. Advanced classes are in high demand, and one of the other big trends is that more and more individuals are seeking certification. Some of the top certification programs that New Horizons provides are Microsoft, Novell, CompTIA, Lotus, and Certified Internet Webmaster.

In addition, increasingly powerful software that can do more than anyone ever dreamed possible is driving students to application-based classes in droves. These desktop applications classes offer hands-on training for the latest versions of the most popular desktop applications used in the business world. New Horizons Computer Learning Centers is able to provide specific, targeted solutions for real-world challenges in business projects.

NEW HORIZONS HAS SOME 40 INSTRUCTORS, 23 CLASSROOMS, AND FOUR LARGE CONFERENCE ROOMS IN THE EXECUTIVE CONFERENCE CENTER ON AMERICAN WAY, SERVING AN AVERAGE OF 3,500 STUDENTS MONTHLY.

J onathan Epstein, Gary Blankenship, and Rod Starns are, in a sense, modern-day storytellers. In an age where consumers are bombarded by countless print and video images daily, the three owners of Running Pony Productions know that today's corporate and promotional videos need to be stronger than ever. And they should know. All three of them spent years in television news departments and, together, have 23 Emmy awards to their names.

Today, they use that skill to help businesses, advertising agencies, and nonprofit clients produce segments that stand out above the typical corporate video. "We've grown exponentially in our brief history, and we've done it without any significant advertising," says Epstein. "I think the market was really ready for a provider that understands that video projects need to change minds and accomplish goals to be successful. We just focus on creating pieces that produce powerful results, and the new clients track us down."

Storytelling for Today's Marketplace

F ounded in 1994, Running Pony provides a wide range of video production and media consulting services. Some clients tap the company for a single component of a project, while many more hire it to tackle an important project all the way from concept through completion. Among the services available from Running

ERIC THOMPSON SMOOTHLY CAPTURES MOVING FOOTAGE USING RUNNING PONY PRODUCTIONS' STEADICAM® SYSTEM.

FROM MEMPHIS TO THE WORLD: THE OWNERS AND STAFF OF RUNNING PONY PRODUCTIONS CREATE CORPORATE VIDEOS SEEN ACROSS THE GLOBE.

▼ LISA WADDELL BUSER

Pony are BetaCam videography, linear and nonlinear editing, location direction and production, video duplicating and archiving, aerial photography, multicamera filming, and mobile uplinks and downlinks via satellite. The company uses these skills and the journalism experience of its team to craft standout corporate and industrial videos, marketing and sales presentations, training and educational videos,

documentaries, infomercials, video news releases, television commercials, and interactive CDs and DVDs.

Running Pony's unique style and expertise have caught the eye of regional and national clients. The company shot a national TV special about Memphis barbecue hosted by NBC's Al Roker, and has completed additional assignments for ABC, A&E, VH1, MSNBC, CNN, the Food Network, and PBS' "Experience America." Additionally, the company provided videographers and video content for the major motion picture *Cast Away* during filming in the Memphis area.

▼ LISA WADDELL BUSER

Creative Solutions, Industry Accolades

B ut perhaps the biggest beneficiaries of Running Pony's skills are the regional and national businesses who use the company's storytelling skills for important communications projects. Running Pony, for example, shot and produced a time-lapse video of the construction of AutoZone Park, and was hired as broadcast/video consultant by the Memphis Redbirds to install and operate the closed-circuit television system in the ballpark.

The company completed a similar time-lapse video of the construction of Belz Enterprises' Peabody Place, and

was nominated for regional Emmy awards for videos on the Regional Medical Center at Memphis' Newborn Center and the AutoZone Park time-lapse project.

Running Pony has won national Telly awards for videos produced for the Hilton Hotel Corporation, Baptist Memorial Health Care Corporation, Special Olympics, Porter-Leath Children's Center, Main Street Hardy (Arkansas), and the Memphis Redbirds. The Baptist Memorial video also took home a national Bronze Anvil award from the Public Relations Society of America.

The firm's long list of repeat clients includes the Memphis Convention and Visitors Bureau, St. Jude Children's Research Hospital, FedEx, U.S. Navy, Memphis Area Chamber of Commerce, Memphis Rock 'n' Soul Museum, and many more.

Ready for the Digital Age

Advanced technology is an important part of the Running Pony equation. "We've purchased some advanced, new digital editing and compression tools and a SteadiCam® camera stabilization rig," Blankenship says. "Having access to the latest technology is important to helping clients maintain a cutting-edge image."

Acquisitions in 2000 also included an additional Sony BetaCam, two Sony digital cameras, and second and third Avid nonlinear digital editing suites. The company has also branched into streaming digital video and web-casts, and hired several new employees, including a digital video and new media specialist to further enhance its capabilities.

Running Pony's investments in digital-age equipment and expertise are paying off. The company, for example, was called on by Elvis Presley Enterprises to produce a webcast seen around the world. Running Pony provided four cameras, on-camera talent, and a technical crew to produce a two-hour live "Vigilcast" of the annual Candlelight Vigil at Graceland, which commemorates the death of entertainer Elvis Presley. Video of the event was uplinked by satellite for distribution across the Web, and was used by television stations and networks across the globe. Viewers from Europe, South America, and Asia responded with more than 2,000 E-mails during the Vigilcast.

"In spite of the big part technology plays at Running Pony, there's no element that is more important than our dedication to compelling, persuasive work," Starns says. "Customers decide to take on video projects because they need a piece that's more powerful than any brochure could be. That's what we deliver, and that's why so many come back time after time."

CLOCKWISE FROM TOP:
RUNNING PONY'S PARTNERS (FROM LEFT) ROD STARNS, JONATHAN EPSTEIN, AND GARY BLANKENSHIP COMBINE THEIR EMMY AWARD-WINNING SKILLS ON EACH VIDEO.

ON LOCATION, THE RUNNING PONY TEAM SHOOTS AN INTERACTIVE MARKETING VIDEO AND DVD.

THE LATEST DIGITAL EQUIPMENT PUTS AN ARRAY OF VIDEO TECHNOLOGY IN THE HANDS OF WRITER/PRODUCER T. LEIGH STARNS.

BLANKENSHIP, FORMER UPI NATIONAL PHOTOGRAPHER OF THE YEAR, FOCUSES ON CAPTURING THE BEST SIGHTS AND SOUNDS TO DELIVER A MEMORABLE MESSAGE.

*M*emphis' role as a national health care center means that patients from all over the world travel to the city for treatment expertise. The city's skilled providers and advanced facilities are also making Memphis a center for health care training. And nowhere is that more clear than at Baptist College of Health Sciences. The intimate and specialized college delivers advanced postsecondary training to passionate students from all over the country.

Baptist College of Health Sciences' students are trained in baccalaureate programs that lead to a bachelor of science degree in nursing or a bachelor of health sciences degree in nuclear medicine technology, medical radiography, radiation therapy, diagnostic medical sonography, health care management, or respiratory care. Small, rigorous, and values-based, the college is preparing health care professionals for careers in advanced, community-focused care for the 21st century.

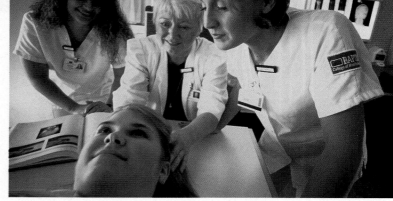

Tradition of Exceptional Training

Education has been a key component in the mission of Baptist Memorial Hospital, Baptist College of Health Sciences' parent organization, since its beginning in 1912. In fact, the hospital opened Baptist Memorial Hospital School of Nursing during the hospital's first year of operation. For more than 75 years, the school offered a nationally recognized diploma in nursing, and its graduates are in a variety of practice and leadership roles throughout the United States and abroad.

Allied health education at Baptist Memorial Hospital began in 1956 with the radiography program. In response to the need for advanced specialization, the nuclear medicine program was added in 1961, the radiation therapy program in 1975, and the diagnostic medical sonography program in 1986. Graduates of these radiology schools are employed in a variety of settings, including specialized areas such as angiography and mammography.

As health sciences continued to become more complex and Baptist emerged as a national leader in a variety of fields, allied health administrators began to design a plan that would enhance the level of education available to students. In 1994, Baptist College of Health Sciences was chartered as a specialized college offering baccalaureate degrees in nursing and health sciences. The college is accredited by the Commission on Colleges of the Southern Association of Colleges and Schools.

"Not many health sciences institutions offer such advanced degrees, but we think it's important to be on par with the level of excellence being practiced all over the city," says Dr. Rose Temple, president of Baptist College of Health Sciences.

Today, students are given what the college calls "higher education with a higher purpose." Focused on offering an exceptional health care education set within a Christian environment, Baptist College of Health Sciences furthers its mission with vast clinical resources, a commitment to critical thinking, high standards of academic excellence, and a focus on lifelong learning.

"Our students are independent thinkers and self-reliant learners who are given assignments that require a high level of self-direction and responsibility," Temple says. "We pride ourselves on graduating articulate health care leaders who value lifelong learning, and are dedicated to healing and restoring lives spiritually, physically, and emotionally within their communities."

Advanced Facilities

Another important piece of the equation is the advanced Baptist College of Health Sciences campus. The primary facility is a 110,000-square-foot center that houses both educational facilities and

AT BAPTIST COLLEGE OF HEALTH SCIENCES, STUDENTS CAN EARN A FOUR-YEAR BACCALAUREATE DEGREE AS A BASIC OR COMPLETION STUDENT MAJORING IN NURSING, RESPIRATORY CARE, OR RADIOLOGICAL SCIENCES. AS PART OF THE BAPTIST MEMORIAL HEALTH CARE SYSTEM, STUDENTS BENEFIT FROM A WEALTH OF CLINICAL RESOURCES AND FACULTY MEMBERS WHO ARE LEADERS IN THEIR FIELDS.

trics, ambulatory care, home health care, and rehabilitation.

Diverse and Nurturing

With an intimate student body of some 500 students, Baptist College of Health Sciences achieves its academic success in part through its 10-to-1 clinical ratio and an average class size of 20. Students come from a variety of races, faiths, and backgrounds. In addition to encouraging academic excellence, this environment also fosters strong interpersonal relationships and ensures that students get individualized attention.

Baptist College of Health Sciences encourages its students' further personal development through community activity. During the 1996-1997 academic year, the college entered into a partnership with the Department of Housing and Urban Development and the City of Memphis to open the HOPE Health Center for the Homeless. The purpose of the center is to address the immediate, nonemergency needs of the homeless, particularly women and children, with the emphasis on health promotion and disease prevention through primary care. The center, which has a full-time staff, also provides an opportunity for interdisciplinary education for students.

For students who want to make a difference in the lives of others, there are few stronger options than Baptist College of Health Sciences. "We offer the best of both worlds," Temple says. "We deliver the advantages of our small size combined with the clinical breadth and depth provided by the renowned Baptist Memorial Health Care system."

THE EDUCATION STUDENTS RECEIVE AT BAPTIST COLLEGE IS HIGHLY PERSONALIZED, AND CLASS SIZES ARE KEPT SMALL, PROVIDING AMPLE OPPORTUNITY FOR INDIVIDUALIZED ATTENTION UNDER THE GUIDANCE OF CARING, COMMITTED PROFESSIONALS.

residence quarters. The center includes classrooms and conference rooms; an auditorium with seating for 250; a nursing skills laboratory; a computer and Internet center; a dormitory with private and semiprivate rooms; and a gymnasium, racquetball court, and swimming pool.

The college's science laboratories are about one block from the main facility. The use of these laboratories allows students to perfect their skills in basic sciences prior to beginning major courses.

A critical component of the college's offering is the vast, double-branch Health Sciences Library. The Health Sciences Library provides services and resources to support the information and education needs of Baptist College of Health Sciences' faculty and students, as well as of the physicians, nurses, and professional staff of Baptist Memorial Hospital.

Baptist College of Health Sciences offers access to exceptional clinical facilities as well. As part of the larger Baptist Memorial Health Care Corporation, the college allows its students access to a wide range of clinical sites and experiences throughout the region. Within the nationally known Memphis medical community are clinical facilities that provide a rich learning environment for students in acute care, neonatal care and pedia-

AT BAPTIST COLLEGE, THE PATIENTS ALWAYS COME FIRST. AND THAT MAKES EVERYONE—FACULTY, STUDENTS, AND HEALTH CARE PROFESSIONALS—A PART OF THE HEALING PROCESS.

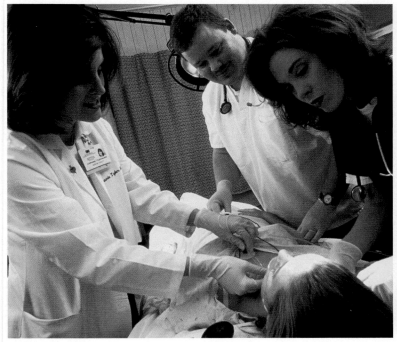

*W*hen Sam's Town Tunica opened its doors on May 25, 1994, the resort heralded a new era in Tunica, Mississippi, just south of Memphis. Sam's Town offered the market's first hotel and casino combination, and immediately set a high standard. Modeled on the Sam's Town property in Las Vegas, Sam's Town Tunica was developed by Las Vegas-based Boyd Gaming, a leader in multifaceted entertainment destinations. ▲ *That expertise*

was clear in Tunica from the beginning. "In Tunica, Sam's Town was more than the first casino with a hotel," says Bill Boyd, chairman of the board for Boyd Gaming and the son of the company's founder. "We brought a philosophy to town that changed the way people saw casinos, and they're still trying to catch up."

The Boyd philosophy calls for a diverse entertainment mix that combines exceptional gaming opportunities with the best restaurants, bars, hotel accommodations, and entertainment.

Something for Everyone

To see the something-for-everyone approach in action, a visitor simply has to step through the front door at Sam's Town. A soaring atrium leads into a massive, two-story casino. With 65 table games—including a room devoted exclusively to live poker, 1,500 slots, and the only live Keno in Tunica—the casino is one of the most fast-paced and exciting around. Sam's Town offers the latest slot machines, including Elvis slots, the popular x-factor games, multidenomi-national games, and "ticket in/ticket out" coinless games.

But what keeps people coming back to Sam's Town is the variety of diverse entertainment options available at the property. And thanks to an additional $21 million renovation in 2001, the facility outshines the competition with more than 1 million square feet of amenities. "That's 90 percent of the property devoted to nongaming entertainment," Boyd says. "That's what makes the Sam's Town experience so exciting and so noticeably different."

In the arena of live entertainment, Sam's Town Tunica shows its commitment with free, live music and dancing at Roxy's Live! The jewel of the Sam's Town entertainment crown, though, is the 1,600-seat River Palace Entertainment Center. The venue attracts the best acts in the industry, including Wayne Newton, LeAnn Rimes, Joan Rivers, Patti LaBelle, Gladys Knight, Bill Cosby, and George Carlin.

Another big draw to Sam's Town is the resort's spectacular dining variety. Twain's offers casual fine dining with a contemporary mix of new and exciting menu items, as well as prime steaks, fresh seafood, and delicate pastas. Twain's inviting bar, two fire-places, private dining room, extra-large wine list, and old-world ambience all contribute to the restaurant's unprecedented appeal.

For heartier appetites, Sam's Town offers the eye-popping Great Buffet. Offering everything imaginable—from Asian delights to Mexican specialties to the fresh seafood that has made Sam's Town dining famous—the Great Buffet is a feast for the palate. It is a feast for the eyes as well, with outstanding artwork, a wall of fire, and a bubbling brook and fountain. Sam's Town also offers world-famous Corky's Memphis barbecue in the country's only Corky's BBQ Buffet.

The list goes on and on. From its 854 luxurious guestrooms to a sparkling swimming pool to 30,000 square feet of banquet space to the adjacent River Bend Links championship golf course, the list of attractions at Sam's Town makes it a first choice for entertainment.

The Best Team in Town

One of 11 Boyd Gaming casinos nationwide, Sam's Town Tunica employs some 1,700 area residents. The area was severely underdeveloped economically before casino gaming arrived in the early

OPENING IN 1994, SAM'S TOWN TUNICA IMMEDIATELY SET THE STANDARD FOR ENTERTAINMENT IN TUNICA.

1990s, and companies like Sam's Town have played a big role in injecting new vitality into the area.

"These are some of the best employees in the country," Boyd says. "Our terrific team is a big part of our ability to offer the best gaming experience in the area." Sam's Town offers a fun and diverse workplace, and employees are encouraged to be proactive when it comes to serving guests. Sam's Town and Boyd Gaming see themselves as an integral part of the community that provides its team members, and the company strives to return the favor.

Sam's Town is a regional leader in community development. The company has contributed more than $150,000 to the area Make-A-Wish Foundation, more than $5,000 to the Blues Foundation, and $50,000 to the Memphis in May festival. The Sam's Town team pulls together to surpass United Way goals every year, and employees have contributed almost $500,000 to the cause.

Sam's Town Tunica has built a Habitat for Humanity house for a

needy family in Tunica, and has provided for a new primary and emergency care clinic in the area. The company works with the area literacy council, hosts a free holiday carnival for its employees' children, and even helped a nearby town buy a fire engine. Boyd has also helped to launch a 10-week operations internship for

University of Mississippi students majoring in accounting, business, or hospitality management.

"We've enjoyed our top spot in the Memphis market, and are thankful to the patrons and team members that make it possible," Boyd says. "It's a relationship we look forward to building on."

SAM'S TOWN IS NOT SIMPLY A CASINO— THE ENTERTAINMENT DESTINATION IS A DIVERSE MIX OF GAMING OPPORTUNITIES COMBINED WITH EXCEPTIONAL BARS, RESTAURANTS, HOTEL ACCOMMODATIONS, AND ENTERTAINMENT.

hen clients walk through the doors of Compass Financial Advisors, LLC, they will hear both southern drawl and Parisian French. They will also see stock prices flashing across computer screens, portfolio analyses coming out of the printer, and insurance quotes spread across desktops. With the flurry of activity happening in one central location, clients might think they are in a huge New York office. But they're not. They're in a small,

independent financial consulting firm in Memphis.

Multiple Services, One Independent Firm

A Memphis success story since its inception in 1994, Compass Financial Advisors today focuses on five major categories of financial consulting: retirement plans, executive compensation planning, group health and welfare benefits, business continuation planning, and wealth planning for high-net-worth individuals and families.

This diversity of function and talent is what makes Compass so unique. According to Tom Wallace Sr., founder and senior partner, insurance/benefit planning and investments go hand in hand. "The same amount of planning, attention to detail, and client communications is necessary in both divisions of our company," explains Wallace.

And with Wallace's more than 30 years of experience in the insurance field and 15 years in investments, many of his clients hire the firm for their companies' benefits needs, as well as for their personal investment planning.

Clients also enjoy the fact that, as an independent firm, Compass does not sell its own insurance or investment vehicles, and therefore gives unbiased advice. "Because of our independence, we choose only the best products and services for our clients, based on their personal needs—not on our own financial interests," Wallace explains. "That is one reason our firm continues to thrive among larger financial companies."

Insurance and Benefit Planning

Compass works with corporations, institutions, and high-net-worth individuals in its insurance and benefit planning division. For private and publicly traded corporations, the company seeks out and compares the very best in group hospitalization and major medical benefits, life insurance, disability, and long-term care products. Compass complements a company's core fringe benefits program with a complete line of voluntary products.

Each year, before a client's contract with an insurance provider comes up for renewal, the Compass team evaluates the plan and compares it on a cost/benefits analysis to those of other insurance providers. "This keeps insurance companies on their toes, because they know that we act as watchdogs for our clients, and that our loyalty is to our clients and not to them," Wallace explains. He adds that clients enjoy the fact that they can call the experienced service team of Compass to eliminate insurance claim problems.

Compass also designs 401(k) and 403(b) plans, equity-based compensation plans, and supplemental executive retirement plans (SERPs). The firm offers expertise in designing business continuation plans to ensure the continuation of a privately held company.

▼ JAY ADKINS

FOUNDED BY TOM WALLACE SR., COMPASS FINANCIAL ADVISORS, LLC IS A MEMPHIS SUCCESS STORY, TODAY FOCUSING ON FIVE MAJOR CATEGORIES OF FINANCIAL CONSULTING: RETIREMENT PLANS, EXECUTIVE COMPENSATION PLANNING, GROUP HEALTH AND WELFARE BENEFITS, BUSINESS CONTINUATION PLANNING, AND WEALTH PLANNING FOR HIGH-NET-WORTH INDIVIDUALS AND FAMILIES.

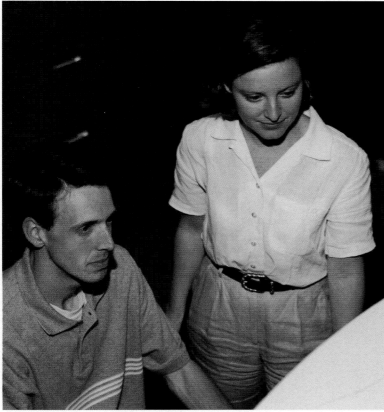

"We treat each client as though he or she were our only client," explains Wallace. "We discuss with all of our clients what their goals are, how they define risk, and what special circumstances they are in. Then we develop well-researched, highly detailed plans that are built around their unique situations."

With this information in mind, Compass helps clients develop investment strategies that take into account their tax situations, wealth transfer planning, corporate responsibilities, and other factors. Regardless of the situation, Wallace insists, the most important aspect of protecting and growing wealth is laying out a solid, personalized plan and aggressively implementing it.

Big-Company Results, Small-Company Care

It is undeniable, today, that there is a myriad of financial services offered both at larger financial companies and through on-line brokerages. Yet, Compass continues to grow because the firm provides the kind of personalized, unbiased expertise and service that other companies can't offer.

The firm's balance sheet is healthy, but Wallace offers his own litmus test for how well Compass is doing: "There is only one bar we use to measure our success: the client's original goal. If we have performed well, but have not met the objectives originally presented to us by the client, we haven't done our job."

And it is this uncompromising commitment to excellence that has earned Compass Financial Advisors, LLC every dollar, franc, and euro that the company manages.

THE KEY TO COMPASS' SUCCESS IS PERSONALIZED PLANNING AND SERVICE. YET THE DIVERSITY OF TALENT AND FUNCTION IS WHAT MAKES THE COMPANY UNIQUE.

COMPASS WORKS WITH CORPORATIONS, INSTITUTIONS, AND HIGH-NET-WORTH INDIVIDUALS IN ITS INSURANCE AND BENEFIT PLANNING DIVISION. FOR PRIVATE AND PUBLICLY TRADED CORPORATIONS, THE COMPANY SEEKS OUT AND COMPARES THE VERY BEST IN GROUP HOSPITALIZATION AND MAJOR MEDICAL BENEFITS, LIFE INSURANCE, DISABILITY, AND LONG-TERM CARE PRODUCTS.

For high-net-worth individuals, Compass also offers general wealth planning and wealth transfer planning. In addition to the risks posed to family wealth by taxes and probate costs, high-wealth individuals face other concerns. "Many parents today, for example, want their children to work, regardless of their financial situations," Wallace explains. "We've helped clients develop incentive trusts that pay heirs contingent on their earned incomes."

Investment Consulting

With high-net-worth clients worldwide and with greater than $450 million to manage, Compass' investment consulting division is thriving. "We now advise a number of European clients, and have expanded our staff to include French, Spanish, and German-speaking professionals," Wallace says.

The key to Compass' success is personalized planning and service.

hen casino gaming hit the Mid-South, many area residents and tourists alike wondered how the new Tunica-area casinos would stack up with the great gaming resorts of the world. When the Gold Strike Casino Resort opened in 1998, gamers' doubts were put to rest. An elegant casino and hotel with luxurious Las Vegas-style amenities, Gold Strike offers visitors an experience every bit as exciting as its counterparts in Las Vegas and Atlantic City.

"Unlike casinos that try to capitalize on the popularity of gaming without making a real investment in the property, we have gone to extraordinary lengths to build and operate a resort property that spares no expense and overlooks no detail," says Clyde Callicott, director of marketing. "For us, there's no other way to guarantee the visitor will have a truly memorable experience."

Attention to Detail

Long before visitors reach the casino, hints of the majesty that awaits them can be seen. The 317-foot-tall, golden hotel tower is one of the tallest buildings in Mississippi and is visible from miles away. The 31-story structure holds more than 1,200 oversized luxury rooms, including 100 regular suites, 20 deluxe suites that are 1,500 square feet each, three business suites, and two 2,000-square-foot suites. Many of the elegant suites offer picturesque views of the Mississippi River.

Featured amenities include the Golden Reflections Spa, which offers an indoor, heated pool, complete with rock formations; Jacuzzis; a health spa; a workout room with a vast array of state-of-the-art exercise equipment; massage therapists; and tanning beds. Other guest facilities include 24-hour room service, complimentary valet service, and a business center. Easy access to the attached casino, dining, entertainment complex, and 900-seat Millennium Theatre is provided.

Other details that enhance the plentiful amenities and make an overnight stay at Gold Strike a pleasurable experience are features such as the beautiful architecture and finishing touches on the building itself. There are rock formations around the pool, exquisite waterfalls, beautiful crystal chandeliers, grand marble floors, and large-screen televisions with cable access. There are also dataports in each room, individual climate control, butler service, wet bars and kitchenettes, a video arcade for guests ages 21 and under, gorgeous flower and greenery arrangements, a complete retail store, covered parking, and, of course, gold, gold, gold—everywhere.

No visit to Gold Strike Casino Resort would be complete without sampling its epicurean selections. The Chicago Steakhouse serves a hearty, classic cuisine of steaks grilled to perfection, chops, and fresh fish. The restaurant has a full bar and wine cellar, as well as a mahogany-paneled dining room. The Courtyard Buffet is European inspired, and features breakfast, lunch, and dinner. The culinary display is

AN ELEGANT CASINO AND HOTEL WITH LUXURIOUS LAS VEGAS-STYLE AMENITIES, GOLD STRIKE CASINO RESORT OFFERS VISITORS AN EXPERIENCE EVERY BIT AS EXCITING AS ITS COUNTERPARTS IN LAS VEGAS AND ATLANTIC CITY.

open-air and casual, and offers a taste of everything. The Atrium Café serves home-style meals that taste like they came right out of Mama's oven. The Food Court provides a number of classic favorites: McDonald's, Front Street Pizza, and the Gold Strike Side Street Deli, as well as a coffee bar.

Convention and banquet facilities can accommodate up to 1,200 people. Large business groups and social events have more than 30,000 square feet of flexible and functional meeting space available to them, with a 10,000-square-foot grand ballroom and four smaller meeting rooms ranging from 500 to 1,200 square feet. Each space can be outfitted with the latest audiovisual equipment, and a large prefunction area is ideal for receptions and registrations. A world-class banquet staff assures delicious food upon request.

Gold Strike's amazing attention to detail makes guests feel like they are living in splendor. Yet none of it would matter without good customer service, which is what Gold Strike Casino Resort values above all else. The company's employees and executive staff are committed to the complete and total satisfaction of each individual guest. From weekend getaways to family reunions, business conferences and conventions, or just a simple night out on the town, Gold Strike Casino Resort's goal is to ensure a successful, pleasurable experience by taking care of all of the details.

Vegas-Style Excitement

Gold Strike Casino Resort delivers a high level of "24k excitement" 24 hours a day. The company provides a true Vegas-style experience and is setting a standard of excellence for Tunica casinos. Over and above the plush, elaborate setting one would only expect to find in Las Vegas, Gold Strike Casino Resort features a complete selection of gaming opportunities. There are 1,457 reel and video slot machines, a poker room, and 50 table games, including blackjack, three-card poker, roulette, Caribbean Stud, craps, and Let it Ride—all housed in more than 50,000 square feet of elegantly designed gaming space.

Since Las Vegas is known for its exciting, headline entertainment, Gold Strike Casino Resort brought it to Tunica with its luxurious, 900-seat Millennium Theatre. The theater has featured performances by Don Rickles, Tony Bennett, Engelbert Humperdinck, Willie Nelson, Howie Mandel, and the Moody Blues.

Personal service, professional attitude, and a polished, plush environment—all of these features combine to make Gold Strike Casino Resort a winner with those in the Memphis area and beyond.

ongenital heart disease occurs in roughly one in 100 children. In the United States, where birthrates are low, it's not unlikely that doctors will see 100 incidents per 1 million people in the general population. But the statistics don't bode so well for families in underdeveloped countries. ▲ "In places like Peru, the birthrate is almost double, which means close to 200 incidents of heart disease per million in the population," says Dr. William Novick,

founder and medical director of Memphis-based International Children's Heart Foundation (ICHF). "In Yugoslavia, 400 to 600 children need heart surgeries each year, and these are the countries least equipped to handle it."

Since the early 1990s, Novick and a growing team of volunteers have been working to do something about this need for heart surgeries, and the results have been nothing short of miraculous. Today, ICHF sends teams all over the world to perform free heart surgery on needy children. Led by Novick, a pediatric heart surgeon, the missions help almost 300 children per year. In all, ICHF has made more than 50 trips to 13 countries, and has completed more than 1,200 operations and more than 10,000 diagnoses.

SINCE THE EARLY 1990S, DR. WILLIAM NOVICK AND A GROWING TEAM OF VOLUNTEERS HAVE DEDICATED THEIR ENERGIES TO HELPING SAVE THE LIVES OF CHILDREN IN NEED OF HEART SURGERIES IN UNDERDEVELOPED COUNTRIES AROUND THE WORLD.

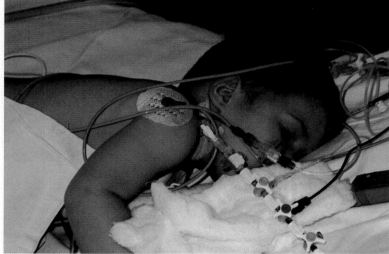

The organization is equally dedicated to training and educating local health care professionals in the visited countries. ICHF gives on-site instruction, and even brings many of these professionals to the United States for advanced study so that they may better serve children in their own countries.

"Saving needy children is our short-term goal," says Novick. "Empowering doctors in these countries to save their own children is our long-term goal. I always say our mission is to make ourselves obsolete in the countries that we serve."

One Heart at a Time

Each ICHF mission lasts about two weeks and entails countless hours of preparation. Volunteers from all over the world and the small ICHF staff work long hours to solicit as many medical supplies as they can.

Dozens of volunteers prepare the equipment and materials that will be used during surgery while the team travels and works abroad. The home team prepares data on children and traveling team members, and develops a package of equipment that must be shipped weeks ahead of time to ensure that the equipment arrives.

This hard work is paying off. In the former Soviet Union, for example, ICHF has been helping children since 1996. On its first trip to Minsk, the team performed operations on 33 children. In addition, ICHF made provisions for two physicians from the First Children's Hospital of Minsk to spend six months in Memphis studying pediatric heart disease and surgery techniques. In 1998, the ICHF team returned to a slightly upgraded hospital, where they currently operate on 150 children each year. ICHF is planning another trip to Minsk in the near future.

The ICHF program for the children of Bosnia began in 1995, when the first young patient was referred for surgery in Memphis. Since then, ICHF has made two trips to Sarajevo and provided operations for 43 Bosnian children. During the initial trip to Sarajevo, the team provided the first pediatric cardiac surgery in the history of the country.

ICHF's first team trip to Croatia occurred in April 1993 and provided 14 lifesaving pediatric cardiac surgical operations. Since the inception of these programs for the children of Croatia with heart disease, ICHF has made 22 trips to Zagreb to provide

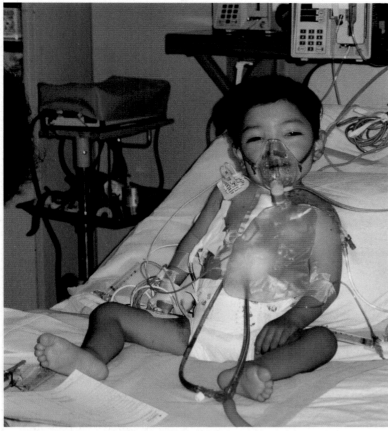

operations, education, upgraded medical hardware, and disposable equipment. The program has provided operations in Zagreb to more than 400 children, and has brought 36 Croatian children to Memphis for surgery since March 1994. In addition, the organization has provided grants for medical training for four Croatian physicians to study at Le Bonheur Children's Medical Center in Memphis.

The list goes on and on. In Ukraine, 55 surgeries were performed and 11 physicians and nurses have been brought to Memphis for training. And in Kazakhstan, 70 children received surgery and eight physicians and nurses were brought to Memphis for training.

So Many Needs

The volunteers and donors are making miracles happen," Novick says. "But we're hardly scratching the service. For example, we've helped 41 children in China so far, where 175,000 kids need surgery."

To help more and more children, ICHF is working harder than ever to secure the funding and equipment needed to help. In spite of the free services provided by physicians and the many donated products, the trips abroad are costly as well, depending on the size of the team and the destination. A typical trip to South or Central America with a 16-member team costs around $35,000. The same trip to China costs some $75,000.

ICHF is also working to renovate the Variety Children's Charity of Memphis Heart House. When completed, the Heart House will serve as a center for visiting health care professionals from all over the world. The facility will provide housing for visiting physicians and nurses, serve as an educational resource center, house a clinical research center, house parents with children in intensive care at Le Bonheur Children's Medical Center, and serve as the worldwide headquarters of the International Children's Heart Foundation.

"If folks send money, I promise to use it all," Novick says with a determined smile. "And if they send supplies, I promise to use them up. We still have a long way to go."

TODAY, ICHF SENDS TEAMS ALL OVER THE WORLD TO PERFORM FREE HEART SURGERY ON NEEDY CHILDREN. IN ALL, ICHF HAS MADE MORE THAN 50 TRIPS TO 13 COUNTRIES, AND HAS COMPLETED MORE THAN 1,200 OPERATIONS AND MORE THAN 10,000 DIAGNOSES.

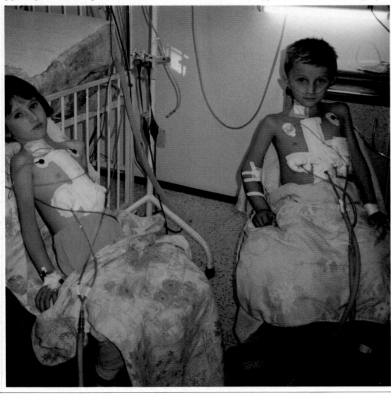

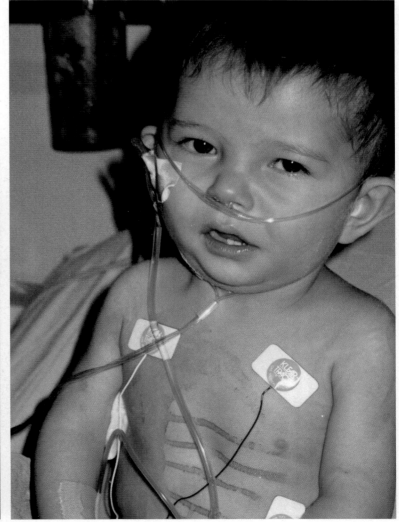

W hen it opened its doors in Germantown in 1995, Borders Books brought a new kind of bookstore to the Memphis area. Nestled on the shady corner of Poplar and Kirby Parkway in the Carrefour Center, the 30,000-square-foot store offers books and music, and complements its massive collection with a staff of knowledgeable and helpful employees. ▲ As a result, the team at Borders' Memphis store helps customers by

directing them to the materials they came in for, making recommendations to browsers, offering special services like computer searches and orders, and even hosting weekly events and readings that celebrate literature and culture.

Serious Service for Serious Readers

B orders began in 1971, when Tom and Louis Borders opened a "serious" bookshop in the heart of Ann Arbor, an academic community in southeast Michigan. The store grew and was soon known regionally as an exceptional bookstore where customers could always rely on a friendly, well-informed staff to find exactly what

they were looking for. The store also had a reputation as a great place for browsing a vast selection of popular and eclectic titles.

The Ann Arbor store was so successful that the Borders brothers decided to open more stores. They focused on suburban markets, where demand for their brand of "serious" bookstores seemed unfilled. Throughout the 1980s, Borders stores opened with great success in markets across the country.

In the early 1990s, Borders began selling music in addition to books. The formula only improved Borders' success, and the company was a national powerhouse in no time. The formula was so successful, in fact, that other

large book chains began to emulate the Borders concept.

Industry observers note that several companies began to open Borders-style book and music superstores at a furious pace, and the market is still expanding rapidly. Since 1991, national bookstore sales have grown from $7.8 billion to more than $10 billion. In 1997, Borders opened its first overseas location in Singapore. In 1998, the company opened three stores in the United Kingdom and one in Australia.

Today, Borders is one of the nation's leading book and music retailers. With more than 300 stores worldwide, Borders Group, Inc., the bookstore's parent company, is now an independent, publicly owned corporation.

A Part of the Memphis Community

I n Memphis, Borders lives up to its national reputation for serving readers with a vast selection and exceptional service. With more than 200,000 book, video, and music titles, the store also stocks more than 2,000 periodicals in 10 different languages from 15 countries. Borders' knowledgeable employees can help customers find the titles they're looking for, and an in-store coffeehouse provides a quiet place to enjoy the purchase.

The Germantown store hosts numerous readings by local and national authors each month, and has a number of weekly programs for readers of all tastes. On Wednesdays and Saturdays at 11:00 a.m., for example, the store hosts a story time for children. And most Friday and Saturday nights at 8:00, musicians perform. A monthly newsletter offers event schedules and reviews of notable titles.

It's no surprise that Borders has proven so successful. The store's attentive eye to the needs and tastes of serious customers will likely continue to fuel growth and success for Borders Books.

NESTLED ON THE SHADY CORNER OF POPLAR AND KIRBY PARKWAY IN THE CARREFOUR CENTER, THE 30,000-SQUARE-FOOT BORDERS BOOKS OFFERS BOOKS AND MUSIC, AND COMPLEMENTS ITS MASSIVE COLLECTION WITH A STAFF OF KNOWLEDGEABLE AND HELPFUL EMPLOYEES.

I like people and I like challenges," Dean Sykes says with a determined smile. "That makes me a perfect fit for the staffing business." Sykes, CEO of Memphis-based Customized Staffing Services, has turned her passion for people and problem solving into one of the city's foremost staffing services. The company has grown remarkably since its founding, and now provides temporary employees, temp-to-perm employees, outsourced

project personnel, and even long-term outsourced workforces with on-site management.

With seven offices in three states, Customized Staffing Services is proving that a commitment to customer service and to doing the job right keeps customers coming back.

Staffing for the New Economy

Today's positions are more demanding and the labor market is tight. Employers are experiencing increasing difficulty when trying to find honest, hard-working, well-trained, dependable employees. So in 1998, Sykes and partner Devorner Tate set out to meet that need with a new staffing company. "There were lots of competitors in the market, but we knew an emphasis on training the employees and serving the customers would pay off," Sykes recalls.

Sykes was right. Her focus on service has made her an indispensable partner for some of the nation's most notable employers. In discussions with clients, Sykes saw that every client was different and that each needed a custom solution. "While we're always glad to provide a temp when a company has an employee out, our real business has become human resources consulting," Sykes says. "We help companies map out ways to save money on staffing, improve performance, and eliminate a lot of the liability and headaches."

Today, Customized Staffing Services solves client problems with employee solutions that may include seasonal workers, project workers, or temp-to-hire workers. The company even offers employee outsourcing—a solution that allows an outside partner to take over payroll, benefits, workers' compensation, and human resources functions for a streamlining employer.

"As our economy becomes more

fast paced and global, companies need to stay flexible in order to compete," Sykes says. "More and more are turning to us for help."

Building on a Good Name

Sykes' colleagues agree that it is her reputation in the industry for honesty, flexibility, and a strong belief in thorough training that has made the company become so strong in such a short time. This reputation has made Sykes' company a popular choice for the most progressive employers, as well as with area employees.

The formula has led to impressive growth. In 1998, Customized Staffing Services had one office. Today, it has seven: two in Memphis, one in Mississippi, two in Chicago, one in Arkansas, and one in Nashville. Customized Staffing Services employs more than 40 people and sends out more than 500 temps each week.

All of the company's offices are busy, and it is not hard to see why. As long as Customized Staffing Services continues to deliver top-notch, well-trained employees as part of a flexible package, the demand is sure to increase.

DEAN SYKES, CEO OF MEMPHIS-BASED CUSTOMIZED STAFFING SERVICES, HAS TURNED HER PASSION FOR PEOPLE AND PROBLEM SOLVING INTO ONE OF THE CITY'S FOREMOST STAFFING SERVICES.

I n March 2000, the first customer stepped onto the lot at Bill Heard Chevrolet in Collierville. Fifty-one days later, the dealership was named the number-one-volume Chevrolet dealer in the Memphis area. The immediate success was no surprise to management at the dealership. ▲ "Cars are usually the second-biggest investment people make, following a home," says Rick McLey, general manager. "They'll drive

extra distance for service and savings. People know that Bill Heard dealerships stand for overwhelming service and savings, and it took no time for them to find where we were."

Built to Serve

The dealership's parent company—Columbus, Georgia-based Bill Heard Enterprises—opened its first dealership in the Memphis area in 1997. As the company's reputation for exceptional prices and personalized service spread, the dealership began to outgrow the location.

Meanwhile, development in the southeast region of the Memphis area continued to grow. A move to Collierville was soon in the works. Construction began on a state-of-the-art dealership, and the facility opened in 2000 with hundreds of cars, an in-house body shop, an

advanced service center, one of the biggest on-site parts warehouses in the city, and a massive yet comfortable customer showroom.

Every inch of the new facility is designed to serve customers better. And service is the core principle

of Bill Heard Chevrolet. "We're confident we beat everybody on price. Our volume gives us the power to guarantee that," McLey says. "But we're one of the few dealerships nationwide that can combine that exceptional price with great personalized service. We go to extraordinary lengths to make sure every customer is satisfied."

In fact, a Bill Heard customer typically receives at least two customer-satisfaction surveys after the sale, to ensure the experience measured up to expectations. This price-plus-service philosophy is one that can be traced back to the founding of the national Bill Heard organization.

A History of Performance

Founded in Columbus, Georgia, in 1919 by William T. Heard, the company opened as Muskogee Motor Company, and sold Hudson and Essex automobiles to area residents. Heard's reputation for competitive prices and honest service was so well known that the

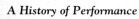

THE SOME 150 EMPLOYEES AT BILL HEARD CHEVROLET COLLIERVILLE ARE DEDICATED TO WORKING TOGETHER TO MAKE THE EXPERIENCE SATISFACTORY FOR ALL CUSTOMERS.

company remained strong even when auto sales all but dried up during the Great Depression.

In 1932, Heard moved to the Chevrolet and Oldsmobile brands. In 1961, Heard's son, W.T. Heard Jr., took the reins of the company and renamed it Bill Heard Chevrolet in honor of his father. W.T. Heard Jr. also set out to tell the world about the company's focus on low prices and personalized service.

Growth took off. The dealerships broke regional records, and Heard expanded with parts divisions. In the 1980s, new Bill Heard dealerships in Atlanta; Huntsville, Alabama; and two in Houston were added to meet demand. In the 1990s, five more Bill Heard dealerships were added—including the original Memphis location—and the company also acquired Oldsmobile and Cadillac franchises.

In 1993, Bill Heard Enterprises was first included in the Forbes 500 list of the largest privately held corporations in the country, and proudly earned its first $1 billion in annual sales in 1995.

Today, the company is the world's largest retail Chevrolet dealer. Bill Heard Enterprises employs more than 2,500 professionals who are dedicated to responding to customers' needs and offering the competitive prices that the company's big volume makes possible.

Serving Memphis and Collierville

From the receptionist to the auto washer to the salesman, it takes dozens of people to sell a car. The some 150 employees at Bill Heard Chevrolet Collierville are dedicated to working together to make the experience satisfactory for all customers.

In addition to volume pricing and personalized service, the company offers a number of other services. The showroom is open until 10 p.m. seven nights a week to accommodate working families. Salespeople, however, can often be seen on the lot well after hours, as all are committed to serving every customer who needs help.

The dealership has extended service hours, and is open from 7 a.m. to 7 p.m. on weekdays and from 8 a.m. to 2 p.m. on Saturdays. And the dealership's in-house body shop is open until 6 p.m. on weeknights

FROM ITS SALES RECORDS TO ITS COMMUNITY INVOLVEMENT, BILL HEARD CHEVROLET IN COLLIERVILLE—LED BY GENERAL MANAGER RICK MCLEY—HAS, IN A RELATIVELY SHORT TIME, CHANGED THE WAY PEOPLE IN THE AREA THINK ABOUT CAR DEALERSHIPS.

and offers 24-hour towing service.

The dealership also knows that there is more to serving a community than simply serving its customers. Bill Heard Chevrolet participates in a long list of Memphis and Collierville organizations, from the NAACP to the chamber of commerce. The company even made a $300,000 commitment to the Memphis Redbirds.

And, in an innovative service program, employees of the dealership spent a day teaching children—and parents—a variety of safety lessons. Families gathered in the company's lot for digital safety photos, fingerprints, and lessons on topics rang-

ing from dog attacks to escaping a fire. The dealership brought out the Sentry Kids SK3000, a system developed for law enforcement that scans a child's fingerprints into a database. The system can take accurate prints from children as young as three months old.

From its sales records to its community involvement, Bill Heard Chevrolet in Collierville has—in a relatively short time—changed the way people in the area think about car dealerships. The company continues to raise expectations and, as it does, is sure to break more and more records for serving its customers.

here is no substitute for the power of education. Whether it concerns an entire community or a single person, education is often the key to success. And no one knows that more than Southwest Tennessee Community College (STCC). Serving the city of Memphis and Shelby and Fayette counties, STCC offers hundreds of programs that enhance careers, fuel industry, and enrich the area's quality of life. ▲ Formed by the 2000 consolidation of

SOUTHWEST TENNESSEE COMMUNITY COLLEGE (STCC) WAS FORMED IN 2000 BY THE CONSOLIDATION OF SHELBY STATE COMMUNITY COLLEGE AND STATE TECHNICAL INSTITUTE AT MEMPHIS.

TODAY, STCC, ACCREDITED BY THE SOUTHERN ASSOCIATION OF COLLEGES AND SCHOOLS TO AWARD ASSOCIATE DEGREES, IS THE LARGEST TWO-YEAR COLLEGE IN TENNESSEE WITH AN ESTIMATED 12,000 STUDENTS.

Shelby State Community College and State Technical Institute at Memphis, STCC has a combined 60 years of educating the Memphis area. The Tennessee Board of Regents, the governing board for both colleges, pursued the consolidation to enhance the programs and services for students and the community, and to better meet the workforce training needs of the Memphis area.

On June 17, 1999, Tennessee Governor Don Sundquist signed Public Chapter No. 510 into law, giving state approval to form the new college on July 1, 2000. Seven transition teams, comprised of faculty, staff, students, and community representatives, were named to address key consolidating areas, including faculty personnel and governance; academic programs; continuing education; student affairs; recruitment, admissions, and policies and procedures; computer information services and business and finance; facilities management and development; and human resources. In addition, numerous task forces met to address specific issues from publication consoli-

dation and mail services to graduation and student activities.

"The teams moved quickly to combine resources for advertising, recruitment, and publications early in the transition process to communicate information about the consolidation and the classes, programs, and services to be offered," says Dr. Nathan Essex, interim president. "In a very short period of time, team members did a tremendous amount of work to ensure that students could have a combined

fall schedule of classes, with some courses offered at certain locations for the first time."

In addition to the transition teams, the Tennessee Board of Regents named a Blue Ribbon Advisory Committee comprised of legislators, community leaders, and chamber of commerce representatives to advise and assist the Board of Regents in the transition process involved in the restructuring of Shelby State and State Tech into STCC.

All the hard work paid off. Today, STCC, accredited by the Southern Association of Colleges and Schools to award associate degrees, is the largest two-year college in Tennessee, with an estimated 12,000 students. A comprehensive, multicultural, public, open-access college, STCC offers a broad range of learning opportunities in technical, career, general, transfer, developmental, and continuing education. STCC prepares students for employment, career advancement, personal enrichment, and college and university transfer.

The college offers academic and technical certificate programs and associate of arts, associate of science, and associate of applied science degrees. In addition, workshops, seminars, and

customized training programs for businesses are offered. The college has two main campuses—one on Macon Cove in East Memphis and one on Union Avenue in Midtown. In addition, the college has five off-campus centers: Fayette Center in Somerville, Gill Center in Memphis, Millington Center at Naval Support Activity Mid-South in Millington, Southeast Center in Memphis, and Whitehaven Center in South Memphis.

New Offerings for a New Economy

While STCC continues as a leader in technical, vocational, and professional education, the college continually adds programs that address the changing needs of area students and employers. Capitalizing on Memphis' emergence as a center for distribution-focused, Internet-based business operations, STCC's Business Administration Department recently announced a new concentration in Electronic Business Management. The program is offered through the Business and Commerce Associate of Applied Science Degree program in the Business Administration Department.

The primary educational objective of the Electronic Business Management concentration is to help students understand how Internet-driven marketplace changes unfold, and to provide them with the skills that will make them important sources of competitive advantage. The new program trains needed specialists for such positions as e-commerce specialist, e-commerce project coordinator, electronic content manager, e-business specialist, and e-commerce senior consultant—positions that will be required to maintain and promote the area's e-businesses.

In addition to the new concentration, STCC also offers a high-tech computer certification program. The college has partnered with an outside provider to teach Certified Microsoft Technical classes. This nighttime program is designed for working professionals who want to increase their skills and value to their employers. Certified instructors teach all classes for the Microsoft Certified Systems Engineer Program for the continuing education unit (CEU) credits with an opportunity to qualify for tuition reimbursement.

To round out its high-tech training, STCC initiates progressive partnerships and public service activities for workforce development and lifelong learning throughout the community. The school even produces proactive, collaborative programs with high schools, technology centers, colleges, and universities.

"Our goal," Essex says, "is to continue our progress toward becoming the college of choice and a national model for technical, career, and transfer education. We're making amazing strides, and are continuing our focus on fostering student success, transforming lives, and strengthening the diverse community."

STCC OFFERS HUNDREDS OF PROGRAMS THAT ENHANCE CAREERS, FUEL INDUSTRY, AND ENRICH THE LIVES OF BOTH THE STUDENTS AND THE GREATER MID-SOUTH COMMUNITY.

A COMPREHENSIVE, MULTICULTURAL, PUBLIC, OPEN-ACCESS COLLEGE, STCC OFFERS A BROAD RANGE OF LEARNING OPPORTUNITIES IN TECHNICAL, CAREER, GENERAL, TRANSFER, DEVELOPMENTAL, AND CONTINUING EDUCATION.

PHOTOGRAPHERS

Owner of Photosynthesis Imaging and a graduate of the University of Memphis, JAY ADKINS specializes in corporate, portrait, and event photography, and has photographed for H&M Company, Compass Financial Advisors, New Horizons Computer Learning Center in Memphis, and other organizations.

Originally headquartered in London, ALLSPORT has expanded to include offices in New York and Los Angeles. Its pictures have appeared in every major publication in the world, and the best of its portfolio has been displayed at elite photographic exhibitions at the Royal Photographic Society and the Olympic Museum in Lausanne.

DAN BALL specializes in portrait, illustration, report, and art photography. His images have appeared in the *Memphis Flyer* and *Memphis Magazine*, and his clients include *Raygun, Maxim,* and V2 Records.

A Memphis-based independent agricultural photojournalist, WILLIAM E. BARKSDALE has photographed and written about Memphis-area agriculture for nearly four decades. He contributes to numerous farm magazines, and his images are used in marketing communications by many firms providing input to the farm market.

REX BRASHER specializes in commercial photography and is co-owner of Brasher/ Rucker Photography. His images have been used by such companies as Coppertone, Maybelline, Dr. Scholls, and Holiday Inn, and he held a one-man art show at the Rainbow Club in London in 1943.

Specializing in aesthetic and documentary photojournalism, JUSTIN FOX BURKS has won several best of show and best of feature awards in the southeast region. Having lived in the Memphis area for most of his life, he has photographed the diverse religious organizations throughout the city.

Owner of API Photographers Inc., WILLIAM CARRIER specializes in people, travel, commercial, and illustrative photography. He has contributed images to such businesses as FedEx and International Paper, and his work has appeared in the Kodak Gallery and the Texas Professional Photographers Association Hall of Fame.

After earning his bachelor of fine arts degree in graphic design from the University of Memphis in 1981, STEVE WILLIS COOK perfected his craft with Brasher/Rucker Photography. After more than 10 years, he took a position as a senior photographer for FedEx and currently produces commercial, industrial, architectural, food, tabletop, and illustrative photography in Memphis.

A location scout for feature films and documentaries, SAJ CRONE has traveled to Inner Mongolia, China, Bali, Singapore, Malaysia, Nepal, India, Greece, France, and Italy. Her clients include Northwest Air, Timna, and the Memphis and Shelby County Film & Television Commission. Her images have been published in *Memphis Magazine, Agenda* magazine, and one of Towery Publishing's previous Memphis books, *Memphis: New Visions, New Horizons.*

Originally from McKenzie, Tennessee, STEVE DAVIS has lived in the Memphis area for more than 25 years. He is self-employed and specializes in location/magazine photography.

KIM ELLIOTT PAULSON is the owner and operator of Fine Grain Photo Lab. She specializes in custom black-and-white printing and processing, and she won the 1999 Print of the Year award from the Memphis Camera Club.

An art director at Towery Publishing, ENRIQUE ESPINOSA earned a bachelor's degree in art history from Rhodes College. He has done freelance photography for various local and regional firms, and his images appear in *Agenda* magazine, as well as Towery's *St. Louis: For the Record* and *Jackson: The Good Life*.

Owner of Stephen Graham Photography, STEPHEN GRAHAM specializes in architecture, interior design, people, lifestyle, and landscape photography, as well as aerial, stock, corporate portraiture, and rural and city images. His work has appeared in publications by A.M.D.G. Architects, Campbell/Manix, Commonwealth Cultural Resource Group, Lerner Publications, Owl Creek Productions, Voyageur Press, and University Business Interiors.

Specializing in children's portraits and black-and-white photography, BARBARA GREENFIELD is a retired elementary school teacher in the New York City school system. A member of the Monmouth Camera Club and the New Jersey Federation Camera Club, she is very interested in graphics and enjoys working in Photoshop.

JOHN HALEY has traveled extensively throughout many second and third world countries, documenting the medical missions of a local children's foundation. While specializing in editorial and portrait photography, he has participated in numerous photo exhibits, ranging from a series of floral images to an in-depth study of a dance group.

Originally from Memphis, BEVERLY HAMMOND considers herself a serious amateur who thoroughly enjoys taking pictures. She specializes in children photography and junk art.

Specializing in commercial, sports, and portrait photography, LARRY T. INMAN is originally from Memphis but has lived all over the United States. A freelance photographer and owner of Inman Images, he has worked with such organizations as the University of Memphis, Memphis Redbirds, International Paper, Memphis in May, Le Bonheur Children's Medical Center, Memphis Visitors & Convention Bureau, the Peabody Hotel, and Memphis Light, Gas and Water.

Owner of Luxora, a company involved in Web development, DARIN IPEMA works in digital photography, videography, animation/special effects, editing, and other digital media. A Memphis resident for more than 20 years, he has done cinematography on two local movies, *Teenage Tupelo* and *The Sore Losers*, and his images have appeared in several Towery publications.

JEFFREY JACOBS produces images for some of the country's largest architectural firms, advertising agencies, product manufacturers, and major publications. Specializing in high-end architectural and interior design photography, he works to create an experience of the environment through interpretive lighting designs.

A former aerospace photojournalist for NASA, DENNIS KEIM now owns dk-studio and specializes in corporate and editorial photography. His work has been featured in several local, regional, and national publications, and his lifestyle photography has appeared in three books: *Huntsville—Where Technology Meets Tradition*, *Huntsville—A Timeless Portrait*, and Towery Publishing's *Huntsville-Madison County: To the Edge of the Universe*.

▼ © JAY ADKINS

Specializing in advertising, corporate, stock, editorial, and fine art photography, JACK KENNER owns Jack Kenner Photography Studio and Take a Closer Look Photographic Gallery. Originally from Memphis, he has participated in numerous photo expeditions to Thailand, Brazil, New Zealand, Kenya, and Tanzania, as well as throughout America and Europe.

A general dentist in the Memphis area, DAN T. MEADOWS specializes in nature photography and has had several images exhibited at the University of Memphis Fogelman Center, Jack Kenner Gallery, Second Floor Contemporary Gallery, and the Germantown Performing Arts Center. He has taken courses and attended workshops conducted by some of the region's finest nature photographers, and has had images published in various magazines and journals.

Having worked as the foreign desk photo editor for Czech News Agency and as the photo editor for a Prague newspaper, W. MICHAEL MOSBY specializes in documentary, editorial, architecture, and portrait photography. He currently serves as the teaching artist for the Memphis Arts Council's art education program.

JUDI PARKS is an award-winning photojournalist living and working in the San Francisco Bay Area. Her work has been collected by museums and public collections in the United States and Europe, and her documentary series, *Home Sweet Home: Caring for America's Elderly*, was recently honored with the Communication Arts-Design Annual 1999 Award of Excellence for an unpublished series. Her images have appeared in numerous Towery publications.

Established in San Diego in 1967, PHOTOPHILE has more than 1 million color images on file, culled from more than 85 contributing local and international photographers. Subjects range from images of Southern California to adventure, sports, wildlife and underwater scenes, business, industry, people, science and research, health and medicine, and travel photography. Included on Photophile's client list are American Express, *Guest Informant*, and Franklin Stoorza.

Originally from New York City, JONATHAN POSTAL has freelanced for such publications as *Vanity Fair*, *Rolling Stone*, and the *New York Times*. He has traveled across the world on assignments for *Time*, *YM*, Liz Claiborne, CBS Records, and others, and has contributed images to *New Orleans Magazine* and advertising accounts. He was the creative director of *Eye Magazine* and won the Memphis Arts Festival's best of photography award twice, and he now serves as photo editor for Towery Publishing.

With images published in several regional publications, DON REBER has worked on assignment for such organizations as FedEx, First Tennessee Bank, Memphis Belle Association, Union Planters, and Radioactive Advertising. Employed by Wolf Camera, he specializes in sports, action, and architectural photography.

© NANCY B. WEBB

Specializing in stock photography of Tennessee and travel photography of the southeast United States, J & D RICHARDSON have contributed images to such travel publications as *Woodall's*, *TL Enterprises*, and *Camping Life*.

With past clients such as the Associated Press, *Newsweek*, *Time*, and *Yankee Magazine*, ROLLIN RIGGS currently covers New England and Connecticut for the *New York Times*. A native Memphian, he specializes in photojournalism and has been the manager of local music act the Bouffants, as well as a book publisher.

A licensed architect, UTTAM SHAH started a business specializing in architectural photography. Several of his images were published in *Memphis Magazine* in conjunction with the 1990 Memphis in May. His work has also been exhibited at the Shainberg Gallery of the Memphis Jewish Community Center, the Buckman Center of St. Mary's Episcopal School, the Fogelman Executive Center, and the Memphis Camera Club's exhibits at the Germantown Performing Arts Center and Christian Brothers University.

A graduate of the University of Memphis, DAVID E. SPARKMAN specializes in fine art, portrait, event, and commercial photography. His images have appeared in the *Memphis Flyer*.

Originally from Alcoa, Tennessee, CINDY STUART graduated from Auburn University and specializes in general, travel, macro, and special effects photography. She has worked in the Memphis area for more than 20 years.

A native of Tupelo, Mississippi, HOPE UIBERALL has lived and worked in the Memphis area for more than a decade. She received a bachelor of science degree in psychology from the University of Tennessee-Martin, and is currently working on her bachelor of fine arts at the University of Memphis.

With a bachelor's degree in architecture from Auburn University, GARY WAGONER is co-owner of Construction Management Plus, Inc., and his clients include FedEx, the Internal Revenue Service, Boyd Gaming, the Town of Tunica, and Fitzgerald's Casino. He is a member of the American Institute of Architects, Construction Specifications Institute, and MENSA.

NANCY B. WEBB has had images published by such organizations as the Mall of Memphis, the Racquet Club, Holiday Inn East, and First Evangelical Church. Originally from Memphis, she enjoys all areas of photography.

A longtime photographer and civil rights chronicler, ERNEST C. WITHERS has witnessed and recorded such events as the Montgomery bus boycott, the death of Medgar Evers, the 1968 Memphis sanitation workers strike, and the aftermath of Martin Luther King Jr.'s assassination. His images have appeared in numerous publications, including *Ebony*, *Jet*, *Time*, and *Newsweek*, and have been part of five travelling exhibits: *Letters March On*, *Appeal to the Ages*, *Good Times in Memphis and Negro Baseball*, *I'm a Man*, and *Picture Tell the Story*.

Other contributing photographers and organizations include Center City Commission, Center for Southern Folklore, Children's Museum of Memphis, Elvis Presley Enterprises, Troy Glasgow, Brian Groppe, Irma C. Idell, Memphis Light, Gas and Water, Memphis Maniax, Memphis Motorsports Park, Brett Patterson, Pink Palace Museum, Playhouse on the Square, Murray Riss Photography, Ross De Alessi Lighting Design, Pat Kerr Tigrett, and Wonders: The Memphis International Cultural Series. For further information about the photographers appearing in *Memphis: Delivering the Future*, please contact Towery Publishing.

LIBRARY OF CONGRESS CATALOGING-IN-PUBLICATION DATA

Memphis : delivering the future / introduction by Frederick W. Smith ; art direction by Brian Groppe.

p. cm. — (Urban tapestry series)

Includes index.

ISBN 1-881096-98-X (alk. paper)

1. Memphis (Tenn.)—Civilization. 2. Memphis (Tenn.)—Pictorial works. 3. Memphis (Tenn.)—Economic conditions. 4. Business enterprises—Tennessee—Memphis. I. Smith, Fred, 1944- II. Series.

F444.M55 M46 2001

976.8'19—dc21

2001035566

Printed in Mexico

TOWERY PUBLISHING, INC.

THE TOWERY BUILDING

1835 UNION AVENUE

MEMPHIS, TN 38104

WWW.TOWERY.COM

PUBLISHER: J. Robert Towery ◆ EXECUTIVE PUBLISHER: Jenny McDowell ◆ MARKETING DIRECTOR: Carol Culpepper ◆ SALES MANAGER: Bill Koons ◆ PROJECT DIRECTORS: Mary Helen Aldridge, Kim Andrews, Mike Bartow, Alexandria Dobkowski, Don Honeycutt, Gigi Phillips ◆ EXECUTIVE EDITOR: David B. Dawson ◆ MANAGING EDITOR: Lynn Conlee ◆ SENIOR EDITORS: Carlisle Hacker, Brian L. Johnston ◆ EDITOR/ CAPTION WRITER: Stephen M. Deusner ◆ EDITOR/ PROFILE MANAGER: Jay Adkins ◆ EDITORS: Rebecca E. Farabough, Danna M. Greenfield, Ginny Reeves, Sabrina Schroeder ◆ PROFILE WRITER: Stinson Liles ◆ EDITORIAL CONTRIBUTORS: Jenifer Barron, Bob Phillips ◆ PHOTOGRAPHY EDITOR: Jonathan Postal ◆ PHOTOGRAPHIC CONSULTANT: Lisa Waddell Buser ◆ PROFILE DESIGNERS: Rebekah Barnhardt, Laurie Beck, Glen Marshall ◆ PRODUCTION MANAGER: Brenda Pattat ◆ PHOTOGRAPHY COORDINATOR: Robin Lankford ◆ PRODUCTION ASSISTANTS: Robert Barnett, Loretta Lane, Robert Parrish ◆ DIGITAL COLOR SUPERVISOR: Darin Ipema ◆ DIGITAL COLOR TECHNICIANS: Eric Friedl, Mark Svetz ◆ DIGITAL SCANNING TECHNICIAN: Brad Long ◆ PRINT COORDINATOR: Beverly Timmons

INDEX OF PROFILES